Knowledge and Business Process Management

Vlatka Hlupic
Brunel University, UK

IDEA GROUP PUBLISHING

Hershey • London • Melbourne • Singapore • Beijing

Acquisition Editor:	Mehdi Khosrowpour
Managing Editor:	Jan Travers
Development Editor:	Michele Rossi
Copy Editor:	Maria Boyer
Typesetter:	LeAnn Whitcomb
Cover Design:	Integrated Book Technology
Printed at:	Integrated Book Technology

Published in the United States of America by
　　Idea Group Publishing
　　1331 E. Chocolate Avenue
　　Hershey PA 17033-1117
　　Tel: 717-533-8845
　　Fax: 717-533-8661
　　E-mail: cust@idea-group.com
　　Web site: http://www.idea-group.com

and in the United Kingdom by
　　Idea Group Publishing
　　3 Henrietta Street
　　Covent Garden
　　London WC2E 8LU
　　Tel: 44 20 7240 0856
　　Fax: 44 20 7379 3313
　　Web site: http://www.eurospan.co.uk

Library of Congress Cataloging-in-Publication Data

Knowledge and business process management / [edited by] Vlatka Hlupic
　　　p. cm.
　　Includes bibliographical references and index.
　　ISBN 1-59140-036-8 (cloth)
　　　1. Knowledge management. 2. Business--Data processing--Management. 3. Electronic commerce--Management. 4. Information resources management. 5. Management information systems. I. Hlupic, Vlatka, 1965-

HD30.2 .K634 2003
658.4'038--dc21　　　　　　　　　　　　　　　　　　　　2002068780

eISBN 1-59140-074-0

British Cataloguing in Publication Data
A Cataloguing in Publication record for this book is available from the British Library.

NEW from Idea Group Publishing

Knowledge and Business Process Management

Table of Contents

Preface i

Section I: Research Issues in Knowledge and Business Process Management

Chapter I 1
Directions and Trends in Knowledge Management Research: Results from
an Empirical Analysis of European Projects
   George M. Giaglis, University of the Aegean, Greece

Chapter II 16
Knowledge Economy: An Overview
   Vlatko Ceric, University of Zagreb, Croatia

Chapter III 33
Simulation Modelling: The Link Between Change Management Approaches
   Wendy L. Currie, Brunel University, UK
   Vlatka Hlupic, Brunel University, UK

Chapter IV 51
Intelligent Agents for Knowledge Management in E-Commerce:
Opportunities and Challenges
   Athanasia Pouloudi, Athens University of Economics and Business, Greece
   Vlatka Hlupic, Brunel University, UK
   George Rzevski, Brunel University, UK

Chapter V 68
Knowledge Management: Analysis and Some Consequences
   Petros A. M. Gelepithis, Kingston University, UK
   Nicole Parillon, Kingston University, UK

Section II: Practical Aspects of Knowledge and Business Process Management

Chapter VI 83
Knowledge Management in Action: The Experience of Infosys Technologies
   V. P. Kochikar, Infosys Technologies Ltd., India
   Kavi Mahesh, Infosys Technologies Ltd., India
   C. S. Mahind, Infosys Technologies Ltd., India

Chapter VII 99
The Learning Enactment of Process Knowledge: An Approach Anchored on
Work Practices
> *Kostas Samiotis, Athens University of Economics and Business, Greece*
> *Angeliki Poulymenakou, Athens University of Economics and*
>   *Business, Greece*

Chapter VIII 118
Brudging the Gap from the General to the Specific by Linking
Knowledge Management to Business Processes
> *John S. Edwards, Aston University, UK*
> *John B. Kidd, Aston University, UK*

Chapter IX 137
Designing Organisational Memory in Knowledge-Intensive Companies:
A Case Study
> *Dee Alwis, Brunel University, UK*
> *Vlatka Hlupic, Brunel University, UK*
> *George Rzevski, Brunel University, UK*

Chapter X 154
Opportunities for Data Mining and Customer Knowledge Management
for Shopping Centres
> *Charles Dennis, Brunel University, UK*
> *David Marsland, Brunel University, UK*
> *Tony Cockett, Brunel University, UK*

Section III: People and Technology: Current Trends in
Knowledge and Business Process Management

Chapter XI 174
Managing Knowledge in a Collaborative Context: How May
Intellectual Resources Be Harnessed Towards Joint Effect?
> *Sajda Qureshi, Erasmus University Rotterdam, The Netherlands*
> *Vlatka Hlupic, Brunel University, UK*
> *Gert-Jan de Vreede, Delft University of Technology, The Netherlands*
> *Robert O. Briggs, GroupSystems.com, USA*
> *Jay Nunamaker, University of Arizona Tucson, USA*

Chapter XII 196
Technical Aspects of Knowledge Management: A Methodology for
Commercial Knowledge Management Tool Selection
> *Nayna Patel, Brunel University, UK*
> *Vlatka Hlupic, Brunel University, UK*

Chapter XIII 217
A Framework for Managing Knowledge in Requirements Identification:
Bridging the Knowledge Gap Between Business and System Developers
Wafi Al-Karaghouli, University of Westminster, UK
Sarmad Alshawi, Brunel University, UK
Guy Fitzgerald, Brunel University, UK

Chapter XIV 238
The Impact of the Knowledge Economy on Leadership in Organisations
Manon Van Leeuwen, Foundation for the Development of Science
and Technology in Extremadura, Spain

Chapter XV 259
The Role of Teams in Business Process Change
Jyoti Choudrie, Brunel University, UK

About the Authors 277

Index 286

Preface

In today's competitive and global business environments, knowledge is recognised as one of the most important strategic assets for modern organisations. In the light of this, knowledge management (KM) continues to receive much attention both from the academic and business communities. With improvements in IT-based systems for handling knowledge, KM is becoming an essential theme of research into business success as well as a subject of new business initiatives. There is a growing emphasis on innovation through 'knowledge work' and 'knowledge workers' and on the leveraging of 'knowledge assets' (Swan et al., 1999).

It is important to note that the effective management of knowledge involves more than simply exploiting the data held on information systems. It also requires attention to the 'softer' parts of the corporate knowledge base, as found in the human and cultural aspects of businesses, particularly the experiences and tacit knowledge of employees. The integration of these 'hard' and 'soft' parts of the knowledge base is believed to be critical to business success, especially in the context of the global digital economy (Hlupic et al., 2002).

So far, the literature has been unable to agree on a definition for the term 'knowledge management' (Brooking, 1999; Malhotra, 1998; Trauth, 1999). The possible reason for this might be that discussions of, and approaches to, the subject are rooted in different academic disciplines and areas of professional expertise. From the *information systems perspective*, for example, KM is often looked upon as synonymous with new forms of 'data mining' and 'warehousing' — the 'hard' tools that allow for sophisticated pattern searches of raw data (Trauth, 1999). From the *innovation management* perspective, a 'cognitive' approach is adopted, which looks at the transfer of explicit and tacit knowledge through product development and organisational change procedures (Kuhn and Abecker, 1997; Nonaka and Takeuchi, 1995; Leonard-Barton, 1995). The *management* literature particularly emphasises the 'organisational learning,' focusing on structures that encourage creativity and knowledge sharing (Ruggles, 1997). It is increasingly evident that approaches to KM research and practice often do not adopt a *multi-disciplinary* view (Hlupic et al., 2002), despite the multi-disciplinary interest in KM (Phillips and Patrick, 2000). Instead, a managerial perspective is often predominant, that does not necessarily accommodate the capabilities of information systems. Sveiby (1999) acknowledges this implicitly when he divides research publications in this field into two categories: 'Management of Information' and 'Management of People.'

Knowledge management and management of business processes are two (often) separated but inseparable areas. Business processes should incorporate activities related to generation, codification and transfer of critical organisational knowledge. On the other hand, knowledge about the key business processes should play an important role in redesigning such processes. Because of such interconnections, this book aims to coin a term *"knowledge and business process management,"* recognising the importance of integrated and interdisciplinary approach to research and practice of managing both knowledge and business processes.

This book is a result of the editor's belief that knowledge and business process management must move towards a more *holistic* approach to nurturing and exploitation of knowledge assets in both 'traditional' and 'virtual' business environments, as well managing business processes from a socio-technical perspective. For this purpose, the book brings together *multi-disciplinary* research and practical expertise in the areas of information systems, knowledge management, systems engineering, e-commerce, business, management and marketing.

The book provides a timely compilation of views on the most recent knowledge and business process management research and practice, contributed by renowned experts from academia and industry. As such, the book provides a significant contribution to the area of knowledge and business process management. The book is divided into three sections, and each section contains five chapters. The first section addresses current research issues in knowledge and business process management. Section Two deals with the practical aspects of knowledge and business process management. Finally, Section Three discusses current socio-technical trends in knowledge and business process management where the particular emphasis is on people and/or technology. The following paragraphs describe in more detail the content of each chapter.

Chapter 1 discusses trends in knowledge management research, based on an empirical analysis of European research projects. The chapter argues that Knowledge and Information Management (KIM) has existed as a separate field of scientific research for almost a decade. The author finds surprising that very few studies to date have been concerned with the identification of the scope and boundaries of the field, as well as the sub-topics and research themes that constitute it. The chapter reports on the results of an empirical analysis of more than 200 EU-funded research projects in Knowledge and Information Management. Using an inductive methodology of pattern matching analysis, a more accurate definition of knowledge management is provided, and an innovative taxonomy of research sub-themes within the 'umbrella' area of Knowledge and Information Management is proposed. Furthermore, a trend towards a gradual maturation of the presently prevailing research paradigm is identified, indicating a need for a 'paradigm shift' that will provide a new direction and vision for future research in the area. The author suggests that targeted future research efforts in the area of knowledge technologies will contribute to the development of the 'next generation' knowledge management systems that will transform the existing 'passive' knowledge repositories into 'active' learning environments.

Chapter 2 provides an overview of issues related to knowledge economy. The author claims that the dramatic development of information and communications technology, the increased speed of scientific and technological progress and the increased global competition led to the growing importance of knowledge and technology for economy. Modern economy, therefore, increasingly includes features of knowledge economy, an economy based on production, distribution and use of knowledge. Also, more and more the growth of companies depends on innovation, and innovation is based on knowledge. The chapter further describes the categorisation and characteristics of knowledge, analyses features of knowledge assets, and describes the reasons for the importance of information and communications technology for knowledge economy. Finally, it describes the production, transmission and dissemination of knowledge, as well as the measurement of knowledge required for providing adequate economic indicators for the new economy.

Chapter 3 investigates several management innovation and change programs including: Total Quality Management, Just in Time, Business Process Re-Engineering, Process Innovation and Knowledge Management, and discusses how simulation modelling could increase their effectiveness. These change management approaches are compared and contrasted, and the applicability of simulation modelling to support the principles of these methods is investigated. The authors argue that there are many similarities among these change management programs, and simulation modelling could be viewed as a missing link between them.

Chapter 4 considers how knowledge management can create new business opportunities in the electronic commerce-based business environments. The authors argue that intelligent systems can offer additional capabilities and advantages for knowledge management in the context of electronic commerce, in comparison with more traditional information technologies. The chapter specifically investigates the potential of intelligent agent-based software for more effective knowledge management for e-commerce-based organisations, adopting the perspective of an SME involved in development of intelligent agents-based knowledge management software. The chapter concludes with a research agenda for knowledge management research in e-commerce.

Chapter 5 investigates the fundamental issues of knowledge management and knowledge market. Although the debate on the nature of 'knowledge' and 'information' is far from settled, in the authors' opinion, it is now taken for granted throughout the academic world that the two notions are related but fundamentally distinct. This result, and its significant consequences, still need to be realised and understood by the great majority of the business world. In the first section of this chapter, the authors briefly comment on some characteristic views of 'knowledge' and 'knowledge management,' and subsequently analyse in-depth the core constituent notion of the latter, that is, knowledge. Furthermore, the authors outline three major consequences of their analysis. The first concerns the limits of management for a certain class of activities involving knowledge. The second concerns the scope and limits of technology for the same class of activities. The third concerns the issue of knowledge market. The thesis the authors develop is that knowledge cannot be taken as a commodity; in other words, the notion of a knowledge market cannot be implemented.

Chapter 6 presents the experience of Infosys Technologies, an IT consultancy based in India, in implementing knowledge management initiatives. The authors claim that the mission of these initiatives is to move the company towards a *"Learn*

Once, Use Anywhere" paradigm. A KM deployment architecture that addresses each of the four focal areas of KM — people, process, technology and content — and uses the proprietary KMM (Knowledge Management Maturity) Model as an underlying framework is described. A description of the Knowledge Shop (KShop), Infosys's integrated knowledge portal, is also given. Furthermore, the Knowledge Currency Unit (KCU) scheme that serves both as an incentivisation and measurement mechanism is described, as well as the role of this scheme in helping to create a knowledge-sharing culture.

Chapter 7 addresses the issues of learning enactment within a single organisation. More particularly, the authors look into theory and provide some empirical evidence regarding the exploration and exploitation of organisational knowledge and capabilities through innovative technological intervention. To this end, the link between work practices and knowledge enactment, knowledge enactment as capability development, capability development in the context of organisational learning, and the role of technology along this course are explored. The study of work practices is anchored on the notion of business processes. The chapter intends to justify the need of contemporary firms to 'manage' knowledge in the context of their business processes, and to establish the main drivers shaping the role of technology in the enactment of learning processes within this perspective.

Chapter 8 also attempts to link knowledge management to business processes. The authors claim that, in general, there is a gap between theory and practical implementation. They believe that this is a particular problem in knowledge management, where much of the literature consists of general principles written in the context of a 'knowledge world' that has few, if any, references to how to carry out knowledge management in organisations. In this chapter, the authors put forward the view that the best way to bridge this gap between general principles and the specific issues facing a given organisation is to link knowledge management to the organisation's business processes. After briefly reviewing, and rejecting alternative ways in which this gap might be bridged, the chapter goes on to explain the justification for, and the potential benefits and snags of, linking knowledge management to business processes. Successful and unsuccessful examples are presented. The authors conclude that linking knowledge management in terms of business processes is the best route for organisations to follow, but that it is not the answer to all knowledge management problems, especially where different cultures and/or cultural change are involved.

Chapter 9 addresses the issue of designing organisational memory in knowledge-intensive companies, where organisational memory is defined as a company's collective expertise and experience that is cultivated through human and technological networks for improving organisational performance. The authors present a case study that has been carried out in a knowledge-intensive company, discuss the key findings from the case study, and propose a framework to assist knowledge-intensive organisations in implementing and managing a corporate knowledge base.

Chapter 10 discusses opportunities for data mining and customer knowledge management for shopping centres. Relying on complex interdependencies between shoppers, retailers and owners, shopping centres are perceived to be ideal for knowledge management study. Nevertheless, although retailers have been in the forefront of data mining, in the authors' opinion, little has been written on Customer Knowledge Management for shopping centres. In this chapter, the authors aim to demonstrate the possibilities and draw attention to the possible implications of improving customer satisfaction, using data mining techniques and an exploratory survey. Aspects of customer knowledge management for shopping centres are considered on the basis of survey results. The objectives of a Customer Knowledge Management system could include increasing rental incomes and bringing new life back into shopping centres and towns.

Chapter 11 discusses managing knowledge in a collaborative context. In particular, it proposes a model describing four conditions necessary for successful collaboration: shared spaces and collaborative culture enable collaboration, whereas goal congruency and resource constraints are required for collaboration to take place. The authors further describe how collaborative technologies have created shared spaces for more efficient and effective collaborative work, and discuss knowledge management activities constraining collaborative culture. The creation of goal congruency and overcoming resource constraints are seen by the authors to be brought about through the creative use of electronic collaboration and simulation technologies. Examples of collaborative contexts in which personalised knowledge is managed are provided, and finally, the chapter concludes with implications and guidelines for managing knowledge in collaborative contexts.

Chapter 12 deals with the technical aspects of knowledge management. The authors claim that one of the repercussions of the continuing popularity of knowledge management is a sudden increase in the number and range of knowledge management tools available on the software market. This can present a problem for organisations that are required to sift through the vast number of tools in the hope of finding one that meets their requirements. Moreover, guidelines describing how to go about selecting a commercial knowledge management tool do not currently exist. The chapter presents a set of guidelines to aid the evaluation and selection of a commercial knowledge management tool. In order to achieve this, a methodology is proposed that outlines factors and issues that could be taken into consideration during the selection of a knowledge management tool. Furthermore, an overview of criteria specific to knowledge management tools that can be used to evaluate and ascertain the features present in a knowledge management tool is also provided.

Chapter 13 reflects on experiences when traditional IT approaches were used to design large IT systems and ended in failure. The main reflections focus on the reasons for system failure and how they relate to the diversity of knowledge, managing knowledge, and the understanding gaps that may exist between the business and the system developers. The study reveals that the understanding gaps mainly result from lack of knowledge of business operations on the developer side, matched by lack of technical appreciation and knowledge on the user side. To help address the knowledge gap problem, a Knowledge Requirement Framework (KRF) employing soft-systems methodology, diagramming and set mapping techniques, is proposed and described.

Chapter 14 discusses the impact of knowledge economy on leadership in organisations. The author claims that as the world economy is moving from the industrial age to knowledge economy, everybody's work will change, affecting the flow of new ideas into enterprises, their management, organisation and procedures. These changes have major impacts on the roles leaders need to play, and on the skills they need. The focus of a leader has shifted towards more intangible issues, being a visionary, a storyteller and a change agent. The chapter reviews the literature on the skills and abilities leaders need to be successful in the knowledge economy, and describes the way in which they need to manage their organisations by managing the organisation's business model, creating a risk-encouraging culture, and by playing different roles.

Chapter 15 addresses the role of teams in the context of business process change. The author claims that the concept of reengineering teams is not new to business process change practice and research. However, frameworks that describe the organisational changes that need to be undertaken in order to establish reengineering teams, in particular, are not available. The chapter proposes such a framework, based on a case study approach. This framework can be used by practitioners and academics to determine beforehand what to expect before the actual re-engineering team is formed. Additionally, the chapter describes the characteristics that surround the planning and design teams. This can be used as a suggestion for organisations in order to decide if they do have the appropriate numbers of individuals within a team. In general, the chapter can serve as a guideline that organisations undertaking business process change in the future can utilise for dealing with the issue of teams.

To conclude, this book provides a unique and timely compilation of multi-disciplinary views related to knowledge and business process management, addressing theoretical and practical aspects from a socio-technical perspective. As such, the book provides a unique contribution to knowledge and business process management research and practice.

REFERENCES

Brooking, A. (1999). *Corporate Memory — Strategies for Knowledge Management*. UK: International Thomson Business Press.

Cortada, J. W. and Woods, J.A (Ed.) (2000). *The Knowledge Management Yearbook 1999-2000*. Boston MA: Butterworth Heinemann.

Hlupic V., Pouloudi A. and Rzevski G. (2002). Towards an integrated approach to Knowledge Management: 'Hard,' 'soft' and 'abstract' issues. *Knowledge and Process Management, The Journal of Corporate Transformation,* 9(0), 1-14.

Kuhn, O. and Abecker, A. (1997). Corporate memories for knowledge management in industrial practice: Prospects and challenges. *Journal of Universal Computer Science*, 3(8), 929-954.

Leonard-Barton, D. (1995). *Wellsprings of Knowledge — Building and Sustaining the Sources of Innovation*. USA: Harvard Business School Press.

Malhorta, Y. (1998). Deciphering the knowledge management hype. *Journal of Quality and Participation,* 21(4), 58-60.

Myers, P. (Ed.) (1996). *Knowledge Management and Organisational Design*. Boston MA: Butterworth-Heinemann.

Nonaka, I. and Takeuchi, H. (1995). *The Knowledge-Creating Company: How Japanese Companies Create the Dynamics of Innovation*. Oxford: OUP.

Phillips, N. and Patrick, K. (2000). Knowledge management perspectives, organisational character and cognitive style. In Edwards, J. and Kidd, J. (Eds.), *Proceedings of the Knowledge Management Conference (KMAC 2000)*, 17-18 July, Birmingham, UK.

Ruggles, R. (1997). *Knowledge Tools: Using Technology to Manage Knowledge Better*, Ernst & Young Center for Business Innovation Working Paper (April 1997).

Sveiby, K. (1999). *What is Knowledge Management?*, [WWW document] URL http://www.sveiby.com.au/Knowledge Management.htm.

Swan J., Newell S., Scarborough H. and Hislop, D. (1999) Knowledge management and innovation: Networks and networking. *Journal of Knowledge Management,* 3(4), 262-275.

Trauth, E.M. (1999). Who owns my soul? The paradox of pursuing organizational knowledge in a work culture of individualism. *Proceedings of the 1999 ACM SIGCPR Conference on Computer Personnel Research*, 159-163.

Acknowledgments

I would like to acknowledge the help of all involved in the preparation and review process of this book, as without this support the project could not have been satisfactorily completed. Particularly, I wish to thank all of the authors for their insight and excellent contributions to this book, and for their enthusiasm for this project. Most of the authors of chapters included in this book also served as referees for articles written by other authors. Deep appreciation and gratitude go to all those who provided constructive and comprehensive reviews. The support of the Department of Information Systems and Computing at Brunel University is also acknowledged, for providing technical resources needed for the completion of this book.

A special note of thanks goes to all the staff at Idea Group Publishing, who gave invaluable contributions throughout the whole process from the initial idea to final publication. In particular, I wish to thank Jan Travers and Michele Rossi for helping to keep the project on schedule. Above all, I would like to thank Mehdi Khosrowpour, for motivating me to accept his invitation for taking on this project.

Last but not least, I would like to thank my husband, son and parents for their unconditional love and support throughout this project.

Eur Ing Dr Vlatka Hlupic, Editor
Brunel Centre for Knowledge and Business Process Management
Brunel University
London, United Kingdom
February 2002

Section I

Research Issues in Knowledge and Business Process Management

Chapter I

Direction and Trends in Knowledge Management Research: Results from an Empirical Analysis of European Projects

George M. Giaglis
University of the Aegean, Greece

ABSTRACT

Knowledge and Information Management (KIM) has existed as a separate field of scientific research for almost a decade. It is therefore surprising that very few studies to date have been concerned with the identification of the scope and boundaries of the field, as well as the sub-topics and research themes that constitute it. This chapter reports on the results of an empirical analysis of more than 200 research projects in Knowledge and Information Management. Using an inductive methodology of pattern matching analysis, a more accurate definition of knowledge management is attempted, and an innovative taxonomy of research sub-themes within the 'umbrella' area of Knowledge and Information Management is proposed. Furthermore, a trend towards a gradual maturation of the presently prevailing research paradigm is identified, indicating a need for a 'paradigm shift' that will provide a new direction and vision for future research in the area. We suggest that targeted future research efforts in the area of knowledge technologies will contribute to the development of the 'next generation' knowledge management systems that will transform the existing 'passive' knowledge repositories into 'active' learning environments.

THE FIELD OF KNOWLEDGE AND INFORMATION MANAGEMENT

In a world of dynamic and discontinuous change, organisations are constantly seeking ways to adapt themselves to new conditions so that they are prepared to survive and flourish in an increasingly competitive environment. The proliferation of the *knowledge economy* (Castells, 1996), emphasizing the value of information as an enabler of competitive advantage, is naturally driving many companies to re-examine the ways they have treated their knowledge assets in the past and to identify ways in which they can exploit them more effectively in the future (Argyris, 1994; Albert, 1997).

In such a landscape, it is not surprising that *Knowledge and Information Management (KIM)* has emerged as one of the most popular strategic change management approaches in the dawn of the 21st century (Davenport and Prusak, 1997; Currie, 1999; Spiegler, 2000). Its supporters argue that organisations may achieve significant competitive advantages by analysing the data and information that often remain unexploited in organisational systems and by transforming them into useful and actionable knowledge. KIM has attracted significant attention in the spheres of both academic research and industrial practice in recent years (Davenport et al., 1998). This is hardly surprising: knowledge is long known to be one of the primary enablers of sustainable competitive advantage in periods of economic turbulence (Nonaka and Takeuchi, 1995). At the same time, the increasing capabilities of contemporary information systems to store, process, and disseminate information and to contribute to its transformation into knowledge, have also served to enhance the role of KIM in organisations.

Despite the wide attention being paid to KIM, the definition of the field (both as an academic discipline and as a managerial application area), together with a clear description of its scope and boundaries, is still a subject of intense debate. A small sample of definitions found both in academic textbooks and business-oriented sources serve to demonstrate the sources of disagreements usually encountered. For example, Starr (1999) defines knowledge management as "*information or data management with the additional practice of capturing the tacit experience of the individual,*" while O'Brien (1999) defines it as "*a tool of enterprise collaboration that facilitates the organisation, management, and sharing of the diverse forms of business information created by individuals and teams in organisations.*" Laudon and Laudon (1998) claim that knowledge management is "*the process of systematically and actively managing and leveraging the stores of knowledge in an organisation,*" while Malhotra (1997) maintains that knowledge management "*embodies organisational processes that seek synergistic combination of data and information processing capacity of information technologies, and the creative and innovative capacity of human beings.*"

Even from this small sample of definitions, the epistemological and ontological basis of KIM as an independent and distinguishable field of research and practice is rather unclear. Some authors see it as an extension of traditional information management, while others view it as the synergistic outcome of combining information management and human creativity. Moreover, some definitions seem to adopt a primarily soft organisational stance and view KIM as a 'process,' while others follow a more technologically oriented hard approach and view KIM as a 'tool.'

Perhaps some of this confusion may be attributable to the fact that the terms 'knowledge' and 'information,' while not necessarily meaning the same thing to everybody, are explicitly or implicitly treated as synonymous in many definitions. Another source of confusion may be the fact that different types of knowledge seem to exist, each with potentially different management require-ments by organisations and individuals. For example, the distinction between explicit and tacit knowledge may prove to be ultimately misleading (Marshall and Brady, 2000), as it tends to split the co-existent and inter-twined types of knowledge into mutually exclusive categories. Finally, a main source of disagreement seems to stem from the use of different analytical lenses to view KIM depending on one's background: researchers from the computer science and information systems fields tend to view KIM as a tool and speak about *knowledge management systems*, while researchers from a management science background usually focus on the *knowledge management process*.

As usual in such cases, the truth is somewhere in the middle: knowledge and information management is an inherently interdisciplinary research field inasmuch as its implementation depends on technological systems and its application depends on user acceptance and embracement (managerial and employee alike). The interdisciplinary nature of the field renders its detailed epistemological study more difficult, albeit at the same time also more important. This chapter sets out on a roadmap to answering these questions through a combination of theoretical and empirical research. The next section identifies the boundaries of KIM by drawing on the relevant literature of the computer science and the management science reference disciplines. Following that, we present the results of an empirical investigation into more than 200 research projects in Knowledge and Information

Management that were funded by the Commission of the European Communities during the years 1998-2001. These projects, most of them still ongoing, amount to a total cost of nearly one billion euro (•1bn), thus representing the largest coherent group of research efforts in the area. Therefore, their analysis can yield extremely interesting findings regarding the major research sub-topics within the 'umbrella' area of KIM as well as indicators of trends and future research directions. These findings are then encapsulated in a novel taxonomy of knowledge management research sub-fields that can serve as an analytical framework when assessing the usefulness and potential contribution of a given area of study within the overall field of knowledge management (including related aspects of information management as well). In turn, this understanding can assist towards formulating policy suggestions for effectively supporting and promoting coordinated knowledge management research for the future.

THEORETICAL ANALYSIS: 'HARD' AND 'SOFT' KIM RESEARCH

As argued earlier, research within the 'umbrella' field of Knowledge and Information Management can generally fall under two broad categories depending on the departing point of the research questions. On the one hand, one research stream draws predominantly on findings from the fields of computer science and information systems, and sees knowledge management as an application area that extends the traditional realm of databases and information management into so-called knowledge bases and knowledge management systems. In other words, this 'sub-area' of KIM is mostly concerned with investigating ways in which technological capabilities can be exploited by organisations in their pursuit of knowledge-driven competitiveness. On the other hand, a separate research stream is approaching the same kinds of problems from a complementary perspective and attempts to tackle the managerial, organisational, and human issues surrounding the successful introduction of knowledge management within organisations. Research under this 'sub-area' of KIM is mostly concerned with investigating ways in which the process of knowledge creation, assimilation, communication, and enactment can be managed by organisations. Table 1 summarises the characteristics and differences between these research perspectives.

'Hard' Research

Knowledge management systems can be thought of as computer-supported tools that address one or more of the following problems related to knowledge and

Table 1: Different research approaches on Knowledge and Information Management (KIM)

	'Hard' KIM Research	'Soft' KIM Research
Driven by	Technological Developments	Organisational Problems
Focus on	Information	Process
Reference Disciplines	Computer Science, Information Systems, Artificial Intelligence	Management Science, Cognitive Sciences, Psychology, Linguistics
Exemplary Outcomes	Knowledge Management Systems, Knowledge Ontologies	Collaborative Work Processes, Employee Empowerment Mechanisms

information management (Ruggles, 1997): *Knowledge Generation, Knowledge Codification,* and *Knowledge Transfer.*

Knowledge Generation refers to the transformation of raw data or summarised information into actionable knowledge. A number of research problems can be thought of as belonging within this area. The first is the problem of *pattern recognition* (Brash, 2000), which is concerned with identifying useful patterns in data so that knowledge may be extracted from them. Questions related to *data mining* are relevant here, as is research in the field of *artificial intelligence* and *knowledge-based systems.* However, other research questions may also be relevant, such as *real-time knowledge capture* and *computer-supported groupware.*

Knowledge Codification is concerned with the process of codifying, categorising, and storing knowledge in an information system. One important research question here is *indexing* (Delesie and Croes, 2000), that is the appropriate data structuring schema to support knowledge discovery. Other relevant questions deal with problems of *knowledge acquisition* and *knowledge representation* (for example, *knowledge ontologies*).

Finally, Knowledge Transfer deals with the exchange of knowledge between individuals and organisations (O'Dell and Grayson, 1998). *User interfaces* in knowledge systems, *technology-based learning,* and *knowledge assessment* (Guns and Valikangas, 1998) are research issues that may be classified under this category.

'Soft' Research

The introduction of a knowledge tool may be a necessary, but it is definitely not an adequate condition of the successful implementation of knowledge management in an organisation (Gill, 1995). To this end, firms need to implement a surrounding *knowledge environment* (Irani and Sharp, 1997) that deals effectively with individual and organisation-wide aspects of managing knowledge as a corporate resource. *Collective learning* (Rzevski and Prasad, 1998), *collaboration and trust* (Constant et al., 1994), and *change management* (Burrows, 1994) are only some of the areas where 'soft' research issues related to KIM may become of importance.

Towards a More Accurate Definition of KIM

The aforementioned differences in departing points, scope, and expected outcomes in much of extant research in Knowledge and Information Management may serve, at least partially, to explain our difficulties when trying to define the area as a scientific field and portray its constituent elements. The differences between 'hard' and 'soft' approaches to KIM research may further mean that a single identifiable research field may simply just not exist. Instead, what we usually term as 'KIM research' may in reality hide two (or even more) separate research fields that, although intertwined and complementary, can be thought of as independent and distinguishable, even if only for analytical purposes.

However, such a hypothesis needs to be backed up by appropriate empirical evidence. To this end, a complementary analysis of empirical nature is needed to identify the pragmatics of ongoing KIM research and contribute towards enhancing our understanding of what the main research problems that constitute what we term as 'KIM research' are. The results of such an empirical analysis of more than 200 ongoing research projects in KIM are presented in the following section.

EMPIRICAL ANALYSIS:
KIM RESEARCH PROJECTS

The discussion that follows is based on the results of the so-called Integrated Programme Portfolio Analysis (IPPA), which is organised by the European Commission at regular intervals in order to provide a strategic overview on the response to calls for research proposals in the area of the 'Information Society Technologies' (IST) programme. The last IPPA exercise, on which this analysis is based, was carried out in July 2001. IPPA is conducted by a group of independent experts and examines the project characteristics from the technical perspective, the time to market, the risk profile of projects related to market dynamics, and so on. In this chapter, the analysis is limited on the part of IPPA dealing with research into Knowledge and Information Management (KIM).

Global Picture

Out of the 1,725 proposals funded by the European Commission in the first six calls of the IST Programme (1998-2001), 316 (more than 18% of the total) were marked as addressing the technological area of '*Knowledge and Information Management*' (KIM). Since this renders KIM the most popular of the technological areas addressed by the programme, it was decided to pursue a more detailed investigation of these projects to identify:

a)   The major research sub-topics and themes that can be grouped under the general heading 'Knowledge and Information Management.'

b)   The trends in KIM-oriented research, as well as the characteristics and directions of promising future research efforts.

c)   Suggestions and recommendations for the effective management of this large-scale research portfolio at the European level.

The KIM projects represent a total funding on behalf of the European Commission of 440 million euro (•440m), while the project participants themselves commit an equivalent amount of money in self-financing the research efforts, thus resulting in a breathtaking amount of nearly one billion euro (•1bn) devoted to European-wide research in Knowledge and Information Management. The sheer magnitude of this amount makes a more detailed analysis of the research outcomes a worthwhile endeavour.

Out of the 316 KIM projects, 235 (or 74.4%) are classified as Research and Technology Development (RTD) projects. This sample of 235 projects was used as a basis for all the analyses presented herein.

Analysing these projects regarding their distribution of projects per Key Action Line (KALs represent the smallest classification unit of research areas in the IST programme) reveals a rather fragmented picture. KIM research projects can be found under no less than 55 different Key Action Lines. The most popular of those is naturally KAL 2.1.2 (Knowledge Management) with 24 projects, followed by KAL 2.2.2/2.2.3 (Smart Organisations) with 17 projects, and KAL 6.1.1 (Future and Emerging Technologies) with 13 projects.

Given the great diversity and dissimilar nature of Key Action Lines that seem to attract Knowledge and Information Management projects, it was felt that the projects might belong to more than one coherent research theme, thus providing an initial indication that our theoretically driven hypothesis discussed in the previous section may prove to be true. It was therefore decided, apart from the overall statistical analysis discussed in the next section, to pursue a more in-depth investigation of the individual projects submitted under the most popular Key Action Lines to identify pertinent research themes and future research directions in KIM.

Project Profiles

The first type of analyses performed on the KIM projects were of the single-variable type, aimed at identifying the project profiles based on a number of characteristics. The KIM projects, as expected, are quite interdisciplinary in nature in terms of the technologies addressed. Figure 1 illustrates the most popular technologies addressed by KIM projects. These include *Visualisation, Virtual Environments, and Image Processing* (14% of projects), followed by *Optimisation Tools and Decision Support Systems* (13%), *Content Authoring Tools* (12%), and *Agent Technologies* (11%). Other technologies that seem to form the underlying basis for research and development in KIM include: *Mobile and Wireless Communications, Middleware and Distributed Systems*, and *Internet Technologies*.

Most of the KIM projects are horizontal in nature, addressing the *Cross Sector/Generic* category, as illustrated in Figure 2. Of the remainder, the interest seems to be almost evenly spread between *Administrations* (13%), *Education and Training* (13%), *Healthcare* (13%), *Cultural* (11%), and *Tourism* (11%).

Figure 1: Technologies addressed in KIM research

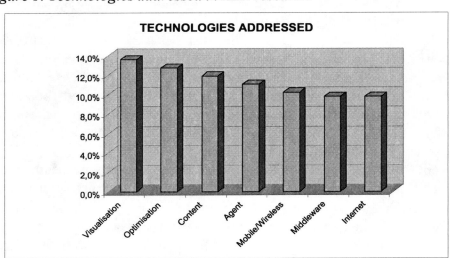

Figure 2: Industrial sectors addressed in KIM research

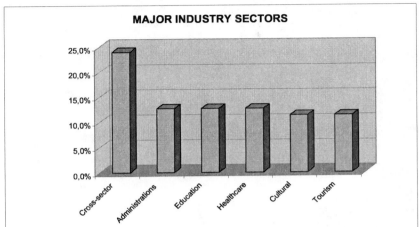

Figure 3: RTD vs. non-RTD Knowledge and Information Management projects

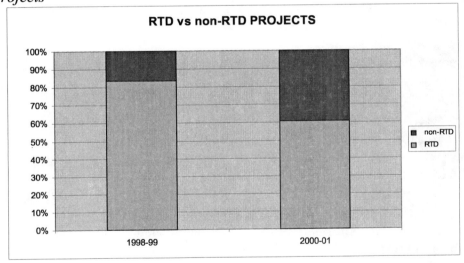

Identifying The Trends

A second-level analysis was then performed to identify major differences between earlier Knowledge and Information Management projects (submitted within 1998 and 1999) and more recent ones (submitted within 2000 and 2001). This comparative analysis yielded interesting results regarding the trends of KIM research through time. Firstly, there is a marked decrease in the number of Research and Technology Development projects, from 84% to 60% of the total, as shown in Figure 3. Non-RTD work in the context of the IST programme refers mainly to

Figure 4: Expected output of KIM research projects

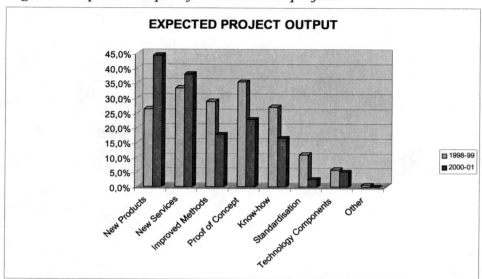

demonstration projects, dissemination and technology transfer actions, studies, and so on.

As the non-RTD work refers mostly to projects that aim at demonstrating the commercial potential of already developed technological solutions, the aforementioned decrease in the number of RTD projects may imply a gradual maturation of KIM as a research field, coupled with a corresponding uptake of more industrial practice-oriented work. This assumption is also supported by other analyses. More specifically, there is a clear shift from more 'revolutionary' project outputs (including proof-of-concepts, improved methods, increased know-how) to rather 'evolutionary' outcomes that are closer to the market (new products and services), as illustrated in Figure 4.

The above might suggest that the area of Knowledge and Information Management is moving towards a gradual assimilation of the prevailing paradigm, as indicated by the fall in research being done. If this is true, a new 'vision' might be required to indicate new research orientations for the future. However, to substantiate this finding and elaborate on what the new vision might be, the next section discusses the results of a detailed analysis of research themes as identified by an analysis of individual KIM projects. This analysis leads us to suggest a novel taxonomy of knowledge management and information management research.

TOWARDS A TAXONOMY OF KNOWLEDGE MANAGEMENT RESEARCH

The aforementioned empirical analysis suggests that a large and rather diverse number of research sub-themes are classified under the KIM research area. For example, in line with the theoretical analysis, a number of projects address corporate knowledge management applications, while some projects address primarily knowledge technologies (for example, technologies for knowledge representation and visualisation). This finding is also consistent with the preliminary results of the theoretical analysis of the literature and suggests that there might be an opportunity for drawing a list of sub-areas within the overall field of Knowledge and Information Management in the form of a taxonomy. It was therefore decided to pursue an exploratory analysis of individual projects to identify the most pertinent research themes and propose a more detailed classification of the KIM category.

To this end, a more detailed analysis was conducted on the KIM research projects. This analysis was based on examining the project scope and objectives as provided by the researchers themselves in the description of each research project. This analysis produced the following outcomes:

- The majority of projects submitted in the Knowledge Management Key Action Line address either the provision of Knowledge Management Services (66%) or the development of Knowledge Management Systems (31%). However, more than half of these projects (55%) do not directly contribute to research and technology development, while some address issues such as ontologies (24%), knowledge visualisation (17%), and semantics (14%).
- The projects submitted in the Smart Organisations Key Action Line address primarily the provision of Knowledge Services (such as knowledge trading) (47%), Application Service Provision (12%), with limited research on knowledge technologies (12%).
- In the Open FET Domain Key Action Line that deals with high-risk long-term research, things are expectedly very different. No common research themes can be easily identified as projects deal with issues ranging from algorithms and data management to neurocomputing and learning (either for humans or machines).
- Finally, the projects submitted under the other Key Action Lines address somewhat different research themes. The majority deals with Information Analysis Methods & Indicators (33%), while some address data mining and data warehousing research problems. Finally, a minority of projects deals with organisational information systems, either in the form of decision support tools or geographic information systems.

Figure 5: Taxonomy for research in knowledge and information management

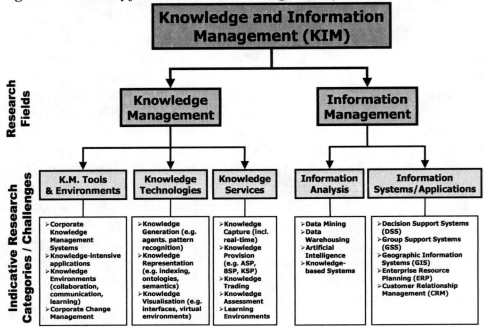

Based on an inductive pattern matching analysis on the above findings, a novel classification for Knowledge and Information Management research is proposed (illustrated in Figure 5). According to this, the KIM area consists of two domains that present different characteristics and research roadmaps: *Knowledge Management* and *Information Management*. Each of these two main research areas can be further divided into a number of more detailed research sub-themes and challenges as shown in the figure.

It must be noted that neither the list of research sub-themes nor the list of research problems and challenges identified in Figure 5 are meant to be exhaustive. Both the fields of knowledge management and information management are very lively research areas, and any attempt to provide anything but an *indicative* list of *current* research problems would be fruitless. Instead, the taxonomy aims to suggest that the portfolio of research issues commonly placed under the KIM 'umbrella' is so complicated and diverse that it deprives KIM of the coherency that should be identifiable in any distinct research field.

At the same time, however, the fact that research in Knowledge Management presents problems and issues that are identifiable from those typically associated with the more 'traditional' field of Information Management does not mean that talking about KIM in general makes no sense. There is a clear need, identified earlier in this chapter, for an interdisciplinary approach to the overall problem of managing information and knowledge as organisational assets. However, we contend that, due to the complexity of this problem, only by a careful analytical decomposition and focused research effort may the research community address the entirety of this overall problem effectively.

CONCLUSIONS

Following a combination of theoretical and empirical research, this chapter has suggested that the research fields of Knowledge Management and Information Management are analytically separable and present distinct research challenges and issues, despite the fact that they are quite commonly treated as synonymous in much academic research and organisational practice.

Furthermore, we have shown that the overall domain of Knowledge and Information Management seems to be at a stage where the prevailing research paradigm has started to present signals of potential weaknesses, since the research community seems to be less focused on research work in recent years. Based on this observation, we may arrive at a conclusion that a paradigm shift may be required. From a research policy perspective, this would present the challenge of identifying the next paradigm, and providing the research community with support to address the research themes necessary to realise this paradigm in the near future.

However, this conclusion should be treated cautiously as significant further research is needed to substantiate it beyond reasonable doubt. Indeed, we have based our observation by examining only research projects being funded by the Commission of the European Communities. Further to the restriction of our sample within the confines of Europe only, this choice presents us with an additional potential bias. The European Commission has a certain viewpoint as to what constitutes 'research,' which is heavily oriented towards applied research and near-commercial tool development. This may explain, at least in part, the bias we have identified towards the lack of basic research and the alleged trend towards less research work being carried lately.

However, the policy implications of our findings remain significant. The challenges associated with the research categories shown in the taxonomy we have suggested are quite different from each other, and some research issues have received much less attention by policy makers (including the European Commission itself) than others. For example, we believe that the *Knowledge Technologies* area has been rather overlooked in comparison with other sub-fields of Knowledge Management. This includes research work in a number of frontier domains such as knowledge representation (including ontological developments and semantics), knowledge visualisation (including interfaces for knowledge presentation and understanding), and knowledge analysis (including agent-based and data mining-based knowledge analyses). Furthermore, in the *Knowledge Management Tools and Environments* domain, an identifiable research challenge exists to drive the development of the so-called 'next generation' Knowledge Management systems that will transform the existing 'passive' knowledge repositories into 'active' learning environments. Further research efforts may address this issue in more detail by explicating the current research challenges within the field of Knowledge Management, and devising research and policy programmes that would address this unbalanced rate of development, which, if left unsupported, will undoubtedly hinder the likelihood of successful Knowledge Management application in organisations.

REFERENCES

Albert, S. (1997). *Managing Knowledge: Experts, Agencies, and Organisations.* Cambridge, UK: Cambridge University Press.

Argyris, C. (1994). *On Organisational Learning.* Cambridge, MA: Blackwell Publishers.

Brash, D. (2000). Developing and validating generic knowledge: An initial experience report. In Edwards, J. and Kidd, J. (Eds.), *Proceedings of the Knowledge Management Conference (KMAC 2000)*, July 17-18, Birmingham, UK.

Burrows, B. (1994). The power of information developing and knowledge based organisation. *Long Range Planning, 27*(1), 142-153.

Castells, M. (1996). *The Rise of the Network Society.* Cambridge, MA: Blackwell Publishers.

Constant, D., Kiesler, S. and Sproull, L. (1994). What's mine is ours, or is it? A study of attitudes about information sharing. *Information Systems Research, 5*(4), 400-421.

Currie, W. (1999). Revisiting management innovation and change programmes: Strategic vision or tunnel vision? *OMEGA: The International Journal of Management Science, 27,* 647-660.

Davenport, T. H. and Prusak, L. (1997). *Working Knowledge: How Organisations Manage What They Know.* Boston, MA: Harvard Business School Press.

Davenport, T. H., De Long, D. W. and Beers, M. C. (1998). Successful knowledge management projects. *Sloan Management Review, 39*(2).

Delesie, L. and Croes, L. (2000). Managing the variability of medical care: Fostering consensus, benchmarking, and feedback. In Edwards, J. and Kidd,

J. (Eds.), *Proceedings of the Knowledge Management Conference (KMAC 2000)*, July 17-18, Birmingham, UK.

Gill, T. G. (1995). High-tech hidebound: Case studies of information technologies that inhibited organisational learning. *Accounting, Management, and Information Technologies, 5*(1), 41-60.

Guns, W.D. and Valikangas, L. (1998). Rethinking knowledge work: Creating value through idiosyncratic knowledge. *Journal of Knowledge Management, 1*(4), 287-293.

Irani, Z. and Sharp, J. M. (1997). Integrating continuous improvement and innovation into a corporate culture: A case study. *The International Journal of Technological Innovation, Entrepreneurship, and Technology Management (Technovation), 17*(4), 199-206.

Laudon, K. C. and Laudon, J. P. (1998) *Management Information Systems: New Approaches to Organisation and Technology.* Englewood Cliffs, NJ: Prentice Hall.

Malhotra, Y. (1997). *Current Business Concerns and Knowledge Management.* Available online at: http://www.brint.com/interview/times.htm.

Marshall, N. and Brady, T. (2000). Knowledge management, knowledge guiding interests, and modes of action: Case studies from complex products and systems. In Edwards, J. and Kidd, J. (Eds.), *Proceedings of the Knowledge Management Conference (KMAC 2000)*, July 17-18, Birmingham, UK.

Nonaka, I. and Takeuchi, H. (1995). *The Knowledge Creating Company: How Japanese Companies Create the Dynamics of Innovation.* Oxford, UK: Oxford University Press.

O'Brien, J. (1999). *Management Information Systems: Managing Information Technology in the Internetworked Enterprise.* New York: McGraw Hill.

O'Dell, C. and Grayson, C. J. (1998). If only we knew what we know: Identification and transfer of internal best practices. *California Management Review, 40*(3), 154-174.

Ruggles, R. (1997). *Knowledge Tools: Using Technology to Manage Knowledge Better.* Ernst & Young Centre for Business Innovation Working Paper.

Rzevski, G. and Prasad, K. (1998). The synergy of learning organisations and flexible information technology. *AI and Society, 12*, 87-96.

Spiegler, I. (2000). Knowledge management: A new idea or a recycled concept? *Communications of the AIS, 14*(3). Available online at: http://cais.isworld.org/articles/3-14/article.htm.

Starr, J. (1999). *KMTool: Ideas for Sharing Knowledge.* Available online at: http://www.kmtool.net/vocabulary.htm.

Chapter II

Knowledge Economy: An Overview

Vlatko Ceric
University of Zagreb, Croatia

ABSTRACT

The dramatic development of information and communications technology, the increased speed of scientific and technological progress, and the increased global competition led to the growing importance of knowledge and technology for economy. Modern economy, therefore, increasingly includes features of knowledge economy, an economy based on production, distribution and use of knowledge. Also, more and more the growth of companies depends on innovation, and innovation is based on knowledge. This chapter presents an overview of knowledge economy. It describes the categorisation and a characteristic of knowledge, analyses features of knowledge assets, describes the reasons for the importance of information and communications technology for knowledge economy, and the economic aspects of knowledge assets. Finally, it describes the production, transmission and dissemination of knowledge, as well as the measurement of knowledge required for providing adequate economic indicators for the new economy.

INTRODUCTION

Influence of knowledge on economic activities has grown considerably in the last three centuries (Drucker, 1993). The first half of the eighteenth century brought the invention of technology, a combination of craft and skill with organised and systematic knowledge. The first encyclopaedia that contained a systematic description of all crafts as well as the first technical schools appeared in the second half of the eighteenth century. These proceedings helped to convert craft into methodology and led to the industrial revolution that caused a radical transformation of society by the use of technology.

In the last quarter of the nineteenth century, Frederick Taylor applied knowledge to the analysis and engineering of work. Taylor's approach resulted in a rapid increase of productivity of about 3.5-4.5% per year, thus knowledge became an important economic resource. Also, as a result of decades of gradual increase of productivity, the standard of living in developed countries increased remarkably. One of the consequences was the increase in funding for education from about 2% of GNP to 10% or more.

In the second half of the twentieth century, systematic application of knowledge in managing production and the service processes, as well as innovation, led to the development of the management function that became essential for further economic progress. An important role of management was to seek out what new knowledge is required to further increase economic output and how this knowledge can be made useful.

In the last two decades, ideas, knowledge and technology became increasingly important to economy. One of the key reasons for this was a dramatic development of information and communications technology that provided a cheap facility for manipulating, storing, distributing and accessing information that led to the growing knowledge intensity of economic activities. Other reasons include increased speed of scientific and technological progress that led to accelerate growth of quantity of scientific and technological knowledge, as well as increased global competition fuelled by globalisation of trade and massive deregulation that led to reduced costs.

The second section of this chapter describes the basic characteristics of knowledge economy and shows how economists treat knowledge in models of economic growth. The third section deals with categorisation of knowledge as well as with the specific characteristics that make it different from tangible goods. The fourth section deals with knowledge of intangible assets and reasons for their increasing significance in contemporary economy. Section five describes reasons for the importance of information and communications technology in knowledge economy, while section six describes the economic aspects of knowledge assets. The next section gives a brief discussion with several examples of knowledge management at a company level. The final section analyses production, transmission and dissemination of knowledge, as well as the measurement of knowledge required for providing adequate economic indicators for the new economy.

BASIC FEATURES OF KNOWLEDGE ECONOMY

Advances in technology and accumulation of knowledge largely determine the economic growth of developed countries. A key driver of growth in modern economy is *innovation* rather than production efficiency; innovation depends on knowledge and also creates new knowledge. Innovative products and services create new markets. Today in the computer industry, 70 percent of revenue comes from products that did not exist two years ago. While approximately 50,000 new products appear every year in the U.S., only a few thousand appeared in 1970 (McKenna, 1997).

Modern economy increasingly includes features of knowledge economy, an economy based on production, distribution and use of knowledge. Knowledge that transforms the economy may come in the form of technological innovation, development of new products and services, software development or complex problem solving.

A growing number of high-skilled knowledge workers, i.e., workers who manipulate symbols rather than machines, are employed in various areas of service economy like education, research and development, consultancy, management or software development. About 85 percent of Americans work in services, with 65 percent of them working in high-skilled areas, and these are the workers that create most of the wealth in modern economy (Wyckoff, 1996). The manufacturing process is also becoming knowledge based so that today intangible inputs, depending upon employee knowledge and skills, account for an average of 70 percent of the value of a car and for 85 percent of the value of hi-tech goods like CDs or chips (The World Economy Survey, 1996).

A range of knowledge-based products appear in the form of knowledge goods, digitised processes, digitised physical goods, and knowledge-enhanced physical goods and services (Choi and Whinston, 2000). Knowledge goods include goods that can be digitised and transferred over computer network, such as magazines, books, photographs or music. Digitised processes are products or services that rely on providers that have specialised knowledge, like Internet-based information search services. Everything that can be digitised and sent over computer network, like news, postcards, tickets, instructions or government forms, is considered as digitised physical goods. Knowledge-enhanced physical goods and services are built around products that cannot be digitised but have some components that are knowledge-based, like control of home security and appliances that is done by software.

On the country level, it is estimated that more than 50 percent of GDP in the major OECD economies are knowledge based (OECD, 1996). The fastest growth of output and employment is in the knowledge-intensive service sectors, such as education, communications and information, followed by high-technology industries such as computer, electronics and aerospace industries. The value added generated by knowledge-based industries in the OECD increased at an annual average rate of seven percent between 1985 and 1994, while the figure for a business sector as a whole was just over five percent.

Advances in technology are related to advances in knowledge that come via advances in science, research and development. Knowledge can significantly affect economic growth when it is embedded in technology that can be used in economic practice. However, new technology has not finished with its invention since inventions typically appear in rudimentary form, as examples of laser, transistor and radio demonstrate. Before new technology can become useful and efficient, it must pass through a long, complex and highly uncertain process including numerous improvements done by different groups of actors (Rosenberg, 1996).

An appropriate government policy is crucial in supporting economic growth by means of scientific and technological development. Such policy has to include support of education, training and research, as well as stimulate interaction between university and industry (OECD, 1996).

For a long period of time, economists realized that economic growth is influenced by knowledge and technology. Nevertheless, traditional models of economic growth correlated production and economic growth with labour, capital, materials and energy, while knowledge was treated as an external influence. It was only a decade and a half ago that economists explicitly incorporated knowledge into general economic equilibrium models in the framework of the endogenous growth theory (Romer, 1994). These models take into account that investments in knowledge can increase the productive capacity of the other factors of production by triggering improvement in organization of production, as well as by introducing new and improved products and services and thus raising returns of investment. However, it is not at all simple to treat knowledge as a production factor since there are serious and not yet completely understood differences in production, exchange and use of knowledge compared with production, exchange and use of conventional production factors.

FORMS OF KNOWLEDGE AND CHARACTERISTICS

A huge quantity of information is constantly being created and stored, but it does not mean that it is automatically turned into knowledge. Information becomes knowledge only when it enables action either by reading and applying it by humans or processing it by machines. Davenport and Prusak (1998) give the following definition of knowledge:

"Knowledge is a fluid mix of framed experience, values, contextual information, and expert insight that provides a framework for evaluating and incorporating new experiences and information. It originates and is applied in the minds of knowers. In organizations, it often becomes embedded not only in documents or repositories but also in organisational routines, processes, practices, and norms."

Codified and Tacit Knowledge

Knowledge appears in two basic forms, as codified and tacit knowledge (Nonaka and Takeuchi, 1995). *Codified knowledge* is knowledge that can be expressed in the explicit and formal way in books, journals, manuals or knowledge bases. This enables efficient and cheap storage, distribution, access, verification and reproduction of such knowledge by means of information and communications technology. This type of knowledge is typically gained by formal education and training.

Tacit knowledge is knowledge that people possess in their minds, and it is difficult to communicate or transform into explicit form. This sort of knowledge often appears as skills or competencies, and it is usually gained by experience or training. A lot of time is needed to be achieved and it is much more difficult to transfer to other people than codified knowledge. An example of tacit knowledge is an expert's understanding of how some complex system operates or how a particular technology can be used in various circumstances. Tacit knowledge is as important for economic purposes as explicit knowledge.

Codified and tacit knowledge are complementary, and one enables creation of the other. Not only that tacit knowledge can be transformed into codified knowledge, but also, by using new codified knowledge, new kinds of tacit knowledge may be developed (Nonaka and Takeuchi, 1995).

Know-What, Know-Why, Know-How and Know-Who

There are several types of knowledge relevant to knowledge economy (Lundvall and Johnson, 1994). *Know-what* is knowledge about facts, and this is the type of knowledge that experts have to possess. *Know-why* deals with scientific knowledge of laws and principles. This type of knowledge is the basis of technological development. Production of this kind of knowledge (research) and its reproduction (teaching) is typically done in organisations like universities. *Know-how* is related to skill, i.e., the ability to do something. This type of knowledge is typically developed and kept in individual firms. *Know-who* includes information about who knows what and who knows how to do what. This type of knowledge is of particular interest in modern economy since it has a need for different types of skills and knowledge that are dispersed in society.

Know-what and know-why are codified knowledge obtained via books, journals, manuals and other knowledge sources or by attending lectures. They are nearest to being market commodities. Know-how and know-who are more tacit knowledge, more difficult to codify or measure. Know-how is normally learned in direct contact between a student and his master, and is further developed through long experience via learning-by-doing. Know-who is typically learned through social practice in informal relations or professional societies.

Characteristics of Knowledge

Knowledge has some characteristics that considerably differ from the characteristics of traditional goods, and complicates its measurement and use in economic models. For example, knowledge remains with the seller even when the buyer has acquired it, so it can be sold to many buyers. Knowledge is not destroyed in consumption, and more units of the same knowledge add no additional value to one that possesses this knowledge. Knowledge also has a spillover effect — learning a task can enhance learning of a new task.

The value of knowledge is not known until it is purchased and used, while for tacit knowledge the value of knowledge is often not known until it is gone. Knowledge can become obsolete, and the lifetime of knowledge is highly uncertain and varies considerably for different types of knowledge. Knowledge embedded in emerging types of products or services that learn or adapt with use undergoes a change each time the product or service is used.

KNOWLEDGE ASSETS

In his seminal book, *Intangibles: Management, Measurement, and Reporting*, Baruch Lev defines knowledge asset (or intangible capital) as a "claim to future benefits that does not have a physical or financial embodiment" (Lev, 2001). He identifies three components of knowledge assets: discovery, organisational capital and human resources, which may appear either independently or in combination. Basic *discovery*-related knowledge assets are research and development (R & D), investment in information and communications technology, patents and innovations. The most important components of discovery are investments in R & D, and they are quite large — e.g., in 1998 R & D-to-sales ratio was 11.1 percent in software companies and 12.1 percent in pharmaceutical companies (Aboody and Lev, 2001). The estimated annual rates of return on R & D investment are also fairly high, between 20-35 percent (Hall, 1993). Contribution of basic research to corporate productivity and growth is found to be substantially larger that the contributions of other types of R & D like product development (Griliches, 1995), with the estimated contribution ratio being three to one in favour of basic research.

Organizational capital incorporates items such as brands, information and communications technology, software or customer acquisition costs. Since there are no reliable data on the investment of a firm in organisational capital, computer capital was used as an approximate measure of organisation capital, since investment in computers can be regarded as the proxy for investment in organisational change. It was shown that each dollar of computer capital is valued in the capital market at almost 10 dollars of the market value (Brynjolfsson and Yang, 1999), and this can be taken as the indicator of the value of organisational capital. Empirical research has proven the strong relation between investments in discovery and organisational capital, and company value and performance.

Although *human capital* (i.e., human resources) is widely regarded as one of the most important components for corporate success, there is no evidence of the existence of significant influence of investments in human capital (e.g., in training or compensation plans) on corporate value. Namely, companies did not publish any quantitative information on human resources, and the survey data does not give enough material for reliable conclusions.

Knowledge assets were created throughout the history of the human race with particular intensity in the period of major inventions like electricity, telephone, transistor and the laser. However, their economic importance exploded only in the last three decades. This explosion is due to the combination of two economic forces, *increased business competition* (market pull) fuelled by globalisation of trade and massive deregulation, and *appearance of information and communications technologies* (technology push), especially the Internet. All these led to the creation of new business models and made knowledge assets a major value driver of business. Modern companies use with intensity internal and external computer networks in order to enable close cooperation between employees, suppliers and customers.

Innovation becomes critical for the survival of companies. The number of professional workers engaged in innovation quite noticeably increased from 3.8 percent of all employees in 1980 to 5.7 percent in 1999 (Lev, 2001). The intensity of knowledge of world-manufactured exports was almost constant between 1970 and 1977, but since 1977 it has progressively increased from an index value of 0.71 in 1977 to 1.04 in 1995 (Sheehan and Tegart, 1998). Also, the economic output of the U.S. economy measured in tons is almost the same as it was a century ago but its real economic value is 20 times larger (Wolf, 1998). The added value is related with intangible components increasingly incorporated in products and services.

THE ROLE OF INFORMATION AND COMMUNICATIONS TECHNOLOGY IN KNOWLEDGE ECONOMY

The rapid development of information and communications technology (ICT) in the last two decades drastically changed the way knowledge is processed, stored, distributed and accessed. New ICT systems for computing, communications, scanning, imaging and storage are continuously being developed. A huge quantity of digitised material appeared and a substantial number of applications were developed. ICT equipment prices dropped dramatically in the last decade, e.g., the annual fall of computer prices was about 12 percent from 1987 to 1994, and about 26 percent from 1995 and 1999. The cost of transmitting one bit of data over a kilometre declined by three orders of magnitude between the mid-1970s and the beginning of the 1990s, permitting much more data to be transmitted over longer distances. All this had a major influence on the economy as a whole.

Digital technologies make processing, storage and accessing of information increasingly cheaper and easier. Huge quantities of information influence the operation of businesses and markets, and lead to creation of wealth through exploitation of information. An exceptionally strong influence of ICT on economy came from the explosive growth of computer networks, the Internet in particular. The Internet and the World Wide Web enable extremely fast and cheap distribution of knowledge (in the form of text, drawings, formulas, computer models, project plans, etc.). The cooperation in development of knowledge on a global scale, as well as distance learning, became a reality for millions of people.

Digitisation and networking also led to massive increase in codification of know-what and know-why parts of knowledge, and caused the shift in balance of the stock of knowledge. The shortage of tacit knowledge appeared, and the skills needed to handle codified knowledge became increasingly important (CSEC, 2000).

Knowledge in digital form can be stored on various media. Tacit knowledge is stored in the human brain, while codified knowledge was traditionally stored in books and journals. In the last 50 years, software appeared as an indispensable new medium for storage of codified knowledge (Armour, 2000). Software has the unique combination of desirable characteristics: it is persistent, quick to update and active. The active property of software means that software, which can easily and quickly be spread over great distances, can be applied to action simply by executing it (examples are technical or scientific calculation, control of plants and project management). Because of its valuable characteristics, a huge and rapidly growing quantity of knowledge from all possible sources is progressively being translated into this medium.

Information and knowledge are used both locally and globally. The main source of local information is legacy databases in companies as well as local networks (intranets), while the main source of distributed information is information stored on millions of servers and accessible via the World Wide Web. While information stored in databases is well structured and mostly textual, information on the Web is unstructured, a mixture of textual and non-textual, and prepared by a variety of individuals and organisations. In spite of this, the Web contains a wealth of useful information. If only one-tenth of the estimated one to two billon Web pages are useful and reliable, this makes the Web a huge information source. Such assumption was confirmed by the development of a library of computer science consisting of a huge number of valuable papers collected on the open Web (Lawrence et al, 1999).

Analysis of the so-called "deep Web" (or "invisible Web") have shown that databases and other sources, that can be reached via their entry Web pages but cannot be searched directly via search engines, are extremely rich. It was found that more than 200,000 deep Web sites presently exist, containing 400-500 times more information than "surface Web" with a three times higher quality (Bergman, 2000). Deep Web sites tend to be narrower, with a deeper content than the conventional Web sites.

In order to enable efficient search for information on the Web, numerous methods and techniques of search were developed and incorporated in search engines. These include text and image search, linguistic and intelligent approaches to search, exploiting the Web hyperlinking structure, software agents or natural language processing (Ceric, 2000). Huge information sources, either stored locally in companies, government and scientific institutions or available via the Internet, contain knowledge that is difficult to discover. Various methods used in data mining and knowledge discovery in databases, such as statistics and machine learning (Fayyad et al., 1996), enable the discovery of information characterisation, clustering of information and relation between different data. These methods are increasingly applied in Web mining, which includes both mining of Web content and Web usage mining (Cooley et al., 1997).

ECONOMICS OF KNOWLEDGE ASSETS

Knowledge assets are exposed to economic laws, just like physical ones. Lev (2001) provides a unified cost-benefit approach to the analysis of knowledge assets, and identified two drivers of benefits from knowledge assets and three cost drivers (value detractors). Value drivers include nonrivalry and network effects, while cost drivers are partial excludability, inherent risk and nontradability.

Value Drivers

Physical or financial assets are rival (scarce), as when someone uses an asset (e.g., computers or credit), it cannot be used by anybody else; also, the more a product is produced, the scarcer will this product be and its cost will be higher. On the contrary, knowledge assets are *nonrival* (nonscarce), since different users can use them simultaneously. For example, the use of specific software by one user does not prevent other users from exploiting it at the same time. Nonrivalry is related with the fact that knowledge assets typically have a large fixed cost and a very small marginal cost (usually related to reproduction and transmission). For example, while the development of complex software requires considerable investments, the cost of producing a CD or sending software over the Internet is negligible. Knowledge assets are therefore not scarce — just the opposite, the more these assets are produced and used, the lower the price. The scalability of knowledge assets is limited only by the size of the market.

The benefits of being a part of the *network* (e.g., mobile telephones network, or network of users of the Corel software suite) increase with the size of the network. A bigger network size increases the usefulness of a network and leads to more applications and better user manuals, helps facilities and lowers prices. Compatibility with the accepted standard is very important since this helps in expanding the network size and in reducing consumer uncertainty (Shapiro and Varian, 1999).

Cost Drivers

Knowledge assets are not without limitations, such as small markets. The principal limitation of knowledge assets is related to difficulties in managing and operating knowledge assets. For example, while the owners of tangible assets can secure them by precisely defined property rights, owners of knowledge assets that heavily invested in their creation cannot completely and effectively exclude others from the benefits of knowledge assets. This phenomenon is called *partial excludability*. For example, companies cannot prevent their employees from leaving the company after they have been given a substantial training. Besides, even when the company has the patent for a product, non-owners can enjoy spillovers due to imitation or copying. The role of management should be to use knowledge management techniques that give optimal benefit from one's own inventions, and also exploit discoveries of others in a legal manner.

The innovation process carries an inherent and considerable *risk* compared with physical or financial assets. A comparative study done by Kothari et al. (2000) has shown that the average earning risk associated with R & D is three times larger than the one associated with physical equipment. Basic research done in the early stage of the innovation process is carrying the highest risk (Rosenberg, 1996).

Promising management instruments for reducing the risk are R & D alliances or diversified portfolios of innovative projects (Lev, 2001).

While physical assets have their market price, there is no organised market for knowledge assets, i.e., they are basically *nontradable*. Nontradability is related with several problems. One of them is the problem with writing complete contracts that specify all eventualities of intangible investments and associated rights and responsibilities of the parties. Two other problems are in tiny marginal costs of producing results of investments in knowledge assets that do not support stable pricing, and problems with property rights for knowledge assets. As for the last problem, up to eight percent of all products and services worldwide are pirated, with costs to the U.S. alone estimated to be $200 billion annually (Lehman, 1996). Recently developed Internet-based markets in knowledge assets may lead to improvement of intangible assets tradability.

PRODUCTION, DISSEMINATION AND MEASUREMENT OF KNOWLEDGE

Production, Transmission and Dissemination of Knowledge

Production of fundamental knowledge is done primarily through basic research at universities and government laboratories, while production of knowledge oriented toward developing technology or creating new products or services is mostly done by applied or commercial research (OECD, 1996). Fundamental knowledge is the foundation for technological development and is regarded as a public good. Governments should therefore subsidise this kind of creation of knowledge in order to enable economic growth. However, the borderline between science and technology cannot be precisely marked; for example, it is well known that the search for a technological solution can trigger the creation of fundamental knowledge.

Knowledge transmission consists primarily of education, and is provided by universities. Properly trained researchers and professionals are necessary for producing and applying scientific and technological knowledge, as well as for further transmission of knowledge. Universities today are confronted with several problems in fulfilling their function: research budgets are decreasing, there is diminishing interest for careers in the field of science and a broad-based education has to be given to a growing number of students.

Knowledge dissemination throughout the economy is essential for stimulation of its wide use and for increasing the contribution of technology to production and service sectors. Knowledge distribution networks based at scientific institutions disseminate knowledge to economic and social institutions, and especially enterprises, that use the knowledge. Partnership between universities and industry helps in efficient transfer of useful knowledge as well as in enabling advanced training required by industry. Companies themselves must become learning organisations and also widely use opportunities of online learning.

Knowledge Measurement

The measurement of knowledge is necessary for obtaining realistic indicators of the economic activity in developed countries. These indicators then serve as guidance for policy decisions by governments and other economic actors. However, knowledge is extremely difficult to quantify and to price, thus indicators of knowledge growth are indirect and partial, and an unknown proportion of knowledge is uncodified and stored only in the minds of individuals (OECD, 1996).

Knowledge measurement is related to several problems. In the first instance, knowledge does not have a fixed volume, and its influence on the economy can vary from a very substantial to a very small one. It is difficult to predict how inputs dedicated to knowledge production will influence knowledge output; measurement of these inputs is also difficult since there are no knowledge accounts equivalent to traditional national accounts. New knowledge is not necessarily an addition to knowledge stock because of the obsolescence of knowledge stock components. Moreover, knowledge may be a flow rather than a stock. Finally, as we have seen in the previous section, the price of knowledge is difficult to stabilise since there are no knowledge markets.

Because of all this, new concepts of knowledge measurement need to be developed for measuring knowledge inputs and outputs, knowledge stocks and flows, knowledge networks and learning. This may include development of additional and improved indicators of acquisition and use of knowledge in industry, analysis of existing patent data, private and social rates of return, knowledge distribution, etc.

KNOWLEDGE MANAGEMENT AT THE COMPANY LEVEL

Success of the knowledge economy depends to a considerable extent on knowledge management at the company level. Davenport and Prusak (1998) have identified the following key factors of success of knowledge management projects: a knowledge-oriented culture, technical and organizational infrastructure, senior management support, a link to economics or industry value, a modicum of process orientation, clarity of vision and language, nontrivial motivation aids, some level of knowledge structure and multiple channels for knowledge transfer. We present several examples of good knowledge management practice.

Knowledge creation requires cooperation of people with different backgrounds, knowledge and experience since such group of people has no routine solutions at hand (Nonaka and Takeuchi, 1995). Matsushita company developed the first automatic bread-making machine by engaging three product divisions with different cultures. These divisions previously made rice cookers, toasters and coffeemakers, and food processors, and had quite different technical expertise. The first group had expertise in computer control, the second in induction heater technology and the third with rotating motors. In order to develop a common language and to start sharing knowledge, the company organized three-day meetings for middle managers, as well as a regular newspaper for factory workers. Such approach helped the company to reach the settled goal.

The second example illustrates management of a company's intellectual capital, and in particular of a company's patents. When Gordon Petrash became Dow Chemical's director of intellectual asset management, Dow had about 29,000 patents that were mostly unexploited since the company was not aware what these patents contained (Interview with Petrash and Stewart, 1994). Therefore, the huge quantity of knowledge contained in these patents was not being used either for the company or as the value that can be sold. Petrash and his group made the evaluation of patents to decide which patents the company could use, which could possibly be sold and which should be discarded. Discovering unused patents of value for the company offers great opportunity for the company, while discarding or selling patents that were of little value for the company saved the company around one million dollars in the first year and a half.

The third example deals with stimulating inventions in the company. 3M company has an excellent record in inventions, since it produces over 400 new products each year, and gets about one-third of its revenues from products that are less than four years old (Davenport and Prusak, 1998). Such success cannot be achieved without intensive knowledge transfer in the company in all phases of invention development, since many people with different knowledge have to cooperate in solving various problems that appear in the process of invention. Researchers in the company can spend 15 percent of their time on personal research interest, and are entitled to apply for research grants and engage other employees in their projects. 3M also organizes regular meetings and an annual three-day knowledge fair where their researchers have the opportunity to meet and exchange ideas and plans. Besides, all researchers have access to the company's online database of technology knowledge. All these create the opportunity for researchers not only to access the knowledge, but also to meet with other researchers and share knowledge and ideas with them.

CONCLUSIONS

The production and the use of ideas and knowledge has increasingly become the source for economic growth in modern economy, strongly influenced by global markets, development of information and communication technology, and rapid scientific progress. Some visible results of knowledge economy are new knowledge-based products and services, intensified personalisation of products and services, Web-based global markets, drastically increased accessibility of information and ability to find relevant information, fast and cheap communication and cooperation on a global scale, as well as online education.

With knowledge becoming the key asset in economy, companies must be reengineered in such a way as to encourage the creation and use of knowledge. Complex organisations of today with highly specialized workers doing simple jobs must be transformed into simpler organisations with flexible, autonomous and highly skilled workers capable of performing demanding and changeable tasks. In order to survive in a demanding and competitive market, enterprises gradually have to become learning organisations with a long-term education and training policy, and an information and communication infrastructure enabling online learning, information access, cooperation and communication. They must establish a system for collection, organisation and maintenance of relevant information, as well as for analysing this information and use data mining techniques for distilling knowledge out of information. The use of knowledge management approaches and techniques needs to ensure appropriate management of sophisticated intangible assets.

Research and educational institutions are confronted with new challenges related to specific characteristics of intangible assets and use of constantly changing information and communications technology. Research institutions have to deal with a lack of appropriate approach to knowledge measurement, i.e., with the need for a new approach in measuring knowledge inputs and outputs, knowledge stocks and flows, knowledge network and learning. Knowledge measurement is necessary for obtaining realistic indicators of the economic activity, and they also serve as guidance for policy decisions by governments and other economic actors. Educational institutions need to find appropriate models for education and lifelong learning, especially online education with minimal or no contact between teachers and students, using information and communications technology.

Policy makers have two basic challenges. First, instead of overestimating the value of individual and direct research and development grants, they must ensure appropriate financing of fundamental public-funding research at university and government institutions, in order to provide its huge indirect value to society and economy (Nelson and Romer, 1996). They also have to give strong support to all stages and forms of education, having in mind the role of education in innovation and formation of knowledge workers. Another major policy-making issue is to combat against widening of the "digital gap" between the poor and the rich. Those who earn most have the best opportunities for education and the best access to information, which gives them the best chance for getting the highest salaries and having the highest job security. Therefore, it is vitally important that access to information and education be equal for everybody; otherwise rich people, regions and nations become richer while poor people, regions and nations became poorer, leading to growing social inequality and instability.

REFERENCES

Aboody, D. and Lev, B. (2001). *The Productivity of Chemical Research and Development. Working Paper.* New York University, Stern School of Business.

Armour, P. G. (2000). The case for a new business model: Is software a product or a medium? *Communications of the ACM, 43*(8), 19-22.

Bergman, M. K. (2000). *The Deep Web: Surfacing Hidden Value. White Paper.* BrightPlanet, accessible online at: http://www.brightplanet.com/deepcontent/tutorials/DeepWeb/.

Brynjolfsson, E. and Yang, S. (1999). The intangible costs and benefits of computer investments: Evidence from the financial markets. *Proceedings of the International Conference on Information Systems*, Atlanta, Georgia, December 1997. Revised April 1999.

Ceric, V. (2000). New methods and tools for the World Wide Web search. *Journal of Computing and Information Technology–CIT, 8*(4), 267-276.

Choi, S.-Y. and Whinston, A. B. (2000). *The Internet Economy: Technology and Practice.* Austin, TX: SmartEcon Publishing.

Cooley, R., Mobasher, B. and Srivastava, J. (1997). Web mining: Information and pattern discovery on the World Wide Web. *Proceedings of the 9th International Conference on Tools with Artificial Intelligence (ICTAI' 97)*, Newport Beach, CA.

CSEC. (2000). *A Primer on the Knowledge Economy.* Prepared by Houghton, J. and Sheehan, P. Centre for Strategic Economic Studies, Victoria University. Accessible online at: http://www.cfses.com/primer.htm.

Davenport, T. H. and Prusak, L. (1998). *Working Knowledge: How Organizations Manage What They Know.* Boston, MA: Harvard Business School Press.

Drucker, P. F. (1993). From capitalism to knowledge society. In Drucker, P. F. (Ed.), *Post-Capitalist Society.* New York: HarperCollins. Reprinted in Neef (1997).

Fayyad, P. S. U., Piatetsky-Shapiro, G., Smyth, P. and Uthurusamy, R. (Eds.). (1996). *Advances in Knowledge Discovery and Data Mining*. New York: MIT Press.

Griliches, Z. (1995). R & D and productivity: Econometric results and measurement issues. In Stoneman, P. (Ed.), *Handbook of the Economics of Innovation and Technological Change*. Oxford: UK Blackwell.

Hall, B. (1993). Industrial research during the 1980s: Did the rate of return fall? Brookings papers on economic activity. *Microeconomics*, 2, 289-393.

HLEG. (2000). The intangible economy impact and policy issues, C. Eustace. Report of the European high-level expert group on the intangible economy. *European Commission*. Accessible online at: http://europa.eu.int/comm/enterprise/services/business_services/publications.htm.

Interview with Petrash, G. and Stewart, T. (1994). Your company's most valuable asset: Intellectual capital. *Fortune*, October 3.

Kothari, S.P., Laguesse, T. and Leone, A. (2000). *Capitalization Versus Expensing: Evidence on the Uncertainty of Future Earnings from Capital Expenditures Versus R&D Outlays*. Working paper. University of Rochester, Simon Graduate School of Business.

Lawrence, S., Giles, C. L. and Bollacker, K. (1999). Digital libraries and autonomous citation indexing. *IEEE Computer*, 32, 67-71.

Lehman, B. (1996). Intellectual property: America's competitive advantage in the 21st century. *Columbia Journal of World Business*, *31*(1), 6-16.

Lev, B. (2001). *Intangibles: Management, Measurement, and Reporting*. Washington, DC: Brookings Institution Press.

Lundvall, B.-A. and Johnson, B. (1994). The learning economy. *Journal of Industry Studies*, *1*(2), 23-42.

McKenna, R. (1997). *Real Time: Preparing for the Age of the Never Satisfied Customer*. Boston, MA: Harvard Business School Press.

Neef, D. (Ed.). (1997). *The Knowledge Economy*. Boston, MA: Butterwords-Heinemann.

Neef, D., Siesfeld, G. A. and Cefola, J. (Eds.). (1998). *The Economic Impact of Knowledge*. Boston, MA: Butterwords-Heinemann.

Nelson, R. R. and Romer, P. M. (1996). *Science, Economic Growth and Public Policy Challenge*. March/April, 9-21. Reprinted in Neef et al. (1998).

Nonaka, I. and Takeuchi, H. (1995). *The Knowledge Creating Company*. Oxford: Oxford University Press.

OECD. (1996). The knowledge-based economy. In *Science, Technology and Industry Outlook*, OECD, Paris. Accessible online at: http://www1.oecd.org/dsti/sti/s_t/inte/prod/kbe.htm.

OECD. (2001). *The New Economy: Beyond the Hype. The OECD Growth Project*. Accessible online at: http://www.oecd.org/oecd/pages/home/displaygeneral/0,3380,EN-home-33-nodirectorate-no-1-33,FF.html.

Romer, P. (1994). The origins of endogenous growth. *The Journal of Economic Perspectives*, *8*, 3-22.

Rosenberg, N. (1996). Uncertainty and technological change. In Landau, R. et al. (Eds.), *The Mosaic of Economic Growth*. Stanford University Press. Reprinted in Neef et al. (1998).

Shapiro, C. and Varian, H. (1999). *Information Rules*. Boston, MA: Harvard Business School Press.

Sheehan, P. and Tegart, G. (Eds.). (1998). *Working for the Future: Technology and Employment in the Global Economy*. Melbourne: Victoria University Press.

The World Economy Survey. (1996). *The Economist*, September 28.

Wolf, M. (1998). The bearable lightness. *Financial Times*, August 12.

Wyckoff, A. (1996). The growing strength of services. *OECD Observer*, 200(June).

Chapter III

Simulation Modelling: The Link Between Change Management Approaches

Wendy L. Currie and Vlatka Hlupic
Brunel University, UK

ABSTRACT

Although change management approaches have been widely discussed in the business and management literature for several decades, not many publications address the role of simulation modelling in supporting these approaches. This chapter investigates several management innovation and change programs, including TQM, JIT, BPR, Process Innovation and Knowledge Management, and discusses how simulation modelling could increase their effectiveness. These change management approaches are compared and contrasted, and the applicability of simulation modelling to support the principles of these methods is investigated. It is argued that simulation could be viewed as a missing link between these approaches.

INTRODUCTION

Organizations continuously need to adapt to new conditions and respond to competitive pressures. As a response to this need for constant change and improvement, various change management approaches have been developed. The subject of managing innovation and change has been widely discussed in the business and management literature for several decades. Every few years, a new management philosophy, method or technique (or panacea or fad) is developed which is believed to enhance business performance (Land, 1996) that emanate from North America and are developed by practicing management consultants.

This chapter investigates five management innovation and change programs: Total Quality Management (TQM), Just in Time (JIT), Business Process Re-engineering (BPR), Process Innovation (PI) and Knowledge Management (KM) in the context of their methodological similarities and suitability for simulation modelling. These change management approaches are discussed in chronological order beginning with TQM and ending with the currently popular Knowledge Management. They are compared and contrasted, and the applicability of simulation modelling to support the principles of these methods is investigated.

The study has revealed that, although these approaches are developed from different disciplinary or functional areas within management, they share a common set of key characteristics. For example, they advocate a company-wide approach to managing change, they seek to change the philosophy or culture of the organization, they are developed largely by management consultancies rather than the academic community, and they are intended to improve business performance. To be successful, they must be top-down led and managed. Simulation models may be used to measure their impact on business processes and performance.

The history of these change management programs shows that, eventually their popularity and applicability declines and they are replaced by 'new' panaceas which, although labeled differently, are in many ways similar to their predecessors. The main objective of all these panaceas is to improve business processes, reduce costs and provide better products and services to customers. This chapter explores the role of simulation modelling in achieving these objectives.

The chapter is structured as follows. First an overview of five management innovation and change programs is given and the concept of simulation modelling is introduced. Subsequently, the suitability of this method to support change management programs is discussed. The five management panaceas are then compared and contrasted from a methodological and simulation modelling perspective, and the conclusions present the main findings of this research and identify future trends in this area.

BACKGROUND RESEARCH

The analysis of the relevant literature reveals that there have been very few comparative studies that consider the use and effectiveness of management innovation and change programs (Currie, 2000). However, one such study by Waterson et al. (1997) analyzed the results of 12 manufacturing practices: Business Process Re-engineering (BPR), Supply-chain Partnering, Outsourcing,

Learning Culture, Empowerment, Team-Based Working, Total Productive Maintenance, Concurrent Engineering, Integrated Computer-Based Technology, Manufacturing Cells, Just-In-Time Production (JIT) and Total Quality Management (TQM).

The study revealed that JIT and TQM were among the most commonly used manufacturing practices. Yet even the most prevalent practices were used either "not at all" or "a little" in over a third of sites (the sample was 564 manufacturing sites across 15 manufacturing sectors ranging from 150 to 1,000 employees). It was further found that improving quality was the main reason given for introducing TQM; cost reduction was given for BPR; and responsiveness to customers was the main motive for introducing JIT. These practices were deemed to be the most successful in achieving their different objectives of quality, cost reduction and responsiveness to customers compared with other practices, although a proportion of companies in each case had experienced failure.

Total Quality Management (TQM)

TQM was first developed by U.S. writers such as Crosby (1979), Deming (1982) and Juran (1986) in the post-war period. It has widespread appeal in both the academic and practitioner communities. This is largely because it offers a company-wide perspective on managing change that includes all members of an organization, from top management to operational and clerical personnel. TQM is sometimes referred to in the literature as an example of Japanese management methods and techniques. Indeed, there was a spate of management books in the early to mid-1980s which linked Japanese manufacturing success with the effective design and implementation of TQM. Such a position led to confusion and misunderstanding since the roots of TQM are found in the U.S., though the theory and practice was later transferred to Japan in the post-war period along with other Western-based management methods and techniques, such as management accounting and practice (Currie, 1994).

TQM is concerned with quality improvement on a company-wide basis. It is a comprehensive approach to improving competitiveness, effectiveness and flexibility through planning, organizing and understanding all the activities and tasks undertaken by people within an organization. The core of TQM is about improving customer and supplier relationships. In this context, customers and suppliers may be either internal or external to the company. For example, a purchasing manager may deal with an external supplier, or an internal accountant may liaise with the sales department of the same company. Whatever the exchange, the notion of suppliers serving their customers is central to the practice of TQM. The key objective is for suppliers to continually seek to improve the way they deal with their customers (internal and external). This is thought to have a positive effect on a company's overall performance as all employees are engaged in the change process. One of the main problems in implementing TQM is that it needs to be a part of company culture, and the changes that it brings are incremental.

Just-In-Time (JIT)

Just-in-Time in general relates to methods aimed at reducing inventory levels. Many authors throughout the 1980s concentrated their attention on the advantages to be gained by incorporating Just-In-Time (JIT) methods and techniques into their production management strategies and operations. The background to much of this interest was a fear that manufacturing in the western world (North America, Canada and Europe, in particular) was experiencing industrial and economic decline. Hayes and Abernathy (1980) argued convincingly that the North American manufacturing industry was being seriously challenged by overseas competitors who could compete more favorably on labor, price, quality and cost. This fuelled further interest in the 1980s with the publication of work, some theoretical and others empirically based, on how industrialized nations could avoid further economic decline (Hirst and Zeitlin, 1989).

As a result of serious economic problems such as rising unemployment, poor investment in education and training, skills shortages, severe global competition for manufacturing goods, lack of investment in new technology, and inefficient manufacturing and production methods and practices, many writers embarked upon research into cross-national comparisons to identify countries, industries and companies with 'world-class' manufacturing strategies (Schonberger, 1986). One conclusion of much of this research was that Japanese manufacturing methods, which included TQM and JIT, which were being used in some of the more successful Japanese manufacturing companies, were producing benefits resulting in greater efficiency, productivity and profitability than could be observed in many U.S. and European manufacturing firms.

Similarly to TQM, JIT was developed in the west and has been adapted by the Japanese to suit their culture (Shingo, 1989). On a comparative level, there is some evidence to show that, in western countries (North America and the UK in particular), the JIT philosophy is perceived in much narrower terms. Gilbert (1989) contends that many commentators on JIT in western manufacturing companies concentrate on a single JIT method or technique, such as inventory control, and so fail to grasp the 'JIT philosophy.' JIT is also discussed in the context of its cost advantages in manufacturing (Voss and Robinson, 1987). As with TQM, there were numerous contributions on the philosophy and practice of JIT from the academic and practitioner communities throughout the 1980s. While JIT continues to be of interest, it too has been somewhat eclipsed by the more recent concepts of BPR, Process Innovation and Knowledge Management.

Business Process Re-Engineering (BPR)

Business process re-engineering (BPR), or *re-engineering*, emerged in the late 1980s and early 1990s as a new approach to managing innovation and change. It was designed to be highly prescriptive since it advocated that managers should constantly seek new and improved methods and techniques for managing and controlling core and service business processes. A more cynical interpretation is that BPR was a euphemism for 'Big Personnel Reductions' (Kavanagh, 1994), as it called for the ambitious restructuring of organizations through *downsizing* and *delayering* of managerial hierarchies and functions. In an article entitled, "Re-engineering work: don't automate, obliterate," Hammer (1990) claims the essence of re-engineering is about 'discontinuous thinking' and the relinquishing of "outdated rules and fundamental assumptions that underlie operations." It is a move away from linear and sequential thinking to a holistic, all-or-nothing, perspective on strategic change in organizations. Managers are criticized for *thinking deductively*. That is, defining a problem and then seeking its resolution by evaluating a number of possible remedies.

As an alternative, Hammer and Champy (1993) make the case for *inductive thinking*. This is to "recognize a powerful solution and then seek the problems it might solve, problems the company probably doesn't even know that it has." Other writers suggest that re-engineering is about serving the external environment through improved customer service and not simply about meeting a narrow range of internal performance targets. Thus, "Re-engineering is a radically new process of organizational change that many companies are using to renew their commitment to customer service" (Janson, 1993). But some writers question re-engineering's claims to radicalism and novelty, and also the notion that organizations can engage in a process of 'collective forgetting,' of wiping the slate clean and starting with *a blank sheet of paper* (Grint et al., 1995).

As opposed to incremental and piecemeal approaches to strategic planning and change, Hammer contends that re-engineering is not a step-by-step, incremental approach. Rather it is a radical innovation and change program. It is intended to *revolutionize* all the components that make up an organization. This includes processes, products, services, people and technologies. Neither is it about *fixing things*, nor propping up a "creaking management process or functional structure" (Kavanagh, 1995). It can be applied in private and public sector organizational settings, and is therefore not simply about improving bottom-line performance. According to its supporters, re-engineering is not simply a quick-fix approach for managers seeking to improve the efficiency of outdated administrative functions, since its fundamental message concerns long-term organizational transformation.

Numerous leading organizations have conducted BPR in order to improve productivity and gain competitive advantage. Yet regardless of the number of companies involved in re-engineering, the rate of failure in re-engineering projects is over 50% (Hammer and Champy, 1993). Some of the frequently mentioned problems related to BPR include the inability to accurately predict the outcome of a radical change, difficulty in capturing existing processes in a structured way, shortage of creativity in process redesign, the level of costs incurred by implementing the new process or inability to recognize the dynamic nature of the processes.

Process Innovation

Perhaps as a result of direct competition with Hammer and Champy (1993), Davenport (1993) developed the concept of *process innovation,* which he claimed was different from process improvement. In short, process innovation was an ambitious management change program designed to "fuse information technology and human resource management" for the purpose of improving business performance. As with BPR, process innovation focuses upon company-wide innovation and change, and is not intended to be a managerial 'quick fix' to resolve short-term functionally based, operational problems. According to Davenport (1993), "Process innovation combines the adoption of a process view of the business with the application of innovation to key processes. What is new and distinctive about this combination is its enormous potential for helping any organization achieve major reductions in process cost or time, or major improvements in quality, flexibility, service levels or other business objectives."

As a response to a competitor in the form of business process redesign or re-engineering (BPR), Davenport argues that the term *process innovation* is more appropriate for encapsulating an ambitious innovation and change program for a number of reasons. Thus, "Re-engineering is only part of what is necessary in the radical change process; it refers specifically to the design of a new process. The term process innovation encompasses the envisioning of new work strategies, the actual process design activity, and the implementation of the change in all its complex technological, human and organizational dimensions." Davenport (1993) outlines a framework for process innovation which consists of five steps (p.24): (i) identifying processes for innovation; (ii) identifying change levers; (iii) developing process visions; (iv) understanding existing processes; and (v) designing and prototyping the new process.

This framework shows many similarities with the work of Porter and Millar (1985) and McFarlan (1984), not to mention BPR as advocated by Hammer and Champy since it invites managers to carefully consider their innovation and change strategies. Along with the previous authors, Davenport's work is prescriptive since it advocates that senior managers should engage in 'process-oriented thinking.' Yet unlike the previous studies, the above framework for process innovation places a greater emphasis on perceiving business activities as a series of interrelated processes, with the recommendation that firms should examine their processes to eliminate or develop new processes. One of the attractions of process innovation is that recent developments in information and communications technologies have led to functional integration between and within companies, suppliers and customers.

Knowledge Management

Knowledge management is the latest (and still popular) change management programme. It is apparent corporate knowledge and knowledge management are becoming increasingly important for modern organizations. In turbulent business environments, one of the main sources of lasting competitive advantage is knowledge (Nonaka and Takeuchi, 1995). Knowledge exists in a variety of places and formats, including databases, intranets, filing cabinets and peoples' heads. Information systems have the potential to assist in the codification, generation and transfer of knowledge. At the moment, however, the majority of knowledge management systems are designed to deal with structured data, where information is directly entered into fields or can be categorised in some manner. This tendency is reflected on the research pertaining to these systems. However, the effective management of knowledge involves more than simply exploiting the data held on information systems. It also requires attention to the 'softer' parts of the corporate knowledge base, as found in the human and cultural aspects of businesses, particularly the experiences and tacit knowledge of employees (Savage, 1996; Starr, 1999).

The concept of knowledge management has emerged due to a change in business trends, which have evolved from an environment that was predictable and incremental, to one that is radical and discontinuous (Nonaka and Takeuchi, 1995). As part of this evolution, Malhotra (1997) describes "knowledge in the minds of organisational members as increasing in value as a resource." However, much care needs to be taken during the information management process, as information overload, often due to the Internet, is thought to be responsible for the sudden proliferation in unstructured data that exists in many organizations (Moad, 1998).

Knowledge management is essentially an organizing principle aimed at, similarly to other change management approaches, satisfying, and where possible, exceeding customer expectations. By providing the right information, to the right people at the right time, knowledge management techniques and software applications enable companies to design their operational processes to be truly dynamic (Malhotra, 1997) and human resources to be truly effective.

The normative literature has been unable to agree on a definition or even the concept of the term 'knowledge management' (Beijerse, 1999; Hlupic et al., 2002). A possible reason for the vagueness and ambiguity is that the word knowledge means different things to different people. An additional factor, which creates confusion, is that there are many different types of knowledge, namely, explicit knowledge where the information is easy to understand and financially tangible, and tacit knowledge which is difficult to document or categorise and is non-financially tangible (Davenport and Prusak, 1998).

Furthermore, even though there are several definitions within the literature, it is increasingly evident that these do not adopt a multi-disciplinary approach. Indeed they often adopt a managerial perspective that does not accommodate the capabilities of information systems. Sveiby (1999) attempts to explain the concept of knowledge management by analysing research publications in this field. He claims that the people involved in knowledge management can be divided into two categories. The first one is where people come from a background which is computer and/or information science oriented who perceive knowledge to be an object and knowledge management refers to 'Management of Information.' The second category consists of people from a philosophy, psychology, sociology or business/management who consider knowledge to be related to processes and knowledge management to be the 'Management of People.' The 'Organisation Level' concentrates its focus on the organisation whereas the 'Individual Level' refers to where focus in research and practice is placed on the individual.

The benefits of knowledge management are apparent and versatile. Sustainable organisational competence is a factor of organisational capacity to create new knowledge through a continual learning process (Argyris, 1994). At present information systems simply support organisational structures to perform the functions of information collection and dissemination. Leveraging companies towards learning organizations requires the synergistic development of information systems with organisational structures and the application of knowledge management principles to enable "intelligent" information processing and utilisation based on user needs and organisational effectiveness (Rzevski and Prasad, 1998).

Having considered an overview of TQM, JIT, BPR, PI and KM, it seems that all of these management innovation and change panaceas offer solutions to ongoing business and managerial problems, and claim to facilitate business improvement. Yet the rhetoric surrounding their success is always more convincing than the reality. Indeed, there are now many criticisms about the lack of success of these panaceas in the workplace. Simulation modelling is therefore considered as a means by which business processes may be analyzed and evaluated, prior to implementing large-scale change.

SIMULATION MODELLING

According to Pidd (1989) simulation modelling can be defined as follows: "The basic principles are simple enough. The analyst builds a model of the system of interest, writes a computer program which embodies the model and uses a computer to initiate the system's behavior when subject to a variety of operating policies." Thus the most desirable policy may be selected.

Simulation modelling could offer a great potential in modelling and analyzing business processes. For example, these models can represent different samples of parameter values, such as arrival rates or service intervals, which can help identify process bottlenecks and suitable alternatives. Simulation models can provide a graphical display of process models that can be interactively edited and animated to show process dynamics.

Business process modelling tools are continuously being released on the software market (e.g., Process Charter, ARIS Toolkit, IDEF, Meta Workflow Modeller, Process Mapping and WorkSmart Analysis). Many of these tools represent business processes by graphical symbols, where individual activities within the process are shown as a series of rectangles and arrows. A majority of software tools for business process modelling have an origin in a variety of process mapping tools that provide the user with a static view of the processes being studied. Some of these tools provide basic calculations of process times. Other, more sophisticated tools allow some attributes to be assigned to activities and enable some form of process analysis. However, most of these tools are not able to conduct 'what if' analysis. Nor are they able to show a dynamic change in business processes and evaluate the effects of stochastic events and random behavior of resources. Simulation modelling, on the other hand, offers wider opportunities for understanding business processes. Simulation software tools are able to model dynamics of the processes, such as the build up of queues. This may be shown visually which enables the generation of creative ideas on how to redesign existing business processes. Some of the examples of simulation modelling tools include ARENA, AutoMod, EDTaylor, SIMPROCESS, Simple++, Simul8 and WIT-NESS. Simulation models of business processes can help overcome the inherent complexities of studying and analyzing businesses, and therefore contribute to a higher level of understanding and improving these processes. In terms of the business environment, simulation models usually focus on the analysis of specific aspects of an organization, such as manufacturing or finance.

There are relatively few examples of using simulation for business process modelling available in the literature. The majority of these publications were written by simulation modelling practitioners rather than business analysis specialists. One article on business process simulation stresses that over 80% of BPR projects used static flowcharting tools for business process modelling. Yet static modelling tools are deterministic and do not enable the evaluation of alternative redesigned processes (Gladwin and Tumay, 1994). The use of business process modelling tools is usually focused on modelling current business processes, without a systematic approach to the evaluation of alternatives. On the other hand, simulation models can incorporate and depict dynamic and random behavior of process entities and resources. A physical layout and interdependencies of resources used in processes under consideration can be shown visually, and the flow of entities among resources can be animated using simulation as a modelling tool.

SIMULATION MODELLING AND CHANGE PANACEAS

Simulation models provide quantitative information that can be used for decision making and can be regarded as problem understanding rather than problem-solving tools. There are several characteristics of simulation that make it suitable for business process modelling (Paul et al., 1998):

- A simulation model can be easily modified to follow changes in the real system and as such can be used as a decision support tool for continuous process improvement.
- A process-based approach (world view) in simulation modelling terminology relates to a time-ordered sequence of interrelated events which describes the entire experience of entity as it flows through the system.
- The flow of information within and between business processes can be modeled as the flow of temporary entities between processing stations.
- A simulation model of non-existing business processes can be developed and used for process design (rather than for redesign).
- Simulation models can capture the behavior of both human and technical resources in the system.
- The visual interactive features of many simulation packages available on the market enables a graphical display of dynamic behavior of model entities, showing dynamic changes in state within processes.
- Simulation model can incorporate the stochastic nature of business processes and the random behavior of their resources.

It could be claimed that the benefits of using simulation for business process modelling are numerous (Profozich, 1998). Simulating the effects of redesigned processes before implementation improves the chances of getting the processes right at the first attempt. Visual interactive simulation models together with a variety of graphical output reports can demonstrate the benefits of redesigned processes which is useful for business process re-engineering approval. Simulation could also be useful for focusing 'brainstorming' meetings, where various new ideas can be tested using a simulation model, and informed decisions can be made on the basis of model results.

Simulation Modelling and TQM

The main objective of TQM is to improve competitiveness and effectiveness through planning, organizing and understanding activities undertaken by people within an organization. Simulation models can incorporate business activities undertaken by employees and provide a graphical display of tasks undertaken by different workers, their duration and sequence, dynamic changes of activities and any potential bottlenecks that can be discovered. As such, simulation models could be used regularly as decision support tools for continuous improvement. For example, a simulation model of a production system could be used for investigating operating strategies that would reduce the size of inventory, machine cycle times, assess various scheduling rules or reduce the level of faults. By doing this, any changes to be done to the real system could be tested on the model to avoid risks of inadequate decisions, and business activities could then be better understood. Other examples of the use of simulation in the context of TQM include benchmarking, process design and product or service design. When changes tested on the model are implemented in the real system, effectiveness of the system should be improved as well as the competitiveness of an organization.

Simulation Modelling and JIT

At the same time as JIT has been viewed as a management philosophy of integrated manufacturing, planning and control in Japan, the western countries often see JIT in the narrow context of inventory control. Simulation modelling can support both approaches to JIT. Real-time models of an integrated manufacturing system could incorporate models of inventory control systems, production design, resource planning and scheduling. In addition, detailed models of inventory control systems can be used regularly to assess the impact of various JIT strategies, the inventory re-ordering policies, optimal levels of inventory and so on. Other applications of simulation in the context of JIT include designing line flow strategy and kanban card system or assessing materials flow.

Simulation Modelling and BPR

Many publications argue that one of the major problems that contribute to the failure of BPR projects is a lack of tools for evaluating the effects of designed solutions before implementation (Paolucci et al., 1997; Tumay, 1995). Mistakes brought about by BPR can only be realized once the redesigned processes are implemented, when it is too late, costly and probably impossible to easily correct such errors. Although the evaluation of alternative solutions may be difficult, this may reduce some of the risks associated with BPR projects. For example, Hlupic et al. (1999) present a business process model of a telephony system of a large multinational company that has been used for determining business processes that needed to be radically changed. The impact of these changes was investigated using the model before the real system was changed.

Simulation Modelling and Process Innovation

Similar to BPR, the essence of Process Innovation is to radically reshape or even transform key business processes to enhance business performance. This approach emphasizes innovation and not just improvement. The focus is on one-time change. Here, simulation models may be developed to investigate key processes to determine innovation strategies, to develop a vision of new processes and to evaluate alternative models of new processes.

Simulation Modelling and Knowledge Management

In the context of knowledge management, simulation models can be used to investigate knowledge management processes, knowledge flow and knowledge processing activities, to simulate missing data needed for knowledge management (e.g., MagentA software), or to evaluate alternative models of knowledge management strategies. Simulation projects usually relate to one-off or continuous study for evaluating knowledge management processes. Models are normally 'people' and information oriented, as the models usually represent the flow of information and knowledge, or could show the effects of new knowledge management practices on business processes. Such models could incorporate human resources and their involvement with knowledge management, and they are not concerned with movements of physical objects within the system.

An important remark to be made here is that simulation modelling cannot be considered equally appropriate for change management approaches. Although possible (as advocated in this chapter), it is more difficult to apply this method for modelling processes that are more abstract and people oriented (as it is often the case in BPR or KM) than for processes that involve physical resources (such as in JIT systems).

CHANGE MANAGEMENT PROGRAMMES: A COMPARATIVE ANALYSIS

A summary of the main ideas on how simulation modelling can support the management innovation and change programs is proven in Table 1. We also compare and contrast the benefits and improvements, similarities and differences, and the role of simulation relating to these approaches.

As Table 1 shows, all five 'panaceas' are concerned with business improvement, albeit using different business drivers. During the 1980s in the U.S. and

Table 1: A comparison of five innovation and change programs

CONCEPT	BUSINESS BENEFITS AND IMPROVEMENTS	SIMILARITIES/ DIFFERENCES	THE ROLE OF SIMULATION
Total Quality Management (TQM)	Quality enhancement, Customer satisfaction, Zero defects, Culture change, Better communications Cost reduction, Flexible working practices	Incremental change, continuous improvement, medium time scale, top-down participation, company-wide scope, medium risk, cultural type of change	Decision support system for continuous improvement, graphical display of physical elements, simulating dynamic changes of the system, communication tool, problem understanding tool, AS-IS vs. TO-BE models, random behavior of system elements captured in models, manufacturing-oriented models, models usually represent the flow of physical objects
Just-In-Time (JIT)	Reduced machine downtime, waste and re-work (of stock) Reduced cost, Fulfill innovation strategy, Improved customer/supplier relationships	Evolutionary change, processual change, medium time scale, top-down participation, cross-functional scope, medium risk, cultural type of change	Decision support system for continuous improvement, graphical display of physical elements, simulating dynamic changes of the system, communication tool, problem understanding tool, AS-IS vs. TO-BE models, random behavior of system elements captured in models, manufacturing-oriented models, models usually represent the flow of physical objects
Business Process Re-engineering (BPR)	Eliminate non-core business processes, Achieve functional integration, Greater worker empowerment	Revolutionary change, on-going frequency of change, long-term time scale, top-down participation, high risk, cultural/cost reduction type of change	One-off study for evaluating strategy for radical change, graphical display of business processes, simulating dynamic changes of the system, communication tool, problem understanding tool, AS-IS vs. TO-BE models, random behavior of system elements captured in models, 'people'-oriented models, models usually represent the flow of information
Process Innovation	Eliminate non-core business processes, Fuse IT and HRM, Encourage cross-functional team building	Radical change, one-time change, long-term time scale, top-down participation, high risk, cultural/cost reduction type of change	One-off study for evaluating innovation to core processes, graphical display of business processes, simulating dynamic changes of the system, communication tool, problem understanding tool, AS-IS vs. TO-BE models, random behavior of system elements captured in models, 'people'-oriented models, models usually represent the flow of information
Knowledge Management	Change business processes as a result of KM initiatives, business improvement, Encourage knowledge sharing	Incremental change, long-term time scale, company-wide participation, low risk, cultural type of change	Simulation models can be used to investigate knowledge management processes, to simulate missing data needed for knowledge management, and to evaluate alternative models of knowledge management strategies. One-off or continuous study for evaluating knowledge management processes, graphical display of business processes, communication tool, AS-IS vs. TO-BE models, 'people'- and information-oriented models, models usually represent the flow of information/knowledge

Europe, there was much concern with quality improvement. While this continues, the more recent approaches of BPR and PI during the 1990s have been concerned with how technology can be used to provide seamless and efficient business processes. While TQM and JIT emphasize the role of 'shop floor' staff in the continuous improvement process, these approaches also assert that top management must fully embrace these change programs if they are to be successful.

Furthermore, all approaches suggest a need for cultural change in an organization, although the time scale, the type of change and associated risks are not the same.

In addition, it is demonstrated that simulation modelling could play an important role in supporting all five approaches. Simulation models could provide a graphical display of physical elements and/or business processes, and capture dynamic changes. These models could be used as communication tools to help people to understand the current processes using AS-IS models, and to evaluate the impact of changes using TO-BE models. Random behavior of system elements can be simulated by models as well as changes to the layout of systems, priorities, sequencing of tasks and human resource management.

One of the major differences between change management approaches in the context of simulation is that models that support TQM and JIT are usually manufacturing oriented. They tend to represent the flow of physical objects (for example, the movement of parts between work centers). But models that support BPR, Process Innovation and Knowledge Management normally deal with the flow of information and how resources may be redeployed. These models are usually 'people oriented' as business processes normally involve human resources.

Writing on the similarities between TQM and BPR, Hammer and Champy (1993) recognized that some people questioned the authenticity of the latter approach and so put forward the view that "Re-engineering and TQM are neither identical nor in conflict; they are complementary. While they share a focus on customers and processes, there are also important differences between them. Re-engineering gets a company where it needs to be fast; TQM moves a company in the same direction, but more slowly. Re-engineering is about dramatic, radical change; TQM involves incremental adjustment. Both have their place. TQM should be used to keep a company's processes tuned up between the periodic process replacements that only re-engineering could accomplish. In addition, TQM is built into a company's culture and can go on working without much day-to-day attention from management. Re-engineering, in contrast, is an intensive, top-down, vision-driven effort that requires non-stop senior management participation and support."

An important observation of the management innovation and change literature is the relative speed at which new 'panaceas' enter the marketplace. As we can see, TQM has many similarities with BPR and process innovation. Moreover, JIT, according to some observers, incorporates many of the concepts and practices of TQM, particularly from a Japanese perspective. The differences between BPR and process innovation are more to do with labeling rather than substance, scope and practice. KM also requires changes in business processes, which are driven both by the use of KM tools (for capturing, generating or disseminating knowledge) and a shift in company culture, which supports company-wide knowledge sharing and dissemination.

In making these points, it is important to adopt a more cautionary perspective on the theoretical and practical value of management innovation and change programs, since a critical and comparative analysis suggests they are largely the products of management consultancy firms which, like other products, have a relatively short shelf life! This is not to totally disparage the value of change programs per se, but to recognize that the business and management literature is fast becoming littered with discarded or once popular business and management 'panaceas.'

FUTURE TRENDS AND CONCLUSIONS

This chapter has investigated five change management panaceas in the context of how simulation modelling may support them. It is apparent that these approaches are differentiated more by labels, ideology and rhetoric, than by a strategic vision which explains their implementation in the business community. To this end, it is difficult to delineate the theoretical and practical boundaries of TQM and BPR, for example. This supports existing research, which shows that the same panacea does not produce identical results across companies operating in the same business sector (Galliers and Swan, 1999). It has been recognized that modelling provides an important means of discovering the essential aspects of the organizational system where improvements will make a real difference in performance as well as providing a sound basis for managing the consequences of the agreed actions (Ackermann et al., 1999). With this in mind, future trends in this area should bring more widespread use of dynamic modelling techniques within the business community.

There are many reasons why simulation modelling should be used as a process modelling tool. For example, a new business process might involve a decision about capital investment that is difficult to reverse. It is usually too expensive to experiment with the real business processes, especially if this involves large-scale organizational change. In many cases the variables and resources for new processes are not determined or understood. The process of simulation model development can facilitate a deeper understanding of some of these issues. The value of simulation depends on the model validity and the likelihood that the results of model experimentation may be replicated and implemented in the real processes.

In addition to modelling business processes to support BPR, Process Innovation and Knowledge Management approaches, simulation modelling could be (and has been) used extensively in a manufacturing sector to support TQM and JIT strategies. In conclusion, we contend that simulation modelling could be viewed as the missing link between these panaceas, particularly insofar as it may help to delineate the boundaries between them and how they may work in practice. In addition, another important benefit of simulation is its ability to provide continuity for change management in companies where the fads seem to come and go.

REFERENCES

Ackermann, F., Walls L., van der Meer, R. and Borman, M. (1999). Taking a strategic view of BPR to develop a multidisciplinary framework. *Journal of the Operational Research Society*, 50, 195-204.

Argyris, C. (1994). *On Organizational Learning*. Cambridge, MA: Blackwell.

Beijerse, R.P. (1999). Questions in knowledge management: Defining and conceptualising a phenomenon. *Journal of Knowledge Management, 3*(2), 94-110.

Crosby, P. B. (1979). *Quality is Free*. New York: McGraw Hill.

Currie, W. (1994). The strategic management of large scale IT projects in the financial services sector. *New Technology, Work and Employment, 9*(1), March, 19-29.

Currie, W. (2000). *The Global Information Society*. Chichester: John Wiley & Sons.

Davenport, H. (1993). *Process Innovation: Re-Engineering Work Through Information Technology*. Boston, MA: Harvard Business Press.

Davenport, T. H. and Prusak, L. (1998). *Working Knowledge: How Organizations Manage What They Know*. Boston, MA: Harvard Business School Press.

Deming, W. E. (1982). Improvement of quality and productivity through action by management. *National Productivity Review*, (Winter), 12-22.

Galliers, R. D. and Swan, J. (1999). Information systems and strategic change: A critical review of business process re-engineering. In Currie, W. L. and Galliers, R. D. (Eds.), *Rethinking MIS*. Oxford: Oxford University Press.

Gilbert, J. P. (1989). The state of JIT implementation and development in the USA. *International Journal of Production Research, 28*(6), 1099-1109.

Gladwin, B. and Tumay K. (1994). Modelling business processes with simulation tools. In Tew, J. D., Manivannan, S., Sadowski, D. A. and Seila, A. F. (Eds.), *Proceedings of the 1994 Winter Simulation Conference*, 114-121, SCS.

Grint, K., Case, P. and Willcocks L. (1995). Business process reengineering: The politics and technology of forgetting. *Proceedings of the IFIP WG 8.2 Conference Information Technology and Changes in Organizational Work*. University of Cambridge, United Kingdom, December 7-9.

Hammer, M. (1990). Re-engineering work: Don't automate, obliterate. *Harvard Business Review, 90*(4), 104-112.

Hammer, M. and Champy, J. (1993). *Re-Engineering the Corporation: A Manifesto for Business Revolution*. London: Nicholas Brearley Publishing.

Hayes, R. H. and Abernathy, W. J. (1980). Managing our way to economic decline. *Harvard Business Review*, July/August.

Hirst, P. and Zeitlin, J. (Eds.). (1989). *Reversing Industrial Decline?* London: Berg Press.

Hlupic, V., Pouloudi, A. and Rzevski, G. (2002). Towards an integrated approach to knowledge management: 'Hard,' 'soft' and 'abstract' issues. *Knowledge and Process Management, the Journal of Corporate Transformation,* 9, 1-14.

Hlupic, V., Patel, N. and Choudrie, J. (1999). The REBUS approach to business process re-engineering. In Kalpic, D. and Dobric, V. (Eds.), *Proceedings of Information Technology Interfaces, ITI '99,* 475-481, June. Pula, Croatia University Computing Centre.

Janson, R. (1993). How re-engineering transforms organizations to satisfy customers. *National Productivity Review,* (Winter), 45-53.

Juran, J. M. (1986). The quality trilogy. *Quality Progress,* (August), 19-24.

Kavanagh, J. (1994). Business process re-engineering. ABC of computing. *Financial Times,* (April 26).

Land, F. F. (1996). The new alchemist: Or how to transmute base organizations into corporations of gleaming gold. *Journal of Strategic Information Systems,* 5, 7-17.

Love, D. and Barton, J. (1996). Evaluation of design decisions through CIM and simulation. *Integrated Manufacturing Systems,* 7(4), 3-11.

Malhotra Y. (1997). *Current Business Concerns and Knowledge Management.* Available: http://www.brint.com/interview/times.htm.

McFarlan, F. W. (1984). New electronics systems can add value to your product and throw your competition off balance. *Harvard Business Review,* (May/June), 98-103.

Moad, J. (1998). In search of knowledge. *PC Week,* (December 7), 111.

Nonaka, I. and Takeuchi, H. (1995). *The Knowledge-Creating Company: How Japanese Companies Create the Dynamics of Innovation.* Oxford: OUP.

Paolucci E., Bonci, F. and Russi, V. (1997). Redesigning organizations through business process re-engineering and object-orientation. *Proceedings of the European Conference on Information Systems,* 587-601. Cork, Ireland.

Paul R.J., Hlupic, V. and Giaglis, G. (1998). Simulation modelling of business processes. In Avison, D. and Edgar-Neville, D. (Eds.), *Proceedings of the 3rd UK Academy of Information Systems Conference,* June. Lincoln, UK. New York: McGraw-Hill.

Pidd, M. (1998). *Computer Simulation in Management Science* (fourth edition). Chichester: John Wiley & Sons.

Porter, M. and Millar, M. (1985). How information gives you a competitive advantage. *Harvard Business Review,* (July/August), 149-160.

Profozich D. (1998). *Managing Change with Business Process Simulation.* Englewood Cliffs, NJ: Prentice Hall.

Rzevski, G. and Prasad, K. (1998). The synergy of learning organizations and flexible information technology. *AI & Society*, 12, 87-96.

Savage, C. M. (1996). *Fifth Generation Management: Co-Creating Through Virtual Enterprising, Dynamic Teaming, and Knowledge Networking.* London: Butterworth Heinemann.

Schonberger, R. (1986). *World Class Manufacturing*. New York: Free Press.

Shingo, S. (1989). *A Study of the Toyota Production System.* Cambridge, MA: Productivity Press.

Starr, J. (1999). *KMTool–Ideas for Sharing Knowledge.* Available: http://www.kmtool.net/vocabulary.htm.

Sveiby, K. (1999). *What Is Knowledge Management?* Available: http://www.sveiby.com.au/KnowledgeManagement.htm.

Tumay, K. (1995). Business process simulation. In Alexopoulos, A., Kang K., Lilegdon, W. R. and Goldsman, D. (Eds.), *Proceedings of the WSC'95 — Winter Simulation Conference*, 55-60. Washington DC, USA.

Voss, C. A. and Robinson, S. J. (1987). Applications of JIT manufacturing techniques in the United Kingdom. *International Journal of Operations and Production Management*, 7(4), 46-52.

Waterson, P. E., Clegg, C. W., Bolden, R., Pepper, K., Warr, P. B. and Wall, T. D. (1997). *The Use and Effectiveness of Modern Manufacturing Practices in the United Kingdom.* ESRC Centre for Organization and Innovation. Institute of Work Psychology, University of Sheffield, S10 2TN.

Chapter IV

Intelligent Agents for Knowledge Management in E-Commerce: Opportunities and Challenges

Athanasia Pouloudi
Athens University of Economics and Business, Greece

Vlatka Hlupic and George Rzevski
Brunel University, UK

ABSTRACT

E-commerce has become a key aspect of the global business environment, causing fundamental changes in markets and organisational structures. This chapter considers how knowledge management, the latest management approach aimed at improving business performance, can create new business opportunities in the new business environment that is defined by electronic commerce. Knowledge management deals with the systematic generation, codification and transfer of knowledge and can be supported by a number of technologies, known as knowledge management tools. It has been argued that intelligent systems can offer additional capabilities and advantages in comparison with more traditional information technologies. This chapter investigates the potential of intelligent agent-based software for more effective knowledge management in the context of e-commerce, adopting the perspective of an SME involved in development of intelligent agents-based knowledge management software. The chapter concludes with a research agenda for knowledge management research in e-commerce.

INTRODUCTION

The importance of knowledge management (KM) as a competitive differentiator is increasingly recognised by both 'traditional' and 'virtual' organisations. A recent OECD report claims that industrial countries are spending as much on intangible knowledge-based investments as on physical equipment (OECD, 1999). There is an expectation that the technical exploitation of knowledge data will improve substantially with the use of intelligent tools that have several additional capabilities in comparison to traditional knowledge management tools, as discussed in this chapter. With improvements in IT-based systems for handling knowledge, knowledge management is becoming an essential theme of research into business success. Yet, it has been argued (e.g., Hlupic et al., 2001; Myers, 1996; Snowden, 1998) that the effective management of knowledge involves more than simply exploiting the data held on information systems. It also requires attention to the 'softer' parts of the corporate knowledge base, as found in the human and cultural aspects of businesses, particularly the experiences and tacit knowledge of employees. There is a growing emphasis on innovation through 'knowledge work' and 'knowledge workers' and on leveraging 'knowledge assets' (Swan et al., 1999).

While some research also makes reference to the organisational context within which the technology will be used (e.g., Delesie and Croes, 2000; Edwards and Gibson, 2000), there is little evidence of whether or how the organisational and technical dimensions have been integrated. The challenges, both technical and contextual, presented in this chapter indicate that electronic commerce creates a new context for knowledge management, not just in terms of the cultural and business environment created, but also in terms of the actual knowledge that is captured, exchanged and exploited. To deal successfully with the latter, it has been suggested that artificial intelligence, and intelligent agents in particular, have a key role to play (Smith and Farquhar, 2000). This chapter will consider how this new technology can be applied in practice. Typically, research in knowledge management would consider the view of the 'client', i.e., how a particular organisation improves its knowledge management practices. Our chapter focuses instead on the ways in which the new context of electronic commerce creates business opportunities for the provider of intelligent technology to support knowledge management. This party, the 'supplier', needs to have a broader view of the new technological and cultural landscape. We access this perspective by researching the case of an internationally oriented SME involved in multi-agent software development used for knowledge management in electronic commerce.

The chapter is structured as follows. The next section presents some of the key organisational and technical challenges for knowledge management, with emphasis on the role intelligent multi-agents and the challenges that electronic commerce presents for knowledge management. Section three introduces the case of an SME involved in development of intelligent agents-based KM software. A research agenda for KM research in e-commerce is then proposed, and conclusions are drawn.

KEY CHALLENGES IN
KNOWLEDGE MANAGEMENT

The literature has been unable to agree on a definition for the term 'knowledge management' (Brooking, 1999; Hlupic et al., 2002; Malhotra, 1997; Trauth, 1999). One reason is that discussions of, and approaches to, the subject are rooted in different academic disciplines and areas of professional expertise. From the *information systems perspective*, for example, KM is often looked upon as synonymous with new forms of 'data mining' and 'warehousing' — the 'hard' tools that allow for sophisticated pattern searches of raw data (Trauth, 1999). From the *innovation management* perspective, a 'cognitive' approach is adopted, which looks at the transfer of explicit and tacit knowledge through product development and organisational change procedures (Kuhn and Abecker, 1997; Leonard-Barton, 1995; Nonaka and Takeuchi, 1995). The *management* literature places particular emphasis on issues of 'organisational learning', especially structures which encourage creativity and knowledge sharing (Ruggles, 1997). It is increasingly evident that these definitions do not adopt a *multi-disciplinary* approach, despite the multi-disciplinary interest in KM (McAdam and McCreedy, 1999; Phillips and Patrick, 2000). Instead, a managerial perspective is often predominant that does not necessarily accommodate the capabilities of information systems. The reverse is also common in research that is intended for a technical audience. We argue that KM must move towards a more *holistic* approach to nurturing and exploitation knowledge assets in both 'traditional' and 'virtual' business environments. In the chapter we demonstrate this in two ways. First, in this section, we give as much attention to the capabilities of intelligent technology as to the context of electronic commerce applications. Second, in the following sections, we demonstrate how technology and context become intertwined in the empirical evidence that our case study provides. Starting with knowledge management tools, this section presents a technological followed by an organisational perspective on knowledge management.

Knowledge Management Tools

Knowledge management tools, as all tools, aim to assist in the completion of a task with ease and efficiency. Ruggles (1997) suggests that KM tools can be divided into three categories, which are believed to represent the primary knowledge activities of most organisations:

- *Knowledge Generation* — the creation of new ideas, recognition of new patterns, the synthesis of separate disciplines and the development of new processes.
- *Knowledge Codification* — the auditing and categorisation of knowledge.
- *Knowledge Transfer* — the exchange of knowledge between individuals, groups and organisations.

The majority of KM tools are designed to deal with *structured* data, where information is directly entered into fields or can be categorised in some manner. Each of these stages presents technical challenges. One important issue is indexing, in other words, the appropriate structuring of data or information to facilitate or lead to knowledge discovery (Delesie and Croes, 2000). Knowledge acquisition and representation can also be difficult to address in KM systems, as they are for knowledge-based systems; they are issues that have been recorded extensively in the expert systems literature (e.g., Doukidis & Whitley, 1988; Firlej & Hellens, 1991; Hart, 1986). With KM systems, the key issue is probably the need to move beyond simple structured data mining towards the capture, mining and manipulation of tacit or unstructured data. Practitioners and researchers alike have identified tacit data as a, if not *the*, corporate resource to be managed and exploited for competitive advantage in the information-intensive economy. In other words, an additional technical challenge for knowledge management is the management of tacit knowledge, which is normally stored and exchanged using unstructured data. Takeuchi (2001) argues that organisational knowledge is created precisely during the time that tacit knowledge is converted to explicit (p. 321). Therefore, a key challenge for the design of KM technology is the identification of patterns (Brash, 2000) in unstructured data that enables reuse of the technology and contributes to system flexibility (Selvin and Buckingham Shum, 2000). There is an expectation that the new generation of KM tools will address this challenge using artificial intelligence (AI) techniques such as case-based reasoning, neural networks and intelligent agents. This chapter focuses on the role of the latter.

Intelligent agents are software objects (special types of computer programs) capable of communicating with each other and reasoning about information contained in messages that pass among them. To justify the adjective *intelligent*, agents must be able to make decisions under conditions of uncertainty, to act upon incomplete information, albeit in a narrow knowledge domain. Key elements of an intelligent agent, which enable it to achieve a limited-scale perception, cognition and execution, are knowledge bases with domain heuristics, simulated simple values and attitudes, and algorithms for reasoning, learning and pattern recognition. Advanced versions of agents can learn from experience and may even have distinguishing personality traits. Standard artificial intelligence techniques may be used for constructing agents, e.g., predicate calculus, genetic algorithms, fuzzy logic and neural networks. However, the experience indicates that the best results are achieved if a very large number of very simple agents is allowed to cooperate and compete among themselves and thus generate "Emergent Intelligence." Agents could be designed to have a particular attitude towards taking risks under conditions of uncertainty. Thus, a team of agents with different risk-taking characteristics emulates a crew of operators with a variety of attitudes to decision making.

Multi-agent systems use multiple intelligent agents and are characterised by distributed problem solving. They contain software objects (agents) capable of exchanging messages among themselves and their users, interpreting the meaning of messages and negotiating decisions. An interesting development in multi-agent systems is an attempt to provide agents with a mechanism for modifying protocols that regulate negotiations, which they conduct among themselves (e.g., Muller et al., 1996). This capability enables agents to incrementally improve their decision-making performance. These capabilities are particularly useful in electronic commerce (as discussed further on in this chapter) where intelligent agents have been taken up. The concept of multi-agent design and control is well developed, although not necessarily articulated in the context of knowledge management. It has been argued that, in this context, the role of artificial intelligence is "giving powerful assistance to people as they solve problems" (Smith and Farquhar, 2000, p.22). This quotation points to the interdependence of technology and the context of use, and supports the idea that the technological challenges mentioned here are witnessed and can only be addressed within a particular organisational and cultural context.

The Knowledge Management Context — Challenges For E-Commerce

Knowledge management, while supported by technology, remains a complex management practice for all organisations—tools will not work unless they can be integrated in the organisational and cultural context. The following paragraphs consider the reasons why this may be the case at four separate but interconnected levels, where KM benefits are realised: the individual, organisational, interorganisational and international levels. Particular emphasis is given to the additional challenges that are present in an electronic commerce context.

At an *individual level*, KM provides organisational members with opportunities and tools to operate, and where possible flourish, in an environment of continuous change. Attention to the individual level signifies acceptance of idiosyncratic knowledge, recognising that personality plays a critical role in the way that people acquire, perceive, value and use knowledge as well as that the creation of knowledge is affected by the world view of the individual (Guns and Välikangas, 1998). This is particularly relevant for the e-commerce context. Specifically, in business-to-consumer e-commerce relations, in contrast to traditional commerce, the customer is not visible and typically not known. The technological awareness of individuals also varies. The potential customer population is large (possibly global) and the 'customer' could have any background (cultural, financial or educational). In knowledge management terms, this presents a business opportunity: customer behaviour can be electronically recorded, therefore can be manipulated and exploited for competitive advantage. Some mechanisms, like cookies, try to contribute to 'learning' more about the customer profile and preferences, although in essence there are several limitations related to the authenticity and interpretation of the data they record. Furthermore, given the technical challenges reviewed previously, it is not clear how organisations can manipulate the vast amounts of data and extract meaningful patterns that could be used for 'mass customisation' or differentiating their products in a global market where first mover advantage is visible and can easily be imitated. Intelligent agents can play a key role here by providing personal attention to the customer, learning and remembering individual preferences, which can be communicated or negotiated as needed. The business implication for the company using the technology is dual: customer service can improve as individual traits are catered for and the company gains knowledge about trends and patterns that can be unveiled from customer choice.

At an *organisational level*, KM supports the streamlining of activities and facilitates improved organisational response to internal and external changes. This often places attention on organisational processes and presents several challenges, not least the difficulty of identifying processes (Nickols, 1998). Huysman and de Wit (2000) have identified several 'traps' that relate to KM at this level:

- *An opportunity trap* — KM will be more effective if it is problem-driven, i.e., if it responds to concerns that are relevant in the particular organisational context, rather than if it is technology-driven or attempting to imitate other businesses, as is often the case.
- *A codified knowledge trap* — It is difficult to record previous knowledge for others to access, especially as new knowledge keeps being created and human actors are busy making sense of the new knowledge and conditions.

- *A management trap* — KM is dominated by management initiatives, but it is unlikely to be effective unless knowledge workers willingly take part in it.
- *The operational level trap* — KM should not be limited to the operational level, in the same way that knowledge exchange processes cannot be limited to this level.

In organisations that use electronic commerce, either partially or fully (virtual organisations), the notion of business processes may be entirely different, as these companies are based on different business models (Tapscott et al., 2000). This complicates the significance of these 'traps' for the networked enterprise and its stakeholders. On the one hand, as business processes are predominantly electronic, they should be more transparent and traceable than in traditional business— thus, information about business transactions is structured and explicit, and this should facilitate knowledge management. For example, it should be easier to create an organisational memory about business transactions and make this readily accessible to knowledge workers. On the other hand, several business processes transcend the boundaries of the organisation, as electronic links to customers, suppliers and other stakeholders make the organisation an extended, networked enterprise. This makes it harder to convert information into knowledge: different organisational settings and therefore different cultural environments, with different sets of tacit knowledge, interact. A related difficulty at this level, which also applies to traditional companies, is that the available data about processes, procedures and resources may be incomplete. This makes it harder to uncover patterns that can lead to knowledge codification and possibly the generation of new knowledge. The use of intelligent agents can be helpful in this respect. Specifically, intelligent agents that are characterised by autonomous learning can use previous history, and learn from it even if the way in which it is interpreted changes at a very fast rate.

Interorganisational and international levels (in many cases, these can be used interchangeably in e-commerce) are therefore more relevant in considering the challenges of the knowledge management context in electronic commerce. At the moment, little is known about the transfer of knowledge at an interorganisational level. Arguably, one of the advantages of KM is that it enables organisations, regardless of size and resources, to compete globally against larger regional trading blocs, tending to reduce economy of scale differences. The problem at this level is that different cultures have different mental models of collaboration or trust (Kidd, 2000). Electronic commerce research acknowledges the importance of trust between trading partners (e.g., Hart and Saunders, 1997; Miles and Snow, 1992; Ratnasingham, 1998; Wilson, 1997) but does not consider how this may relate to knowledge creation and transfer in-between different stakeholders. In more mature and structured interorganisational relations, such as outsourcing, KM has yet to receive appropriate attention (Currie and Pouloudi, 2000). The potential role of multi-agents, at this interorganisational level, is in their ability to represent business partners in the networked enterprise and conduct negotiations on their behalf. They can be also utilised for business-to-business types of transactions, operating, for example, in the context of supply chain dealings. Both roles entail technical and organisational issues. From a technical perspective, the use of multi-agent systems eliminates the need for the selection and implementation of optimal algorithms, which is a complex endeavour. Agents will negotiate what to do next in every particular situation, based on local information and a set of general rules, without any need for optimisation algorithms to be programmed into the system in advance.

From a business perspective, the situation is rather complex because it is at present not clear which rules, roles and responsibilities apply in a legal context that is not well defined. Despite the progress in electronic commerce legislature, several issues remain to be resolved at a global scale for transactions occurring entirely in electronic format or crossing national boundaries (see for example Timmers, 1999, pp.171-174, for an overview of key legal and regulatory issues in the European Union and the USA).

Electronic commerce, by its very nature, combines a business with a techno-logical environment, as transactions occur electronically. It is obvious from the discussion in this section that it offers a good opportunity to illustrate the interde-pendence of technical and organisational (often *inter*-organisational) factors in knowledge management. In the next section we consider the technical and business environment of a recently established company that develops, supplies and supports multi-agent software, and serves as a case study for considering the potential of intelligent agents for knowledge management in e-commerce.

EMPIRICAL INSIGHTS
FROM THE USE OF MULTI-AGENTS
FOR KM IN E-COMMERCE

Following from the previous discussion on the interrelations of technical and organisational factors related to knowledge management in electronic commerce, this section presents how these are witnessed in practice. For our description we adopt the perspective of a small enterprise that has strong links with Brunel University. This allows an 'insider view' to the opportunities and challenges it faces in providing multi-agent support for knowledge management in electronic com-merce. Starting with a description of the company and its multi-agent software, the section leads on to a discussion of the role of intelligent agents in knowledge management, which serves as a guide for proposing a broader agenda for research in this area.

The Company

The company was established in October 1999 to exploit multi-agent research but it has a long history of informal existence marked by previous international collaboration among its founders. Although its physical premises are in the UK, it is largely a virtual corporation with researchers, system designers and programmers collaborating over intranets and the Internet. For example, the main activities related to software development are carried out in Russia. The company aims to become "virtual" and to sell its products and services mainly though the Internet. In doing so, it would become an e-commerce-based organisation selling products and services that support e-commerce. In practical terms, this means that the company has the advantage that it understands from its own experience the challenges of integrating work processes across different cultural settings, hence it is able to exploit this knowledge for providing better products and support to its customers as well.

The corporation has a flat structure, where, as described on the company's web site, "teamwork dominates every aspect of corporate life." Also, the corporation considers intellectual capital to be its key asset. Consequently, knowledge management is important for the company not just as a product but as a competitive differentiator: the company is its own customer. For example, organisational memory is facilitated by the company's own knowledge management software. Similarly, the company culture is maintained through an extensive electronic network. The company is currently in the process of extending the functionality of its web site for procurement and selling its product and services. Plans for e-commerce include using the company's web site for selling, in large volumes, scaled down multi-agent tools and shells to small-to-medium software developers around the world.

Capabilities of Multi-Agent Software

Agents are trained (have access to knowledge) rather than programmed to do a particular job. Advanced versions of agents can learn from experience and have distinguishing personality traits. They can be, for example, risk-averse and this will influence their negotiating behaviour. The principal element of multi-agent systems, which enables them to achieve a limited-scale perception, cognition and execution, is an Ontology, which contains knowledge about the domain in which the system operates. To keep the Ontology simple, the domain of agent activity has to be reasonably narrow. The second component of the system is the Engine, shown in Figure 1.

A key advantage of this architecture is that modifications are easy because the agent code is reusable, multi-agent engines are expandable and the Ontology can be updated by operators without any knowledge of computer programming using

Figure 1: The engine of a multi-agent system

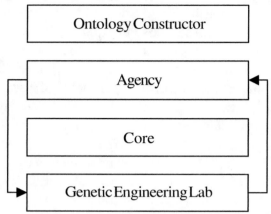

a visual tool called Ontology Constructor. The Agency in the above diagram is the space where agents are created and where they work (negotiate), the Core is a set of run-time algorithms enabling parallel work of a very large number of agents and the Genetic Engineering Lab is a place where the performance of agents is monitored and modifications are made to their "genetic code" to improve their performance (e.g., to negotiate more aggressively, or more carefully).

Multi-agent systems are perceived to be cost-effective; each agent has a limited intelligence yet the overall intelligence of a "swarm" of agents is quite impressive. This is because agents cooperate with each other and make decisions through negotiations. Agents act upon locally available information with great speed, but always respect general policies and rules. They consult each other and they bargain with a view to maximising the overall value of the process they are controlling, rather than furthering their own individual interests. In other words, multi-agent systems behave as an effective team, and the effective teamwork results in an emergent performance, a performance that far exceeds the sum of performances of individual team members. The inherent advantage of multi-agent systems is that they work on the principle of a free market. Agents match supply to demand, and if the perfect match is not possible, they negotiate special deals to achieve partial matching.

Supporting Knowledge Management for E-Commerce

In the context of electronic commerce, agents improve the performance of portals and web sites by providing visitors with an intelligent, personalised, one-to-one service. In particular, they communicate with each visitor as an individual, recognising specific needs and expectations. They also recognise visitors when they return to the site. In addition to this customer relationship management role, multi-agents match portal offerings to visitors' demands rapidly and effectively, and negotiate discounts and special deals on behalf of their clients. From a knowledge management perspective, they continuously analyse available data in the background, with a view to discovering, preserving, maintaining and updating knowledge about each visitor. Discovering and managing knowledge through the use of agents can be directed both to the business environment (customers, competitors, investors, administrative and legal factors, new technologies, etc.) but also to the client's own business processes (cost-effectiveness of human and technological resources, organisational structures, business culture, geographical locations, etc.).

The competitive differentiator of a Multi-Agent Knowledge Management System is based on effective clustering algorithms that enable rapid discovery of knowledge, which as discussed in previous sections can be 'buried' in unstructured data. The key to the effectiveness is the use of multi-agent technology, which provides distributed intelligence to help the process of clustering. Principles and rules of clustering, which are obeyed by agents, are in the first instance entered into the system ontology by knowledge management experts. The system is designed to enable operators without knowledge of computer programming to modify and update clustering principles and rules and thus influence the system performance. The company's selling point is that this system is much less expensive than a typical data mining system and far more effective (e.g., as it enables knowledge exploitation of unstructured data) and user friendly. A unique aspect of the system's user friendliness is the capability to provide the user with a graphical representation of clustering results so that stronger links between data elements appear clearly.

It is worth noting that clustering becomes a self-organising process. As new data become available to the system, the clusters of knowledge are re-evaluated and reconfigured, allowing for a dynamic interpretation of business results. Furthermore, the system can provide patterns without 'knowing' much about the data. This means, on the one hand, that the system may highlight relationships between data that is not obvious, even to the knowledgeable human agent, thus unveiling real competitive edge issues for their clients. On the other hand, the clustering process becomes faster if human agents define restrictions for the clustering processes, based on their capability to interpret meaningful associations among data elements. This dilemma between speed and scope of data analysis illustrates the interplay of technical capabilities and organisational priorities. The human agent can improve the efficiency of the technology by a good understanding of the context, which can lead to a better definition of Ontology as well as a more insightful interpretation of the data analysis results. Obviously, the responsibility for the translation of results in appropriate business policies lies also with the human agent.

DISCUSSION AND IMPLICATIONS FOR RESEARCH IN KNOWLEDGE MANAGEMENT FOR E-COMMERCE

The interactive character of electronic commerce enables information (and, hence, knowledge) sharing across organisational entities or individuals, often across national boundaries. Through their electronic commerce interactions and transactions, companies acquire much information that can easily be stored and exploited (as the data is usually in electronic form). However, few users of electronic commerce have considered using this information as a basis for understanding and managing their organisational knowledge better. The potential benefits of more effective knowledge management in the context of e-commerce are apparent for both organisational processes and interorganisational relations, and we argue that multi-agent technology has an important role to play in this area. In the previous section we saw how a software house exploited their multi-agent software for knowledge management in electronic commerce for the company and the company's clients.

Electronic commerce is a unique environment for knowledge management, not only because it uses the Internet as a platform but also because the data available to users of e-commerce become dated very quickly as the electronic market changes at a rapid pace. Therefore 'traditional' information technologies cannot deduce knowledge for the future exclusively from past data because of dynamic changes in the turbulent global economy. Companies that aim to support knowledge management in electronic commerce environments have to investigate novel ways of managing and exploiting the individual, organisational and interorganisational knowledge. Intelligent multi-agent technologies can provide a technological solution for dealing with the uncertain conditions of this context, manipulating incomplete or ill-structured historical data.

At the moment, both research and practice of knowledge management in e-commerce are in their infancy. For example, there are a number of problems that we have identified in current practice as well as in the theoretical understanding of KM, namely:

- the variety of theoretical approaches to KM and the lack of consensus in the literature about what constitutes KM and how effective KM can be achieved;
- the limited availability of empirical reports to support these approaches and provide guidance for further improvements in KM practice;
- the lack of KM tools and the differences in the support that existing tools provide to user organisations;
- the lack of awareness about KM opportunities for both traditional and virtual organisations, either because of technical limitations of the available tools or

because user organisations are unable to identify or communicate their needs for more effective KM and the organisational structures that will support them; and

- the lack of substantial research effort to investigate technical and social aspects of KM in e-commerce environments.

As a result of these problems, it is not surprising that the appreciation of the challenges and necessity to integrate technical and organisational aspects of KM, which we believe is critical for more effective KM, is at best incomplete. As yet, there is no generic model of KM grounded in empirical research, which companies or industrial sectors can use as a basis for organising and managing their information resources. Such a model could allow organisations to leverage their core competencies and key skills. Both organisational and technical issues of KM raise significant challenges. However, it is also evident that, even though they are often separated in the literature, in a practical context they are inseparable as they inform and influence each other. We argue that research in KM should reflect this synergy of organisational and technical issues. Research needs to be directed towards understanding how these areas limit or enhance the competitive benefits of KM theories and models — what this new way of working entails with regard to skills, organisational structures and operations.

In other words, the implementation of a KM tool will not result in a 'knowledge environment' if other knowledge activities are not supported. For instance, knowledge transfer is unlikely to occur if the organisational culture was one of *hoarding* information (Clegg and Palmer, 1996; Irani and Sharp, 1997; Walsham, 1995). Moreover, in order to combine the expertise of key stakeholders, new forms of working — such as 'cross-functional teams' — may be needed (these may include, for instance, consumer behaviour experts, database marketers and IT experts). These issues have been recognised for some time in the innovation literature (Madhaven and Grover, 1998), although this has not been investigated in the context of e-commerce.

In addition, there is a lack of published empirical work in this area and there is a lack of tools that organisations can utilise and adapt for KM activities in both traditional and virtual business environments. Similarly, evaluation measures for any available tools are lacking. The investigation of the product and approach followed by the case company considered in this chapter provides some insight in the potential of intelligent agents for KM in electronic commerce but clearly presents a specific, sole experience of a recently established company. More research is needed to provided a more in-depth understanding of the way in which companies respond to knowledge management, and in particular to the use of KM technologies to exploit and enhance their electronic commerce activities. We argue that important areas for further research in this area include the following aspects.

First, in order to inform technological improvements, it is necessary to investigate and evaluate knowledge management tools (including multi-agent-based tools) in real e-commerce environments. This should result in a better understanding of the potential and current limitations of such tools, leading, in turn, to specification of requirements for further development of such tools. Second, in order to improve knowledge management at the strategic level in the use of electronic commerce, it is necessary to identify main barriers and driving forces for knowledge management in e-commerce. This involves defining what knowledge is relevant in the context of e-commerce and how it can be captured, stored, refined and applied. A related aspect is the identification of critical success factors for effective knowledge management in e-commerce-based environments, including research on organisational structures that support knowledge management in e-commerce. Third, knowledge management provides an opportunity to improve organisational practices and processes. Therefore, future research should investigate issues related to teamwork, leadership, culture, incentives and motivation for knowledge management, identifying ways for integrating knowledge management into the daily workflow and particularly the types of reward structures to support knowledge sharing and collaboration. An important dimension of this research is exploring how knowledge management can lead to individual and organisational learning as this will lead to sustainable competitive advantage.

CONCLUSIONS

This chapter has discussed the potential of intelligent agents for knowledge management in e-commerce, using insights from an SME providing such knowledge management tools. The chapter emphasised that technical, organisational and interorganisational aspects need to be considered in parallel for providing useful solutions for organisations doing business electronically. The research setting described in this chapter could stimulate interest for identifying opportunities for competitive advantage for e-commerce user organisations from better KM and threats from KM practices in a business context. A number of future directions of research in this area have been identified on that basis. Our main recommendation is for considering the future of technology within the context in which it will be applied.

REFERENCES

Brash, D. (2000). Developing and validating generic knowledge: An initial experience report. In Edwards, J. and Kidd, J. (Eds.), *Proceedings of the*

Knowledge Management Conference (KMAC 2000), 170-177, July 17-18, Birmingham.

Brooking, A. (1999). *Corporate Memory–Strategies for Knowledge Management*. UK: International Thomson Business Press.

Clegg, S. R. and Palmer, G. (1996). *The Politics of Management Knowledge*. London: Sage Publications.

Currie, W. L. and Pouloudi, A. (2000). Evaluating the relationship between IT outsourcing and knowledge management. Journal of Change Management, *1*(2), 149-163.

Delesie, L. and Croes, L. (2000). Managing the variability of medical care: Fostering consensus, benchmarking and feedback. The case of drug prescription patterns among Belgian home practitioners. In Edwards, J. and Kidd, J. (Eds.), *Proceedings of the Knowledge Management Conference (KMAC 2000)*, 80-87, July 17-18, Birmingham.

Doukidis, G. and Whitley, E. A. (1988). *Developing Expert Systems*. Lund: Chartwell-Bratt.

Edwards, J. and Gibson, P. R. (2000). Knowledge management using CSCW in global strategic alliances and joint ventures via the Internet. In Edwards, J. and Kidd, J. (Eds.), *Proceedings of the Knowledge Management Conference (KMAC 2000)*, 376-384, July 17-18, Birmingham.

Firlej, M. and Hellens, D. (1991). *Knowledge Elicitation: A Practical Handbook*. New York: Prentice Hall.

Guns, W. D. and Välikangas, L. (1998). Rethinking knowledge work: Creating value through idiosyncratic knowledge. *Journal of Knowledge Management, 1*(4), 287-293.

Hart, A. (1986). *Knowledge Acquisition for Expert Systems*. London: Kogan Page.

Hart, P. and Saunders, C. (1997). Power and trust critical factors in the adoption and use of electronic data interchange. *Organization Science, 8*(1), 23-41.

Hlupic, V., Pouloudi, A. and Rzevski, G. (2002). Towards an integrated approach to knowledge management: 'hard,' 'soft' and 'abstract' issues. *Knowledge and Process Management*, forthcoming.

Huysman, M. and de Wit, D. (2000). Knowledge management in practice. In Edwards, J. and Kidd, J. (Eds.), *Proceedings of the Knowledge Management Conference (KMAC 2000)*, 324-333, July 17-18, Birmingham.

Irani, Z. and Sharp, J. M. (1997). Integrating continuous improvement and innovation into a corporate culture: A case study. *The International Journal of Technological Innovation, Entrepreneurship and Technology Management (Technovation), 17*(4), 199-206.

Kidd, J. (2000). Us and them: Obstructing knowledge management in MNEs. In Edwards, J. and Kidd, J. (Eds.), *Proceedings of the Knowledge Management Conference (KMAC 2000)*, 397-410, July 17-18, Birmingham.

Kuhn, O. and Abecker, A. (1997). Corporate memories for knowledge management in industrial practice: Prospects and challenges. *Journal of Universal Computer Science*, 3(8), 929-954.

Leonard-Barton, D. (1995). *Wellsprings of Knowledge — Building and Sustaining the Sources of Innovation*. Boston, MA: Harvard Business School Press.

Madhaven, R. and Grover, R. (1998). From embedded knowledge to embodied knowledge: New product development as knowledge management. *Journal of Marketing*, 62(4), 1-29.

Malhotra, Y. (1997). *Current Business Concerns and Knowledge Management*. Available: http://www.brint.com/interview/times.htm.

McAdam, R. and McCreedy, S. (2000). *A Critical Review of KM Models in the Learning Organisational*, 6(3), 91-100.

Miles, R. and Snow, C. (1992). Causes of failure in network organizations. *California Management Review*, (Summer), 53-72.

Muller, J. P., Wooldridge, M. and Jennings, N. R. (Eds.). (1996). *Intelligent Agents III, Agent Theories, Architectures and Languages*. Reading, MA: Springer-Verlag.

Myers, P. (Ed.). (1996). *Knowledge Management and Organisational Design*. Boston MA: Butterworth-Heinemann.

Nickols, F. (1998). The difficult process of identifying processes. *Knowledge and Process Management*, 5(1), 14-19.

Nonaka, I. and Takeuchi, H. (1995). *The Knowledge-Creating Company: How Japanese Companies Create the Dynamics of Innovation*. Oxford: OUP.

OECD. (1999). *The Science, Technology and Industry Scoreboard: Benchmarking the Knowledge-Based Economies*.

Phillips, N. and Patrick, K. (2000). Knowledge management perspectives, organisational character and cognitive style. In Edwards, J. and Kidd, J. (Eds.), *Proceedings of the Knowledge Management Conference (KMAC 2000)*, 90-102, July 17-18, Birmingham.

Ratnasingham, P. (1998). The importance of trust in electronic commerce. *Internet Research: Electronic Networking Applications and Policy*, 8(4), 313-321.

Ruggles, R. (1997). *Knowledge Tools: Using Technology to Manage Knowledge Better*. Ernst & Young Center for Business Innovation Working Paper (April 1997).

Selvin, A. M. and Buckingham Shum, S. (2000). Rapid knowledge construction and dissemination: A case study in corporate contingency planning using collaborative hypermedia. In Edwards, J. and Kidd, J. (Eds.), *Proceedings of the Knowledge Management Conference (KMAC 2000)*, 48-58, July 17-18, Birmingham.

Smith, R. G. and Farquhar, A. (2000). The road ahead for knowledge management: An AI perspective. *AI Magazine*, (Winter), 17-40.

Snowden, D. (1998). A framework for creating a sustainable knowledge management program. In Cortada, J. W. and Woods, J. A. (Eds.), *The Knowledge Management Yearbook 1999-2000*. Boston, MA: Butterworth-Heinemann.

Swan, J., Newell, S., Scarborough, H. and Hislop, D. (1999). Knowledge management and innovation: Networks and networking. *Journal of Knowledge Management*, 3(4), 262-275.

Takeuchi, H. (2001). Towards a universal management concept of knowledge. In Nonaka, I. and Teece, D. (Eds.), *Managing Industrial Knowledge: Creation, Transfer and Utilization*, 314-329. London: Sage.

Tapscott, D., Ticoll, D. and Lowy, A. (2000). *Digital Capital: Harnessing the Power of Business Webs*. Boston, MA: Harvard Business School Press.

Timmers, P. (1999). *Electronic Commerce: Strategies and Models for Business-to-Business Trading*. Chichester: John Wiley & Sons.

Trauth, E. M. (1999). Who owns my soul? The paradox of pursuing organizational knowledge in a work culture of individualism. *Proceedings of the 1999 ACM SIGCPR Conference on Computer Personnel Research*, 159-163.

Walsham, G. (1995). Interpretive case studies in IS research: Nature and method. *European Journal of Information Systems*, 4, 74-81.

Wilson, S. (1997). Certificates and trust in electronic commerce. *Information Management & Computer Security*, 5(5), 175-181.

Chapter V

Knowledge Management: Analysis and Some Consequences

Petros A. M. Gelepithis and Nicole Parillon
Kingston University, UK

ABSTRACT

Although the debate on the nature of 'knowledge' and 'information' is far from settled, it is now taken for granted throughout the academic world that the two notions are related but fundamentally distinct. This result, and its significant consequences, still need to be realised and understood by the great majority of the business world. In the first section of this chapter, we briefly comment on some characteristic views of 'knowledge' and 'knowledge management,' and subsequently we analyse in-depth the core constituent notion of the latter, that is, knowledge.

In section two, we outline three major consequences of our analysis. The first concerns the limits of management for a certain class of activities involving knowledge. The second concerns the scope and limits of technology for the same class of activities. The third concerns the issue of knowledge market. The thesis we develop is that knowledge cannot be taken as a commodity; in other words, the notion of a knowledge market is not implementable.

WHAT *IS* KNOWLEDGE MANAGEMENT?

Attitudes towards 'knowledge management' (KM) have fluctuated widely since the term first appeared. At first, it was highly and sharply inflated, then a deep, albeit less sharp, disillusionment trough followed until recently. Now, a slightly upward leading slope has started to take form. This should not come as a surprise given the wide disagreements, in both the academic and business worlds, concerning both the term 'knowledge management' and its central constituent notion: 'knowledge.'

To start with compare the following three conceptions of KM that appeared in the *Financial Times* in November 1999.

"The systematic management of the knowledge processes by which knowledge is created, identified, gathered, shared and applied." (Newing, 1999).

"[Knowledge management] Is about spreading information throughout a corporate body." (Dempsey, 1999).

"The management of commercially valuable information." (Vernon, 1999).

What these conceptions exemplify is that KM is perceived in two substantially different senses: a) as synonymous to information management; and b) as distinct from it.

The former sense is the case, knowingly or unknowingly, in the majority of firms dealing with knowledge management. This mistaken identification is what Malhotra (2000) terms the information-processing paradigm to knowledge management. The business world needs to realise that the notions of 'knowledge' and 'information' are substantially different from each other. It follows that firms also need to realise that certain activities cannot be just renamed and expect successful resolution by the application of old techniques and approaches. As Gupta and Govindarjan (2000, p. 71) remark:

"A gap exists between the rhetoric of knowledge management and how knowledge is actually managed in organizations."

To be precise, the gap that exists is between the rhetoric of knowledge management and *what* is actually managed in organizations. And *what* is actually managed in the vast majority of companies is anything but 'knowledge'.

The latter of the two senses introduced above is *now* taken for granted throughout the academic world and by some major pioneering organisations like

Slumberger and Nucor Steel. Such acceptance though has not led to a much-needed clarification of their foundations, that is, of the core constituent notions of 'knowledge' and 'information'. The rest of this section aims to contribute to the foundational clarification of the notion of 'knowledge'. For a summary presentation of the major views on information as well as a rudimentary theory of information and some of its consequences, see Gelepithis (1997).

Before proceeding with our task, we should stress that epistemology (i.e., the study of knowledge) is a vast area that has been studied for 2,500 years by the greatest minds in philosophy and, increasingly, by scientists in disciplines like psychology, neuroscience, and Artificial Intelligence (AI). This fact is ignored by or unknown to the great majority of books and papers on knowledge management, creating a distorted picture of the issues involved and hence of the appropriate solutions. To illustrate our point we present the following four viewpoints.

The easiest way out of the nexus of problems surrounding knowledge, without really addressing any, is exemplified by Newing's (1999) definition above in which knowledge is taken as something self-explainable or something we all know about and therefore is in need of no explanation at all. I would avoid commenting on such an approach. Let us concentrate on three views by, more or less, well-known workers in knowledge management who do accept not only the importance of the distinction between information and knowledge but also the need to explain what knowledge is.

Borghoff and Pareschi (1998, p. v) write:

"Information consists largely of data organised, grouped, and categorized into patterns to create meaning; knowledge is information put to productive use, enabling correct action. Knowledge is quite different from information, and managing knowledge is therefore decisively and qualitatively different from managing information. Information is converted into knowledge through a social, human process of shared understanding and sense-making at both the personal level and the organizational level."

This viewpoint, however unintentionally, gives the impression that there are no problems in an area beset with significant issues. For instance, what about all that information that is *not* put to productive use? Is knowledge creation, however viewed, a manageable process? Why yes or no? Could human knowledge be shared through the use of information and communication technologies (ICT) or even of AI techniques? How information is actually converted into knowledge is a big, significant, and wide open issue.

Consider now a different viewpoint as exemplified by Davenport and Prusak (1998, p. 5):

"Knowledge is a fluid mix of framed experience, values, contextual information, and expert insight that provides a framework for evaluating and

incorporating new experiences and information. It originates and is applied in the minds of knowers. In organisations, it often becomes embedded not only in documents or repositories but also in organizational routines, processes, practices, and norms."

This view restricts knowledge to informal expertise and assumes the incorporation of values. However valuable tacit knowledge is, it is definitely not the full story. The reader may juxtapose this view with the following two classification schemes attempting to specify what types of knowledge are most important for an organisation.

First according to Savage as quoted in Skyrme (1999):

* Know-how — a skill, procedures.
* Know-who — who can help me with this question or task.
* Know-what — structural knowledge, patterns.
* Know-why — a deeper kind of knowledge understanding the wider context.
* Know-when — a sense of timing, and rhythm.
* Know-where — a sense of place, where is it best to do something.

The second classification, due to Quinn, Baruch, and Zien (1997, pp. 2-3), structures the knowledge of an enterprise into the following five levels of increasing importance:

* Cognitive knowledge (or know what) — the rules and facts of a discipline.
* Advanced skills (know how) — the capacity to perform a task sufficiently well to compete effectively.
* System understanding (know why) — understanding the interrelationship and pacing rates of influences among key variables.
* Motivated creativity, discovery, or invention (care why) — the capacity to interrelate two or more disciplines to create totally new effects.
* Synthesis and trained intuition (perceptive how and why) — the capacity to understand or predict relationships that are not directly measurable.

It is interesting to note that both schemes accept the importance of the notions of understanding and sense (i.e., meaning) in, at least, some cases, but choose not to address the foundational issues involved.

We come now to our preliminary analysis of the nature of 'knowledge.' First, a couple of remarks and a disclaimer. The debate on the nature of 'knowledge' is far from settled and it is well beyond the scope of this chapter to review it. Equally, our analysis is only intended as a first draft outline contribution rather than a fully fledged theory of knowledge. For a philosophical and AI perspective on 'knowledge,' the reader is referred to Pollock (1986) and Newell (1990) respectively.

All theories (more accurately conceptions or schools of thought) of knowledge are based on the notion of belief. Where they differ is their stance on the justifiability of a belief.

We part with this tradition. Our basic building blocks are: a) the notion of meaning; and b) the process of understanding. Specifically, our thesis is that knowledge is the end result of the communication and understanding processes. The previous sentence seems to contradict the one immediately preceding it. It does not; it is coded for brevity and needs to be expanded in order to be clarified. First, both understanding and communication involve meaning. Second, there are two kinds of knowledge: individual and collective. As a first cut, individual knowledge is the end result of the understanding process; and collective knowledge is the end result of all communication processes among the members of a community. We now need to provide appropriate definitions of the related processes of understanding and communication so that proper definitions of individual and collective knowledge can also be given.

Although there had been general agreement that 'communication' involves sharing and 'understanding' (see, for example, Cherry, 1957; Ogden and Richards, 1923; Rogers 1983, 1986), no one had, *axiomatically*, defined them until Gelepithis (see 1984 for the overall framework and detailed argument, 1991 for a summary and a major key consequence). In what follows, we repeat those definitions and proceed with our analysis.

Definition of communication:

- H_1 communicates with H_2 on a topic T if, and only if: (i) H_1 understands T {Symbol: $U(H_1T)$}; (ii) H_2 understands T {Symbol: $U(H_2T)$}; (iii) $U(H_1T)$ is describable to and understood by H_2; and (iv) $U(H_2T)$ is describable to and understood by H_1.

Definition of understanding:

- An entity E has understood something, S, if and only if, E can describe S in terms of a system of own primitives (i.e., self-explainable notions).

Let us now develop a rudimentary theory of knowledge by clarifying and expanding some of the basic notions of our axiomatic system.

First, one's own primitives may refer to any idea, expression, belief or whatever someone may use to think. Second, primitives are of two kinds: linguistic and non-linguistic. It follows that such primitives may be either formal or informal. Usually, they are informal. Primitives may also be implicitly referred to. It is obvious that what may be a primitive for one person may not be a primitive for another. Even more to the point, what may be a primitive for one may be a complex idea for another. For example, 'water' was a primitive for my grandmother but it is not a primitive for those knowing that 'water' is really H_2O. It follows that since one's understanding depends on *one's* own primitives, it may well vary very significantly from person to person depending on the system of primitives reached by each person on a particular topic by a certain time. Also, since one's primitives may change with time, one's understanding may change as well. Compare, for example, a toddler's primitives with those of a quantum physicist with respect to the notion of electricity (for a discussion, see Gelepithis 1995). In summary, one's understanding depends both on time and on one's primitives. Or, more accurately, it depends on one's own primitives, which in turn depend on time. With these remarks we move on to our definition of *individual* knowledge:

Knowledge of *a topic T* for an entity E at time t, is the end result of E's understanding at time t.

It follows that:

Knowledge of E at time t is *the system* of understandings that E has reached by that time.

This we call E's knowledge system at time t or equivalently, E's *individual* knowledge at time t (symbol, $K_{e,t}$). Obviously, $K_{e,t}$ is a subsystem of E's semantic system at time t (symbol $S_{e,t}$). Where, $S_{e,t}$ is the system of all meanings that E has acquired, or has produced, by that time.

Let us see now some further important characteristics of one's individual knowledge, which follow from our analysis so far. First, *individual knowledge* is both structured and extremely rich. Second, there is a single most important characteristic of both individual human knowledge and of human semantic systems: they both change and, crucially, their changes are unpredictable.

So far we considered only individual human knowledge. There is of course collective human knowledge, which may take two forms: shared (e.g., common beliefs); and shareable (e.g., books, databases). This distinction may be seen better when considering organisational knowledge (sometimes known as organisational memory). Organisational knowledge may refer to two fundamentally different types. First, it may refer to employed individuals and their individual knowledge. This is the most valuable type and the one that the company has no real power over it. Second it may refer to an organisation's databases (whether electronic or paper-based); as such it should better be termed organisational archives. The characteristic of the second type is its static nature. This is in sharp contrast to the claim of writers like Davenport and Prusak (1998, p. 25) that: "[i]n contrast to individual knowledge, organizational knowledge is highly dynamic: it is moved by a variety of forces."

Although extremely interesting, a discussion of collective human knowledge would take us far beyond the scope of this chapter; we, therefore, just make explicit a point we shall use later on. Namely, given the relation between understanding and communication, one easily deduces that individual and collective knowledge necessarily both overlap and they are fundamentally distinct. As a result, both types of human knowledge have both formal and informal elements.

The above definitions and remarks provide a rudimentary but useful body of knowledge. Let us see what consequences do follow from this.

OUTLINE OF CONSEQUENCES

We present three major consequences of our rudimentary theory concerning:

a)   *The limits of management for a certain class of activities involving knowledge.*

b)   *The scope and limits of technology for the same class of activities.*

c)   *The issue of knowledge market.*

The first consequence is both obvious and unlikely to be pleasing. The expression 'knowledge management', when it is not misleadingly used to refer to the management of information, is a misnomer since no-one can manage something that takes place inside another one's mind. Let us clarify this point. As we have seen in the previous section, human knowledge may be partitioned in the way (illustrated in Figure 1).

Where the hyphenated arrow stands for the fact that shared human knowledge is essentially individual human knowledge that is common to more than one human. Furthemore, individual human knowledge is the result of one's complex, internal process of understanding. As such it is not manageable. What we are left with then is shareable human knowledge. Such knowledge in a variety of media (e.g., electronic, paper-based) is fundamentally static and, as it stands, meaningless. In other words, information. It needs to be interpreted by a human to be useful in any way. Such interpreted information becomes internalised and subsequently may provide part of the constituents for further knowledge creation (e.g., innovation). There it is where the management of a company—not knowledge management— can help. It can facilitate the creation and mobilisation of the available intellectual

Figure 1: Major partitionings of human knowledge (see text for the meeting of the hyphenated arrow)

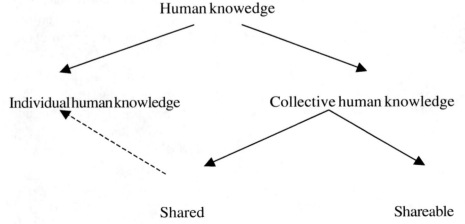

capital (that is, human resources) required for any knowledge-creation activities. Equally, it can create, sustain, or, even better, develop further the appropriate environment that would nurture such activities. This can be extremely valuable but it has nothing to do with managing knowledge.

It is worth noting that those widely accepted as pioneers in what is now called 'knowledge management' (e.g., Itani, 1987; Nonaka 1991) did not talk of knowledge management. Their emphasis was on human resources and how they could be best nurtured so that they can be mobilised and innovate. Nonaka, for instance, talked about the knowledge-creating company and how it could be managed, not about KM. It follows that a more appropriate name for the field would be knowledge nurturing. But that would be, probably, too much to be expected from those managers whose professional behaviour is still, exclusively, hard-science based.

Talking about mobilisation of invisible assets and the knowledge-creating company, Itani and Nonaka identified the key issues needed to be addressed. For our purposes we shall focus our attention to the Identification, Creation, Acquisition, and Sharing of Knowledge or KICAS for short. Their solution is far from clear. Actually, we believe that there cannot be a solution in the traditional sense of the word since they refer to the ongoing, dynamic, and creative processes necessary for the solution of any kind of humanly solvable problem rather than to problems themselves. As such, and taking into account the key characteristics of knowledge as outlined earlier, managers need to become themselves the 'couriers' and, most importantly, the communicators of knowledge within their company. This is, in essence, the major new activity of what Hansen and Oetinger (2001) call T-shaped managers.

The first consequence referred to the limits of *management* for a certain class of activities, namely, the KICAS nexus of issues and the need for managers to refocus their activities. The second consequence concerns the scope and limits of *technology* in dealing with the KICAS issues. Without loss of force for our argument, we shall focus on two of the four issues, namely, the creation and sharing of human knowledge. These are the issues emphasised by organisational and management scientists like Nonaka and Takeuchi (1995), Quinn et al. (1997) — under the name diffusion for knowledge sharing — and Skyrme (1999) — under the name knowledge networking for the same issue.

Our second point may best be seen if we start with some historical remarks. The earliest, but neither easy nor permanent, way to solve the KICAS nexus of problems has been to attract the appropriate human(s). This practice, of all organisations, individuals, and states, is still the best *prerequisite* to the solution of the KICAS nexus of problems. Slowly, the development of networks of knowledgeable people started — sometimes in the form of schools of thought like the

Platonic Academy and the Aristotelian Lyceum—and gradually were turned into what we now call Universities or Learned Societies. More recently, companies with sufficient resources started developing their own dedicated resources in the form of R&D departments. Usually, the objective of such divisions is the development of appropriate technology for the benefit of the company. Sometimes the objective was more general, such as developing aids to innovation. Instances are the Myers-Briggs type indicator and the Herrmann Brain dominance instrument (see Leonard and Straus, 1997, for discussion and references).

Most recently, the use of ICT and increasingly AI is at the forefront of developments facilitating innovation and providing solutions to aspects of the KICAS set of problems. Books and edited collections describing models or technological tools for enhancing human interaction or a human's ability to deal with the exponential explosion in exploring one's semantic structure abound (e.g., Quinn et al., 1997; Borghoff and Pareschi, 1998; Skyrme, 1999). What is common in all these developments is that despite the increasing use of artificial aids, the human remains in the loop. We cannot do without her too (see, for instance, Cross and Baird, 2000; Senge and Carstedt, 2001). Let us take a closer look.

In principle, AI/ICT can provide solutions to the following three types of problems:
- Overall integration of information and knowledge sources and tools.
- Identification of appropriately specified information through the use of Search Engines.
- Formalisation of certain aspects of Human Knowledge through R&D in Knowledge representation, and reasoning.

AI/ICT systems though, cannot, on their own, either create or share knowledge. This is a point that is very often overlooked with serious negative consequences. Let us briefly see the reason for these intrinsic limits of the AI/ICT systems.

Such systems may be distinguished into two categories (Gelepithis, 2001). The first category is characterised by tools employing representational systems, which are eventually human-based. Human-based AI systems, whether creative or not, are, *at best,* axiomatic systems with in-built procedures for the handling of the system's premises. At worst, they are ad hoc systems capable of providing a cost-effective and, quite often, enhanced solution with respect to their human counter-parts. A better solution, nevertheless, does not constitute creation of new knowledge. In the best-case scenario, they are capable of producing consequences some of which are bound to be new. Such a capability is of course very desirable but it is ultimately checked and evaluated by humans. In other words, *novel* human knowledge could only be created by humans; creative AI systems, even in principle, can only create *new consequences of existing* knowledge. Creation of novel human knowledge is species-specific.

It should be noted that although humans are the only creators of *novel* human knowledge, ICT and in particular AI can facilitate the creation of such knowledge through the development of tools enabling: (a) increased connectivity within the semantic system of humans; and (b) increased and enhanced human-human communication. I believe the latter is what Skyrme (1999) calls knowledge networking.

The second category — say R — not yet developed but feasible, will be characterised by systems possessing their *own* representational systems, that is, by representational systems independent of the language of another kind of system — say human. Such systems will be able to create novel knowledge, but such knowledge will not be necessarily understood by humans. To be precise such knowledge will be understandable by humans only to the extent that it will be formalised. This is a point that need not concern us here though and we shall not expand on it (for more information on the two fundamental categories of representational systems, the reader is referred to Gelepithis (1995)).

We come now to our third consequence: a knowledge market is not implementable. The first thing that any knowledge market would need is a system that would measure knowledge. This is a requirement that, probably, the great majority would agree on but nobody has, so far, proposed a solution to it. Of course, no solution yet does not imply no solution ever. In what follows we first present two claims and one argument for the implementability of a 'knowledge market', and subsequently we briefly outline our argument against.

The first viewpoint may be termed the 'blind faith to market forces' approach. According to this, the situation in trying to create a knowledge market is problematic but: "Given time, market forces will undoubtedly take care of the situation" (Burton-Jones, 1999, p. 221). The second viewpoint may be termed the 'shifting the goalposts' approach. Its extreme form is illustrated by Gamble and Blackwell (2001, p. 185). They remark: "It is almost axiomatic in management that what you cannot measure you cannot manage." Unfortunately, the next step they go to is to create a metric for a "knowledge management initiative." No comments.

An almost acceptable 'shifting the goalposts' viewpoint has been put forward by Davenport and Prusak (1998). They first introduce the elements of a 'knowledge market' and subsequently they discuss its inefficiencies and pathologies as well as ways to overcome them. For the purpose of this chapter, we focus our attention on their presentation of the characteristic elements of a 'knowledge market'. Their starting point is that knowledge markets exist although not as "pure" markets (i.e., markets that operate solely in economic terms). On that basis they try to establish the elements for a good knowledge market. They see three:

"first of all, to recognize that market forces exist; second, to try to understand how it functions; and third, to make it more efficient" (ibid, p. 26).

On market forces they distinguish three players: buyers, sellers, and brokers. The problem is that the object of their transactions although named to be knowledge is, essentially, information. The two notions are related, but as we know, they are fundamentally distinct. Their next step is the mechanism of the knowledge market, that is, its price system. They claim that a price system for a knowledge market revolves around the notions of: money, reciprocity, reputation, altruism, and trust. In a nutshell they recognise that money is far from adequate and believe that reciprocity, reputation, and altruism (these three in diminishing degree), as well as their combinations, constitute the substitute for money. Since transactions involving reciprocity, reputation, and altruism do not constitute payment in the traditional monetary sense of the term, they are forced to introduce the notion of trust as the necessary factor for the workings of such a market. But trust is one of the goods (the other two are loyalty, and truth-telling), cited by Nobel Laureate Arrow (1974, p. 22), which "cannot, in principle, be taken as commodities in the market sense."

Linking knowledge to truth or truth-telling is an avenue worth taking and fully exploring but it is well beyond the scope of this chapter. Instead, we briefly outline here why a 'compromised' knowledge market of the sort that Davenport and Prusak have considered cannot really function by commenting on the first two elements of their methodology. In other words, we assume that markets require two elements for their existence. First, an object to be transacted among their players. Second, a price system as its mechanism for the transactions. Let us see why these two requirements are not applicable in the case of knowledge.

Attaining knowledge is a process whereby the start and end points are difficult if not impossible to define. The expert is knowledgeable in his particular field because of an integration of a number of factors such as factual information, experience and intuition. This process is ongoing, and even when a knowledgeable state is achieved the learning process still continues. Therefore knowledge is a special state or process which cannot be seen as a commodity. Davenport and Prusak's (1998) buyers, sellers, and traders cannot trade in knowledge but only in information.

When an expert gives some advice or judgment, we are gaining information that is based on his or her knowledge. We may say that the more knowledgeable the expert, the more valuable the information gleaned. Therefore what companies should be aiming to do is create the environment that allows the knowledge process and state to be achieved. The information resulting from such environments can be marketed. It is important to make the distinction between the two. Information can be treated as a commodity but the knowledge environment that produces the information is not subject to market forces.

Some may argue that 'knowledge' markets have existed, at least since humans started exchanging goods they produced themselves, for any good produced was bound to involve the use of some 'knowledge' at some point in the production process. Nevertheless, what was traded was the good produced, not the 'knowledge' involved in its production. The reason is simple. The 'knowledge' involved in the production of goods was but one element of a complex internal process. In those earlier times, that process was simply beyond any sort of measure. It is still today, and it will be tomorrow, because it involves too many tacit elements. The formal-informal boundary will keep shifting, creating ever larger areas of formalised knowledge and, at the same time, revealing larger areas of informal knowledge. Again a full discussion of this point exceeds the confines of this chapter.

Goods are there to be checked, compared against similar ones, and eventually assigned a price. Goods are objective entities persisting, more or less invariably, through considerable time intervals. Human knowledge, both individual and collective, changes. What is more, it changes unpredictably. No manager would wish to purchase a car that could be turned into a 10-meter boa constrictor. Seriously now, what should be the value of the 21st century equivalent of Newton's laws? How much should one pay for that imperceptible, yet consciously made, grimace that reveals a no-purchase of company-X? Human knowledge is not a rose, a cup, or a massage.

ACKNOWLEDGMENT

We would like to thank the anonymous reviewer for his or her constructive comments. Taking them into account was a useful exercise and resulted in a better chapter.

REFERENCES

Arrow, K. (1974). *The Limits of Organization*. New York: W. W. Norton & Company, Inc.

Borghoff, U. M. and Pareschi, R. (Eds.). (1998). *Information Technology for Knowledge Management*. New York: Springer.

Burton-Jones, A. (1999). *Knowledge Capitalism: Business, Work, and Learning in the New Economy*. Oxford: Oxford University Press.

Cherry, C. (1978). *On Human Communication: A Review, a Survey, and a Criticism* (third edition). New York: The MIT Press.

Cross, R. and Baird, L. (2000). Technology is not enough: Improving performance by building organizational memory. *Sloan Management Review, 41*(3), 69-78.

Davenport, T. H. and Prusak, L. (1998). *Working Knowledge: How Organizations Manage What They Know*. Boston, MA: Harvard Business School Press.

Dempsey, M. (1999). The need for vigilance in the information battle. *Knowledge Management, Financial Times Survey*, (November 10), 2.

Gamble, P. R. and Blackwell, J. (2001). *Knowledge Management: A State of the Art Guide*. Kogan Page.

Gelepithis, P. A. M. (1984). *On the Foundations of Artificial Intelligence and Human Cognition*. Ph.D. Thesis, Brunel University, England.

Gelepithis, P. A. M. (1991). The possibility of machine intelligence and the impossibility of human-machine communication. *Cybernetica, XXXIV*(4), 255-268.

Gelepithis, P. A. M. (1995). Revising Newell's conception of representation. *Cognitive Systems, 4*(2), 131-139, (Special issue on Representation).

Gelepithis, P. A. M. (1997). A rudimentary theory of information: Consequences for information science and information systems. *World Futures, 49*, 263-274.

Gelepithis, P. A. M. (2001). *Intelligent Systems Volume 1: Knowledge Representation, Social and Psychological Impact of Artificial Intelligence*. Athens, Hellas: Stamoulis Editions, Averof st. (In Greek).

Gupta, A. K. and Govindarajan, V. (2000). Knowledge management's social dimension: Lessons from Nucor Steel. *Sloan Management Review, 42*(1), 71-80.

Hansen, M. T. and von Oetinger, B. (2001). Introducing T-shaped managers: Knowledge management's next generation. *Harvard Business Review*, (March), 107-116.

Itani, H. (1987). *Mobilizing Invisible Assets*. Boston, MA: Harvard University Press.

Leonard, D. and Straus, S. (1997). Putting your company's whole brain to work. *Harvard Business Review on Knowledge Management*, 109-136. Boston, MA: Harvard Business School Press.

Malhotra, Y. (2000). Knowledge management and new organization forms: A framework for business model innovation. In Malhotra, Y. (Ed.), *Knowledge Management and Virtual Organisations*. Hershey, PA: Idea Group Publishing.

Newell, A. (1990). *Unified Theories of Cognition*. Boston, MA: Harvard University Press.

Newing, R. (1999). Connecting people: Both through IT and face-to-face. *Knowledge Management, Financial Times Survey*, (November 10), 2.

Nonaka, I. (1991). The knowledge-creating company. *Harvard Business Review on Knowledge Management*, 21-45. Boston, MA: Harvard Business School Press.

Nonaka, I., and Takeuchi, H. (1995). *The Knowledge-Creating Company.* Oxford: Oxford University Press.

Ogden, C. K. and Richards, I. A. (1923, 1956). *The Meaning of Meaning.* New Jersey: Harcourt Brace and Co., Inc.

Pollock, J. L. (1986). *Contemporary Theories of Knowledge.* Hutchinson.

Quinn, J. B., Baruch, J. J. and Zien, K. A. (1997). *Innovation Explosion: Using Intellect and Software to Revolutionize Growth Strategies.* New York: The Free Press.

Rogers, E. M. (1983, 1986). *Elements of Diffusion* [Extracts from Chapter 1 of Rogers, E. M. (Ed.) (1983), *Diffusion of Innovations*, 3rd ed., New York: The Free Press.] In Roy, R. and Wield, D. (Eds.), *Product Design and Technological Innovation.* Open University Press.

Senge, P. M. and Carstedt, G. (2001). Innovating our way to the next industrial revolution. *MIT Sloan Management Review, 42*(2), 24-38.

Skyrme, D. J. (1999). *Knowledge Networking: Creating the Collaborative Enterprise.* Oxford: Butterworth Heinemann.

Vernon, M. (1999). Enhancing links to the customer. *Knowledge Management, Financial Times Survey,* (November 10), 10.

Section II

Practical Aspects of Knowledge and Business Process Management

Chapter VI

Knowledge Management in Action: The Experience of Infosys Technologies

V. P. Kochikar, Kavi Mahesh and C. S. Mahind
Infosys Technologies Ltd., India

ABSTRACT

This chapter presents the detailed architecture that Infosys has deployed for implementing KM internally, and the company's experiences in using that architecture for managing its knowledge. A brief historical perspective of the evolution of the Infosys KM effort is discussed and a description of the Infosys Knowledge Shop (KShop), Infosys's integrated knowledge portal that we have built, is given. The real test of the maturity of any organizational initiative is when it becomes invisible, a part of the normal way people work. The aim of the KM initiative is thus to move towards a culture where knowledge sharing is built into the organizational fabric. The chapter elaborates on one key mechanism that has been devised to help create such a sharing culture — the Knowledge Currency Units (KCUs) scheme. Some of the key challenges and success factors the company has faced are discussed, and the approaches used to manage those are described.

INTRODUCTION

Today's organizations face a strategic landscape that is characterized by changing technology, rising stakeholder expectations, shifting competitor profiles and the emergence of new markets. The need to stay competitive in such an environment throws up immense challenges, and leveraging well on knowledge — internal as well as external to the organization — is a key imperative. Knowledge Management (KM) has thus, in recent years, acquired increasing management focus.

A central tenet of KM is to raise the speed and quality of learning, decision-making and customer service at the level of the organization as well as the individual. By institutionalizing best practices existing in pockets, facilitating greater reuse and helping better virtual teamwork, KM also raises the organization's ability to deliver higher quality and achieve faster time-to-market. Overall, KM also reduces risk and makes the organization more robust to thrive in a changing environment.

Given that most KM programs must start out with modest resources, a KM strategy must be optimized to extract the greatest effectiveness from these resources. A key success factor is getting the optimal emphasis on each of the four focal areas — people, process, technology and content — right from the early stages (see, for example, Davenport and Prusak, 1998). The specific emphasis laid on each of these is a function of the organizational culture and business context.

Infosys Technologies Limited (*NASDAQ: INFY*) is an IT consulting and software services organization headquartered in Bangalore, India. Founded in 1981, the company's revenues in 2001 were $413 million, having grown at a compounded rate of 70% over the preceding decade. The company primarily services Fortune 1000 clients located in North America, Europe and the Asia-Pacific. Infosys has consistently been rated among India's leading wealth-creators, and recorded a net profit of $131 million in 2001, representing 32% of revenues. It was the top-ranked Indian company in the *Review 200* listing compiled by the *Far Eastern Economic Review,* and has been rated the most respected company in India by, among others, *Business World* and the *Economic Times*. The company operates globally, with eight development centers in India, five in North America and one in the UK, and has 10,500 employees on its rolls.

The mission of Infosys' KM effort is to ensure that all organizational learning is leveraged in delivering business advantage to the customer. The objectives are to minimize effort dissipated in redoing learning that has already happened elsewhere, and ensuring that Infoscions (as employees are called) in contact with the customer have the collective knowledge of the organization behind them. The company thus aims to move towards a *"Learn Once, Use Anywhere"* paradigm. Infosys uses the proprietary KMM, or Knowledge Management Maturity model (Kochikar, 2000a), a staged maturity framework, to underpin its KM strategy.

Infosys has devised and implemented a KM deployment architecture that has been found to work well. This chapter presents the detailed architecture that Infosys has deployed for implementing KM internally, and the company's experiences in using that architecture for managing its knowledge. While each company's KM journey is unique, we believe that sharing information about our architecture and experiences will prove useful to other organizations venturing along the KM path. Equally important, we believe that sharing the *process* by which we arrived at the architecture that is most optimal in our context holds meaningful lessons for other organizations seeking to define their own KM implementations. Thus, we also present here a brief historical perspective of the evolution of the Infosys KM effort.

A description of the Infosys Knowledge Shop (KShop), Infosys's integrated knowledge portal that we have built, is given. The real test of the maturity of any organizational initiative is when it becomes invisible, a part of the normal way people work. The aim of the KM initiative is thus to move towards a culture where knowledge sharing is built into the organizational fabric. We elaborate on one key mechanism that has been devised to help create such a sharing culture — the Knowledge Currency Units (KCU) scheme. This narrative also brings out some of the key challenges and success factors we have faced, and describes the approaches we have used to manage those.

KNOWLEDGE @ INFOSYS–
A HISTORICAL PERSPECTIVE

The company started small but has grown explosively over the last 10 years, and now has operations spread out across multiple locations spanning the globe. The effective utilization of the company's knowledge base has always been seen as pivotal to success. Factors that have driven this belief include:

- *The quality imperative*: The primary mechanism for raising the quality of services delivered to the customer is the institutionalization of best practices residing in organizational pockets — a process which needs the sharing and adoption of these practices across departmental interfaces.
- *The revenue productivity imperative:* The constant search to provide greater value for each dollar spent by the customer means the company must raise the level of reuse; the cost and effort of redoing something that has been done earlier — and relearning something that has been learned earlier — grow less affordable.
- *The risk reduction imperative:* Diversifying into new technologies, domains, geographical areas and services means that the organization must learn new ways of doing things; managing changes in team composition resulting from attrition and personnel movements require that as much knowledge as possible be documented.
- *The market awareness imperative:* As customers as well as competitors become increasingly global, the company needs to have efficient mechanisms to pull in learning from new environments.

- *The growth imperative:* Maintaining a consistently high pace of growth means an ability to rapidly enable new recruits on technology, process and cultural issues; it also needs the definition and dissemination of scalable processes that support the delivery of high-quality software and consulting.
- *The virtual teamwork imperative:* Increasingly globalized operations and rising customer expectations have meant a more complex execution model, often requiring teams that are spread across continents to collaborate in delivering a single software service. Such *virtual teamwork* represents a microcosm of the issues arising in KM, needing good technologies to support communication and collaboration, and a mindset of working with co-workers who may be situated in different time zones, and who may possibly belong to different cultures.

Driven by the above imperatives, several practices have been evolved at Infosys for ensuring the effective sharing and use of knowledge. While many of these pre-date the formal term 'Knowledge Management,' they can nevertheless be retrospectively classified as practices that sought to implement the spirit of KM.

In 1992, the company felt the need for an organization-wide repository that would enshrine experiential learning gained during the execution of software projects, and make it available for 'posterity.' The Education & Research (E&R) department was charged with the responsibility of developing and managing such a system. The system developed by E&R, christened the Body of Knowledge (BoK), was initially implemented by means of a simple, homegrown software application. The BoK system envisaged entries being contributed by Infoscions, with a lightweight review mechanism to screen their content, applicability and presentation aspects. A pre-defined template required a declaration that the work was experiential, and that it did not violate third-party Intellectual Property Rights (IPR) — in case the IPR belonged to a third party such as the customer, clearance from that party was mandatory. In 1997, this system was re-hosted as a web-based application with HTML content, and made available on the then-fledgling intranet. The application — at the time the first to be developed in Infosys that was based on web technologies — featured an easy-to-use interface with search utilities. Incentives for contribution were also defined, as were mechanisms to publicize contributions.

Given the knowledge-intensive nature of Infosys's business, a clear understanding of its 'knowledge capital' has always been considered essential. Traditional financial statements are notoriously ill-equipped to reflect this intangible form of capital. Infosys has adopted a model for evaluating its intangible assets. The methodology used is based on Dr. Karl-Erik Sveiby's Intangible Assets Monitor framework (Sveiby, 1997).

By late 1998, the company was multi-locational and had reached an employee strength of 5,000—which meant that it was no longer possible for people to rely on informal mechanisms for identifying 'experts' to be consulted for knowledge inputs at various stages of project execution. It was decided then that E&R would develop a knowledge directory, to be christened the *People-Knowledge Map* (PKM), which would provide pointers to experts within the organization. Before implementing this directory, two fundamental questions needed to be answered. The first was, would the registration of experts in this system be mandatory—i.e., would every employee who met certain pre-defined criteria for 'expertise' on a given subject be entered into the system? After extensive debate and considerable thought, it was decided to make registration purely voluntary, with incentives to promote it. The rationale behind this was that mandatory registration, while ensuring large numbers of registrants, would be unlikely to guarantee a very high degree of commitment to respond on the part of the registrant (unless responding too was made mandatory, which would be unlikely to guarantee a high quality of response!). Voluntary, incentivized registration, on the other hand, would be likely to attract a small number of highly enthusiastic registrants, thus ensuring that the credibility of the PKM system remained high.

The second question to be answered was, at what level of granularity would these experts register? Existing taxonomies, such as those of the IEEE, the ACM, the Dewey Decimal system and various other taxonomies used by the academic and research communities, were considered, but none was found to fit our requirement. Some of the reasons: the 'top levels' of standard taxonomies are too general, yet do not encompass many areas that we needed—for example, vertical domains, culture, etc.; most standard taxonomies have large portions that are not relevant to Infosys's business; many latest terms are not yet included in them; and, these are generally taxonomies of concepts, which do not contain many proper names (of products, technologies, etc.) that are important for our purposes.

The solution was to develop a proprietary *knowledge hierarchy*—a multi-level taxonomy of topics that represented knowledge in the Infosys context. At the time of definition, the hierarchy consisted of about 780 nodes, with the top level being *Technology, Methodology, Project Management, Application Domain* and *Culture*, and deeper levels representing a finer grain of topics. The PKM application developed featured an intranet-based interface that supported registration of or search for experts. Users could also see profiles of experts and contact them to satisfy their knowledge needs.

The company-wide intranet, called *Sparsh*, has acted as a central information portal since its inception in 1996. The intranet consists of about 10,000 nodes, spread throughout the global development centers (DCs), and marketing offices. Official policies, press releases and articles, and web-based in-house information systems are available from the home page. Sparsh also links project, Practice Unit, department and personal web pages. Protection from external intrusion is achieved by means of firewalls.

The company's e-mailing system, which every Infoscion has access to, supports bulletin boards for official announcements as well as technical and personal discussions. The technical bulletin board has been a vibrant knowledge exchange forum in its own right, generating discussions on technical topics.

A web-based *virtual classroom,* also developed and managed by E&R, has been deployed on the intranet, and allows access to various courses. This system incorporates a discussion forum where participants can post and respond to course-related queries.

Practices that have worked are also propagated through regular seminars and best-practice sessions, held both within units and organization-wide. There were also a few other knowledge-sharing practices and systems employed by various organizational units, primarily for use within their units.

An Organization-Wide KM Initiative

The formal KM initiative was born in late 1999 when Nandan Nilekani, president and COO, decided that all the knowledge-sharing mechanisms that had existed until then needed to be synergized under a common umbrella, with a clearly articulated vision and strategy for implementation. Widespread consultation and debate helped define the vision, which was *to be an organization...*

- ..where every action is fully enabled by the power of knowledge;
- ..which truly believes in leveraging knowledge for innovation;
- ..where every employee is empowered by the knowledge of every other employee;
- ..which is a globally respected knowledge leader.

Knowledge Management Adoption — A 'Maturity' View

The first step towards the development of a conceptual framework for implementing KM at Infosys was to define a *knowledge life cycle* as consisting of the following stages:

Knowledge Acquisition is the stage where the knowledge is first generated/ absorbed by any organizational unit. *Knowledge Sharing/Dissemination* implies packaging the knowledge/expertise in a form fit for use, and delivering it to the point of use, at the time of use. Sharing may be synchronous — direct person-to-person, or asynchronous — through capture, storage and subsequent delivery. *Knowledge Reuse* represents the stage where the knowledge/expertise shared is actually put to use for performing a task.

In any given organization, each of these stages of the knowledge life cycle can exhibit varying degrees of maturity. Rising maturity of each of these life-cycle stages implies an increase in the overall maturity of KM in the organization. It is therefore possible to map a given degree of maturity of each of these stages to an overall level of maturity of KM of the organization. This is the concept behind the Knowledge Management Maturity model, which characterizes each maturity level of KM in terms of the efficacy of each of the three stages of the knowledge life cycle.

The KMM model, which draws philosophically from the Software Engineering Institute's CMM (Capability Maturity Model) (SEI, 1993), thus envisages five stages of KM maturity — *Default, Reactive, Aware, Convinced* and *Sharing*. It is worth noting that in the model:

- A given maturity level implies a certain level of organizational capability (from level 4 onwards, quantitatively) subject to the prerequisites being met.
- Each maturity level clearly maps on to the company's business goals (i.e., the meaning of each level in business terms is clear).

The concept of maturity level of KM thus helps an organization achieve two aims:

- It provides a framework which an organization can use to assess its current level of KM maturity.
- It acts as a mechanism to focus, and help prioritize, efforts to raise the level of KM maturity.

For further details of the Infosys KMM Model, the reader is referred to Kochikar (2000a). We now proceed to explain the architecture that was developed for deploying KM in the organization.

THE KM DEPLOYMENT ARCHITECTURE

As said earlier, deploying KM needs the four major areas of People, Content, Technology and Process to be addressed. In order to understand the most optimal distribution of effort in the Infosys business and cultural context, a detailed survey of various constituencies within the organization — from top management to programmer level — was carried out, and several rounds of discussion of the draft architecture helped converge on the final architecture that is described below. Detailed analyses of the issues faced in the process of evolving this architecture are discussed in Kochikar (2002a, b).

The People Architecture

The people architecture defines the roles and responsibilities for various aspects of the KM implementation. The distribution of responsibilities must strike the right balance between functions that will be managed by a central group, and those that will be performed in a decentralized way. Infosys has chosen a 'facilitated decentralized approach,' which envisages the following: the technology architecture management for KM — development, deployment and maintenance — is done by a central KM group. All stages of the content management process are anchored by the KM group — creation of internal content however must happen in the field, and is facilitated by the KM group.

The conception and implementation of the KM strategy is also anchored by the seven-member central KM group. The group has two sub-groups — one each to oversee KM research and content management, and technology architecture development and maintenance — each headed by a manager. A third managerial role — that of the brand manager — has responsibility for internal publicity and promotion. The research and content management group includes a knowledge content editor whose primary role is to anchor the content management process. Other roles — *practice champions* who devote time to facilitation of content generation, reviewers and *Gurus* — are part time and played by appropriately identified individuals from across the organization.

In the early stages of a KM effort, providing the right incentives is a key success factor. The reward and recognition program for KM at Infosys revolves around the *Knowledge Currency Unit* (KCU) scheme. The scheme incentivizes authors, reviewers and users of knowledge. Authors earn KCUs when their documents/ artifacts are accepted for publication in the KM repository. Subsequently, each time a document is used, the user can award KCUs which accrue to the author's KCU account. The user of a document can give on-line feedback on its utility, and suggestions for improvement. The effort spent by subject area experts on reviewing documents for publication also earns KCUs.

Employees thus build their KCU accounts, whose balance is a measure of their involvement in knowledge sharing. Accumulated KCUs can be redeemed for digital gift certificates that can be used at a specified Internet-based mall.

A successful KM incentive program must, however, go beyond material rewards, and public recognition is a powerful form of motivation. KShop features a *KCU Score Board* that gives visibility to top knowledge sharers. Periodic *Knowledge Summits* are held to celebrate knowledge-sharing activities, and publicly recognize and reward leading knowledge sharers.

The Content Architecture

The content architecture specifies how knowledge assets are organized for ease of retrieval. Eighteen distinct content types have been identified, a few examples being white papers, case studies, FAQs and web site reviews. Experiential learning is encapsulated in the form of Body of Knowledge (BoK) documents, which constitute a key content type in the current architecture — BoK entries existing in the legacy BoK system have been migrated to the new architecture. The four-level *knowledge hierarchy,* initially developed in 1998-99 as described earlier, has been expanded and now contains just over 1,200 topics or subject areas — the explosive growth of Internet technologies alone has contributed over 300 topics. To facilitate easy retrieval, each document is tagged by one or more paths through this hierarchy. Thus, a white paper on the eXtensible Mark-up Language (XML) would be tagged by the path *Technology>Internet/E-Commerce Technologies>XML*. A graphical view of a section of the hierarchy is shown in Figure 1.

Associated with each document is a *composite KCU rating,* which factors in the KCUs awarded by subject matter experts to the document at the time of reviews, those awarded by users over the document's life cycle, and also the frequency and recency of its use. The composite KCU rating is thus a market-determined indicator of document quality.

Documents are also tagged by the audience role(s) for which they are most suitable, and by security parameters that limit access to a desired subset of the audience.

Figure 1: A partial few of the knowledge hierarchy, showing a subset of topics

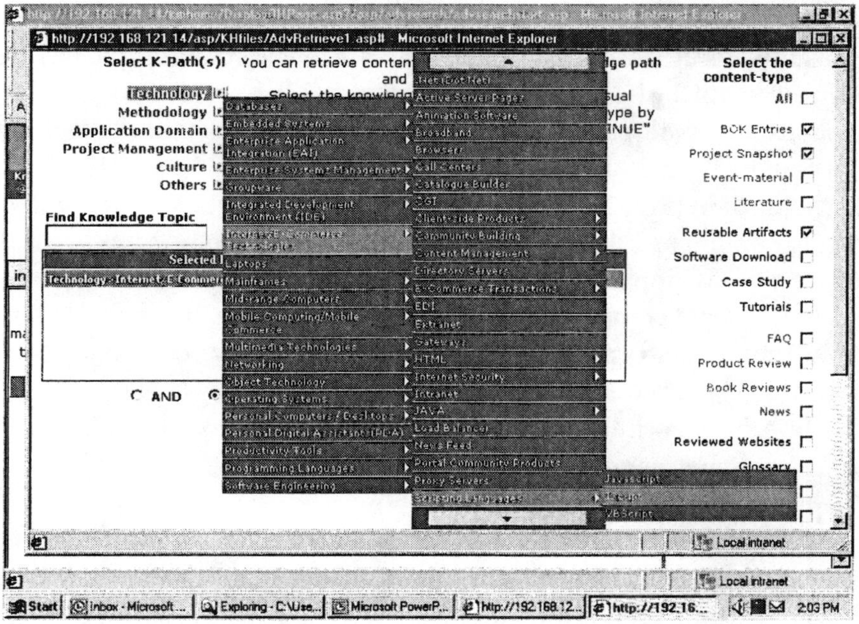

Figure 2: Homepage of knowledge shop, the Infosys knowledge portal

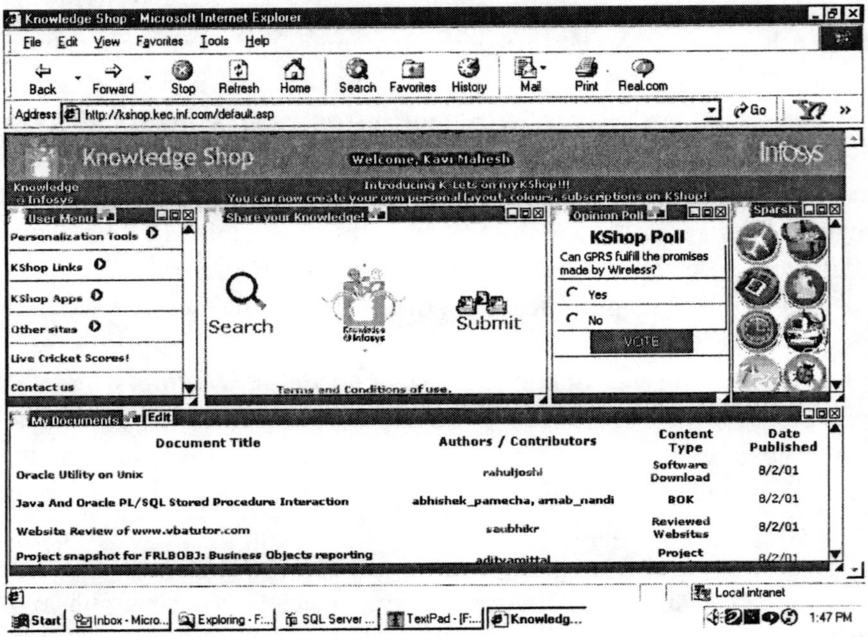

The Technology Architecture

The Infosys Knowledge Shop (KShop) (Figure 2) provides all of the basic functionality expected of a knowledge portal as well as several applications that are customized to suit the Infosys business processes. Each of the 18 distinct content types has its own home page, which describes the kind of knowledge represented by that content type, and displays the top ranking (by composite KCU rating) documents in the repository of that content type. An advanced search engine helps users find content by knowledge paths, keywords, content types or the other parameters by which content is tagged. Content retrieved is displayed in decreasing order of composite KCU rating — the system thus aims to assist the user in sifting through a possibly large number of documents that may meet the search criteria specified.

KShop, built entirely by the KM group's technology team, also includes basic features such as an on-line document submission facility, a review and publication workflow, several ways of showcasing new and popular content, threaded discussion forums and on-line chat rooms. KShop supports interfaces that allow users to award KCUs to authors while rating their documents, and for KCU account redemption. KShop also hosts the revamped People-Knowledge Map expert locator application.

Several other incentives are offered for employees to use KShop on a daily basis. It provides live feeds of stock quotes and sports scores. Its homepage (Figure 2) can be personalized by each user to create their own *myKShop*, with a customized layout, sizes and colors. In addition, they can 'subscribe' to content by defining the content types and knowledge paths of their interest. Subscribers can see latest content additions that match their subscriptions when they visit the home page. They can also choose to be alerted to additions matching their subscriptions by e-mail at a frequency of their choice. The portal serves about 20,000 requests a day. Each access is also logged so that KM activity can be tracked by parameters such as location, practice unit, department or project.

KShop runs on five PCs, each of which acts as a server. Conventional wisdom has it that an enterprise-grade knowledge portal for a large company must run on high-end, "server class" machines running expensive software such as application servers. Our experience has thus shown that an effective and scalable technology infrastructure can be built for knowledge management without expensive hardware or special KM software products.

Satellite Repositories

The Technology architecture (Figure 3) distributes content storage and management by implementing locally managed content repositories that act as satellites to the central KM repository. The rationale behind this satellite repository system is to permit specialized groups in the organization to own content relevant to their areas. However, the user interface is seamless — a search on KShop's

Figure 3: Technology architecture of knowledge shop

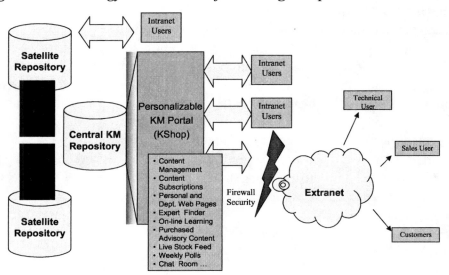

home page retrieves content irrespective of whether it is located in the central repository, or on one of the satellites.

Back-End Data Integration

A variety of corporate data is drawn into the knowledge portal periodically by tight integration of its database with various corporate databases. Employee data, including contact information, location and current project assignment, are synchronized with the corporate HR database on a weekly basis. Data on encashment of KCUs (which are taxable perquisites!) are integrated with the payroll system so that appropriate taxes can be deducted.

The Process Architecture

The process architecture includes processes that are internal to the KM Group and which are used in the management of various KM functions, and those that are developed and deployed to facilitate KM in the field. The content management process comprises different stages such as review by identified internal experts, streamlining and editing, publishing, certification and maintenance. About 170 documents are submitted to KShop each month, and go through a two-tier review process — the first stage of review happens at the content editor's desk where conformance to usability, styling and IPR norms are checked. The second stage of review is done by subject matter experts, and checks for content quality, relevance and utility.

Other defined processes include those for publicity, branding, reporting and benefits measurement. Since the Infosys KM effort is relatively young, ensuring that outdated content is updated or removed is not yet a priority. However, a content maintenance process has been defined, and will use the KCU mechanism to identify documents that potentially qualify for revision or 'retirement.'

A key focus on the process front has been to minimize the overhead associated with creating content. Tweaking existing business processes to facilitate knowledge sharing, and automating certain types of content generation have been two solutions to this vexing problem. For example, 'project snapshots' are now generated 'on the fly' from existing databases containing project management and employee data, thus obviating the need for manual compilation of these snapshots.

In addition to its reward and recognition role, the KCU scheme also provides a mechanism for quantitative management of the KM processes. One aspect of quantitative management is the composite KCU rating mentioned earlier. KCUs are also used as metrics in the measurement of KM benefits and for measuring the level of KM activity in any organizational unit. The average rate of KCU generation is currently 8,000 per month.

EFFECTIVENESS AND BENEFITS
OF KM AT INFOSYS

There are, in general, three forms of evidence that can be used in assessing the benefits of a KM program — anecdotal, survey-based and metrics-based. Evolving metrics-based methods to measure benefits is the most challenging — tracing business benefits attributable to knowledge-sharing, defining appropriate metrics, ensuring that the data required to compute the metrics is available, are some of the challenges involved.

In an internal survey based on a sample size of about 600, more than 99% of the respondents said that they believe KM is essential for the company; 79% said the knowledge-sharing environment in the company encouraged the documentation of knowledge for future use; 87% asserted that whenever possible, they tried to reuse existing organizational knowledge rather than start from scratch.

Content submission to the company's knowledge repository has increased nearly 10 fold since the transition from the BoK system to the organization-wide integrated KM implementation. A document is downloaded/viewed by users of KShop every two work minutes. The survey also revealed that users had received distinct benefits from the knowledge-sharing environment that is prevalent in the company:

• More than 80% believe that their team's quality of work and productivity have improved, while 70% said good knowledge-sharing practices had helped in delivering tangible benefit to customers.

• 73% felt they saved more than one person-day in the last six months by using the existing knowledge architecture, with 14% saying they saved more than eight person-days (and 13% saying they saved nothing). Three-quarters said that when needed, they were easily able to tap organizational knowledge in doing their work.

Our approach has been to measure in quantitative terms the impact of knowledge sharing on traditional indicators of project performance, using the KCU mechanism. Several projects have also been able to quantify savings in dollar terms, and also report various other benefits such as improved quality, faster turnaround times, etc. These projects are showcased during the periodic knowledge summits, thus allowing other projects to appreciate the relevance and potential benefits of knowledge sharing.

Up until the date of writing this, 185 employees have crossed the figure of 100 KCUs earned, with eight having crossed the figure of 1,000 (a measure of the vibrancy of the initiative is the fact that, during the time gap of two months between the two revisions of this chapter, the above figures went up from 102 and three, respectively!).

OTHER KM INITIATIVES AT INFOSYS

Apart from defining a greenfield architecture for managing knowledge, a successful KM strategy must usually also integrate existing knowledge-sharing mechanisms and collimate them so that they do not result in duplication or lack of visibility of effort. The satellite repository mechanism described earlier is an example of how the Infosys KM strategy has accommodated the need of groups that maintain specialized knowledge to continue to retain ownership of that knowledge. This section brings out illustrations of how the specific KM needs of a few other groups are addressed.

Infosys's Banking Business Unit (BBU), which provides software products and surround solutions to banks, has a knowledge base — "TechOnline," accessible from the internet home page, www.infosysinbanking.com — that serves to meet the reference needs of its customers, partners and employees at customer sites. This system is linked to the same database into which the global helpdesk logs calls and solutions, thus ensuring the solutions are current. Knowledge gained about the customer, product and deployment scenario is recorded and baselined in a version control system.

As a second example, an offshore development center within Infosys, dedicated to a large telecommunications client, has also developed a customized KM strategy. This center's client is acutely sensitive to intellectual property issues, and requires the center to be isolated from the rest of the Infosys network by a firewall — an artificial barrier to KM. This center thus uses a separate instance of KShop, tailored to its specific needs, which include a focus on the telecommunications domain and the use of local newsgroups.

Newsgroups have been found to be effective in supporting interaction with the client and Infosys communities, as well as between project members. The newsgroups, averaging about 40 posts a day, have contributed to the identification and growth of subject matter experts, reduction in bug-fix time and increase in productivity. Project processes have been tailored to include KM as a stated objective. This center has also included KM in its internal project reviews and performance appraisals.

ACHIEVING THOUGHT LEADERSHIP IN KM

The Infosys KM effort, featuring somewhat seminal aspects in concept as well as in implementation, has received its share of attention from practitioners and researchers worldwide. The KM architecture, the proprietary KMM model and Infosys's experiences in implementation have been published and presented at several academic and industrial events worldwide (see, for example, Kochikar,

2000b; Kochikar and Raghavan, 2000). There have also been several invited presentations and discussion sessions with several companies, including customers, with heartening feedback. The initiative also features in the curriculum at two business schools. An affirmation of Infosys's success on the knowledge-sharing front has been the fact that the company was featured as a finalist for the 2001 **MAKE** (*Most Admired Knowledge Enterprises*) awards (Chase, 2001). Infosys was among the 37 companies worldwide that qualified to reach the final round.

In addition to internal implementation, Infosys has also found considerable interest evinced by customers for possible KM services. A prototype of a productized KM solution has been built for a world-leading software product company. The customer has been quoted as saying that the decision to contract Infosys for this engagement came as a natural choice, after seeing the internal KM implementation at Infosys. Infosys has also carried out a KM implementation for a Fortune 250 Personal Computer manufacturing company, with a focus on managing their customer knowledge. The expected benefits of this system were retaining the customer for life, and creating the ability to conduct focused marketing campaigns to get higher return on each advertising dollar spent.

GETTING THERE — CREATING A SHARING CULTURE

Creating a culture of sharing is governed by principles that have much in common with Metcalfe's law — as more people grow convinced of the benefits of participating in the knowledge-sharing movement, it becomes easier to convince still more people to buy in. Thus, as long as steady progress is made on the road towards achieving greater sharing, the pace of adoption accelerates with time. Once a 'critical mass' of users has been reached, the movement reaches a take-off stage beyond which it becomes self-sustaining, without significant effort being devoted to publicity and promotion. Until this stage is reached, however, considerable effort needs to be focused on promoting the initiative. For this reason, the KM group has a full-time brand manager, whose mandate is to constantly promote KM with a view to pushing it higher on the agenda for every quarter of the organization. Over time, as the initiative matures, the brand manager's role is expected to evolve towards sustenance of the initiative. Similarly, as KM becomes part of the organizational fabric, we expect more of KM to happen as an integral part of a variety of roles across the organization, without needing additional staff dedicated to KM.

ACKNOWLEDGMENTS

The authors gratefully acknowledge the guidance and support received from Nandan Nilekani, Kris Gopalakrishnan and S. Yegneshwar in making the Infosys KM initiative a reality. None of the work described here would have happened without the able work put in by the KM team — K. R. Shyamprasad, V. Mahesh, B. Padma, S. Veena and R. Einith. We also acknowledge M. Haragopal, K. Kavitha, G. Lakshmanan and Ashish Goal for the matter included in the section titled, "Other KM Initiatives."

REFERENCES

Chase, R. L. and the KNOW Network. (2001). *2001 Most Admired Knowledge Enterprises*. Available at http://www.knowledgebusiness.com/make/index.asp.

Davenport, T. H. and Prusak, L. (1998). *Working Knowledge: How Organizations Manage What They Know*. Boston, MA: Harvard Business School Press.

Kochikar, V. P. (2000a). The knowledge management maturity model–A staged framework for leveraging knowledge. *KMWorld 2000 Conference*, Santa Clara, CA, USA. September 13-15.

Kochikar, V. P. (2000b). *Learn Once, Use Anywhere. Knowledge Management Magazine*, *4*(1). UK: Ark Group.

Kochikar, V. P. and Raghavan, S. (2000). Managing knowledge in the e-organization: The IT perspective. *Proceedings of ICEIS 2000, The International Conference on Enterprise Information Systems*, July 4-7. UK: Stafford.

Kochikar, V. P. (2002a). Creating the KM infrastructure at Infosys: The technology challenge. *IIMB Management Review*, *13*(4), 104-110.

Kochikar, V. P. (2002b). *Building an Organizational Architecture for Knowledge Sharing: Challenges Faced*. Working Paper, Infosys Technologies Ltd.

Software Engineering Institute. (1993). *The Capability Maturity Model*.

Sveiby, K.-E. (1997). *The New Organizational Wealth: Managing and Measuring Knowledge-Based Assets*. San Francisco, CA: Berret-Koehler.

Chapter VII

The Learning Enactment of Process Knowledge: An Approach Anchored on Work Practices

Kostas Samiotis and Angeliki Poulymenakou
Athens University of Economics and Business, Greece

ABSTRACT

This chapter is concerned with issues of learning enactment within a single organisation. More particularly, we look into theory and we provide some empirical evidence regarding the exploration and exploitation of organizational knowledge and capabilities through innovative technological intervention. To this end, we explore the link between work practices and knowledge enactment, knowledge enactment as capability development, capability development in the context of organizational learning and the role of technology along this course. Our study of work practices is anchored on the notion of business processes. It is in the intentions of this research to justify the need of contemporary firms to 'manage' knowledge in the context of their business processes, and to establish the main drivers shaping the role of technology in the enactment of learning processes within this perspective.

INTRODUCTION

Knowledge-based theories of the firm have been systematically concerned with the socio-economic behavior of contemporary organizations in terms of strategy, structure, core capabilities and routines. Dominant in these firm features are the notions of knowledge and learning, which are being proposed as prerequisites for sustainable development as much for economic systems as for individual organisations (Lundvall & Jonson, 1994). Moreover, the proliferation of technology imposes new challenges on the knowledge perspective as an explanatory and normative element of firm behavior. The interplay among knowledge, learning and technology encapsulated in the popular term 'knowledge management' are largely thought to drive the 'knowledge-based' economy.

As 'management' of knowledge we consider both an organizational capability and an organizational practice. The intensive knowledge characteristics of organizational capabilities suggest their strong attachment and specificity to the environment where they have been developed. Applications of Information and Communication Technology (ICT) can enable and strengthen the utilization of firm specific resources, knowledge in our case, within the scope of existing work practices. These notions, elaborated *inter alia* in the *learning ladder* framework by Andreu and Ciborra (1996), form our theoretical baseline when we study not only the influence of ICT on the development or support of organizational capabilities, but also the institution of ICT as an organizational capability itself.

The research builds upon three major theoretical streams: knowledge (and learning) enactment, organizational capabilities development and technology (ICT)-enabled organizational change (situated). We consider the change brought forward by the adoption of technology, specifically dealing with the management of operational knowledge, as being closely associated with the organization's business processes. The notion of 'business process' has been earmarked as a key element for reshaping firms' competitive behavior and strategic orientation (Galliers, 1987; Scott Morton, 1991). As thinking 'strategically' about the organization of work in terms of business processes has become an increasingly common approach, we have set as the objective of our research to consider the effects of extending this perspective to explain phenomena related to learning enactment within an organization. For the purposes of the research described in this chapter, a business process is a narrative abstraction of work practices and in many cases the reference point for updating organizational and systems' designs.

Empirical work described in this chapter, still in its initial stages, is based on a longitudinal case study. We monitor a Retail Bank in a state of rapid business development and intense innovative behavior. Knowledge management is being considered for adoption by this organisation as a practice that could facilitate the sustainable development of new products and services, and, beyond that, the transition to a radically different set of operational arrangements. Specifically, the organization under study has recently established an electronic banking division that is responsible for the creation of new electronic banking services and their promotion to existing and new clients. Ultimately, the strategic orientation of this organization is (in their own words) "to become a virtual service provider."

In tandem with these developments, the bank is proceeding with the development of an experimental knowledge management infrastructure. This infrastructure consists of a technological solution and a set of guidelines related to the management of its adoption. This initiative, the focus of the research, targets knowledge enactment requirements both at the functional level, where the clients interact with bank employees, and at the tactical-strategic level, where the design and implementation of the new e-banking services and products is taking place.

In what follows we discuss first relevant approaches related to knowledge, knowledge enactment, capabilities development and the role of technology in organizational learning. Then, we turn to the case setting and we discuss its characteristics and learning requirements. Our interpretations are largely driven by Andreu and Ciborra's discussion regarding the role of ICT in the learning process. More specifically, we study how organizational capabilities and knowledge can be part of a learning process anchored on the work practices of the organization, and how ICT applications can affect the enactment of learning processes.

KNOWLEDGE AND CAPABILITIES: CONSTITUENTS OF THE LEARNING PROCESS

Central to the discussion about the role of Information Technology in the work context of the organization is the learning process associated with its introduction, appropriation, embodiment and use. Learning occurs in terms of using a new technology, combining the technology with existing work practices and therefore supporting them, but most importantly in terms of allowing situated reconfigurations of the existing work arrangements to evolve (Orlikowski, 1996). Innovative technologies are seen to stimulate more this learning process and thus to invoke organizational change. We regard knowledge as the factor stimulating innovative technological re-tooling, which in turn effects the organizational processes of capabilities development, abstracted from the organizational routines and work practices in place.

Knowledge Enactment in Organizations

For many, knowledge assets are seen to constitute the very basis of post-industrial economics. Boisot (1998) sustains that technology, competences and capabilities, each in their own way, are manifestations of a firm's knowledge assets operating at different levels of organization. In each of these manifestations, knowledge is inherently implied in both explicit and tacit forms. The emergent challenge is how to address knowledge in individuals and in organizations. The 'management' of knowledge implies, in our view, knowledge enactment and work contextualization, without which it is difficult to conceptualise and express the value of knowledge assets for the organization. We discuss this assertion by looking into the constitution of knowledge as an individual and as an organizational asset.

The concept of knowledge implies more than an accumulation of information, rather it is an *organized* collection that reflects the intentions of the humans who create it and interpret it (Laudon et al., 1996). Thus, knowledge should be treated not as a factor simply put into use in problem solving, but as a key feature impacting the performance of the organization (Starbuck, 1992).

Attempts to 'organize' knowledge for industrial purposes reveal a variety of aspects and categories identified in the organisational literature. Aspects of knowledge such as its nature (knowledge as an object, or as a process), its context (i.e., social, organisational, group, individual) and its location (i.e., routines, intellectual capital, symbols, etc.) have been discussed by a variety of scholars. The distinction between tacit and explicit knowledge has a prominent position in this discussion. Explicit or codified knowledge is the knowledge that is objective and rational and can be expressed in a formal and systematic language (Nonaka, 1994; Nonaka et al., 2000). Explicit knowledge is very often codified in a written form such as manuals, brochures, standardized procedures, etc.

Polanyi encapsulates the meaning of tacit knowledge in the phrase "We know more than we can tell' (1966). Tacit knowledge is subjective, experiential and hard to formalise and communicate. Tacit knowledge has a personal quality; it is deeply rooted in action and understanding, involves both cognitive and technical elements, and is non-transferable without personal contact (Nonaka, 1994; Nonaka et al, 2000; Senker, 1993).

Blumentritt and Johnson's (1999) framework for categorising knowledge places the primary emphasis on the degree of difficulty in *transferring* knowledge. They distinguish four different categories of knowledge:
- *Codified knowledge*, equivalent to information. The knowledge has been made explicit by a human and it is in a readily transferable form.
- *Common knowledge*, knowledge that is accepted as standard without being formally explicit.
- *Social knowledge*, knowledge about cultural and interpersonal relationships; knowledge of social links and shared values.
- *Embodied knowledge*, tacit knowledge related to experience, background and skills of a person.

According to this framework, the transfer of codified knowledge involves the smallest degree of difficulty while the transfer of embodied knowledge is the hardest task. The knowledge flow and transfer is an important issue basically at the functional level of the organization, but moving up the organizational structure knowledge becomes more complex and difficult to capture.

Capabilities and Their Development

Capabilities and competences are prominent in the literature dealing with the 'strategic exploitation' of knowledge. Strategic thinking and the quest for growth are seen to require organisations to develop firm-specific patterns of behavior, i.e., difficult to imitate combinations of organisational, functional and technological skills (Teece et al., 1997). These unique combinations create *competencies* and capabilities, and take place as the firm's intangible knowledge is being applied in its business behavior (and more specifically in its value-adding business processes).

Knowledge in the tactical and strategic management levels of the organization is manifest also in the form of capabilities and competences. Boisot (1998) defines competences as the organizational and technical skills involved in achieving a certain level of performance in the production, while capabilities depict the strategic skill in the application and integration of competences. Slightly differently, Nanda (1996) defines capabilities as the potential input from the resource stock to the production function. The development of capabilities lies upon the appropriate utilization and combinations of internal and external resources. Competitive advantage stems from the firm-specific configuration of its intangible knowledge, through which it adds value to the final product/service (Schumpeter, 1942; Penrose, 1959; Grant, 1996; Coombs and Richards, 1991; Teece, 1982, 1984).

Knowledge, Capabilities and the Learning Process

Against a background of rapid change in their environment, firms are being urged to anchor their strategy so that it focuses not on organizational routines but on dynamic capabilities. Organizational routines are symbolic static perceptions that firms create for their operations, be they functional, tactical or strategic. A routine reflects the static behavioral models employed by the organization for the execution of its tasks, nowadays increasingly organized around business processes. However, static representations and routines entail sufficient amount of tacit knowledge generated by the recursive execution of tasks along different business situations. Internal validation mechanisms transform this knowledge initially to a shared mindset of operation and further to a conceptual model for it.

Similarly to Kim's (1993) distinction of operational and conceptual learning, we sustain that the transformation that is inevitably taking place is a learning process that utilizes tacit knowledge embedded in existing work practices as they are being routinized. Learning associated with routinization knowledge leads eventually to higher levels of understanding of the work arrangements in the organization (conceptual learning). The 'by-products' of conceptual learning are capabilities.

Capabilities consist of more dynamic (flexible) working and behavioural patterns, allowing the organization to change rapidly.

The association of knowledge with the process of new capabilities development has already raised sufficient interest and is highlighted in the work of Leonard Barton (1995), and Andreu and Ciborra (1994) among others. According to Leonard-Barton, the capabilities-building process is sustained and nurtured by four groups of organisational activities that help the creation and the diffusion of knowledge:

- shared creative problem-solving to produce current products;
- implementing and integrating new methodologies and tools, to enhance internal operations;
- formal and informal experimentation, to build capabilities for the future; and
- learning from outside the organisation.

Barton's model is quite generic; it deals with the role of knowledge creation within the scope of organizational and technological innovation. Barton's approach does not provide detailed insights into what takes place as work practice knowledge is transformed into capabilities (the objective of our study). The *learning ladder* of Andreu and Ciborra (1994) is more forthcoming in this sense (Figure 1). Their model refers to three learning loops that explain how work practices are involved in the transformation of organizational resources to capabilities and then to core capabilities.

Figure 1: Learning loops in capabilities transformation process (Source: cCiborra and Andreu, 1994)

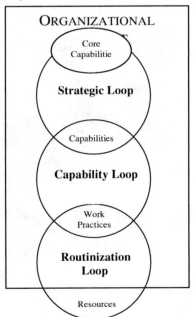

The first learning loop deals with *mastering the use of standard resources within work practices*, which then leads to the evolution of the work practices themselves. Changes in the work practices impose changes in the existing resources, and similarly the use of new resources can convey new work practices. Learning enactment is the iterative interaction between resources and work practices in this mode of learning.

The second learning loop addresses the *development of capabilities through the exploitation of existing work practices*. Capabilities suggest the cumulative concentration and combination of knowledge regarding the execution of the work practices along different business situations. They are more abstract than work practices and describe the ability and knowledge of the organization to perform specific tasks. The continuous improvement and refinement of organizational routines constitutes capabilities-driven learning enactment.

In the final learning loop, *capabilities obtain strategic significance and are thus transformed into core capabilities*. What makes core capabilities 'strategic' is that they point to the organisation's ability to redress its mission in accordance with competitive challenges coming from the external environment. Core capabilities define which capabilities are necessary for the firm's success and why, while capabilities contribute to some extent to the development of the core capabilities by addressing the inner dynamics of the firm. In this mode of learning enactment, the role of the competitive environment is extremely important as it dictates the value and devaluation of core capabilities.

KNOWLEDGE IN WORK PRACTICES: BUSINESS PROCESSES, PROCESS KNOWLEDGE AND THE LEARNING LADDER OF ANDREU AND CIBORRA

The literature on organizational knowledge and learning, as shown in the selective review provided in this chapter, is littered with implicit or explicit references to work practices. While the key role of work practice in the study of knowledge and learning in organizations emerges as a common theme, in our view more work is needed on the elaboration of this relation. For example, literature is not offering sufficient detail on how work practices could be conceptually organized in a sufficiently generic fashion that is relevant for organizational learning action. Models related to the study of the organization of work (e.g., task analysis) usually address its execution and not its knowledge and learning dimension. Unanswered questions multiply when technology is factored in as an increasingly important element of organizational learning. The design of appropriate systems requires, *inter alia*, models related to information and functionality that can feed and support learning enactment.

The organization of work is firmly anchored on the structure of the organization. Currently, hierarchical and functional decomposition-oriented models of organizational structure are being abandoned at an increasing speed. The notion of 'business processes' seems to have captured the interest of firms, across industry sectors, in their quest for more flexible and responsive work designs (Davenport,

1993). In this sense, we opted to exploit the business process concept in our learning-oriented study of work practices. We consider business processes as the organizational manifestations of work practices and routines that take place within firms. We argue that the scope of the business process construct can be broadened to become a rich unit of analysis for organisational learning studies. Moreover, as 'business processes' are becoming a standard in the vocabulary of re-organisation and systems integration initiatives within firms, we expect to reap the effects of familiarity when we approach our empirical setting under this perspective.

Therefore, we have applied the business process concept as the descriptive instrument for work practice. As such, and in order for it to serve our learning-oriented analysis purposes, a business process comprises *activities and tasks* carried out by organisational *actors* and *resources* (information and other) involved in the execution of these activities and tasks.

We turn now to discuss how business processes could be embedded within the Andreu and Ciborra *learning ladder* framework in terms of knowledge and capabilities. As suggested by this framework, we approach the learning (capability development) process in three levels. Each level corresponds to a different aspect of the learning process. The first concerns the *improvement of the efficiency of work practices by mastering the use of standard knowledge resources* to alleviate apparent difficulties encountered within business processes. The main emphasis here is on improving the operational efficiency of business processes. The second learning aspect refers to *potential changes in the nature of the work practices and organisational routines leading to the change in the business process itself* but also to possible identification of new 'peripheral' capabilities. Combination and integration of work practices and processes is possible at this stage. The final aspect, significantly harder to operationalise, refers to the generation of new core capabilities as a result of increased awareness of the evolution course of capability development in the organization. Needless to add, we expect a continuous interplay among these three aspects of learning in the organizational reality.

THE ROLE OF ICT
IN THE LEARNING PROCESS AND THE
OBJECTIVES OF THIS RESEARCH

In Andreu and Ciborra's analysis, information and communication technology is considered as a resource that could actually take part in the learning enactment as a component of capabilities. The role of technology changes across the three learning aspects discussed above. This is particularly due to the nature of computer-based information systems seen by the authors to contribute to learning in each case. The discussion is anchored on the *services* that different types of information systems offer to actors. Routinization learning occurs in the use of operational and productivity information systems that the organization has in place; as the requirement in this case is the management of resources and their integration with functional routines. Moving up the learning ladder, information systems involved in the learning process become more sophisticated and include problem-solving support applications, collaboration systems and personnel training. Zuboff's terminology (1988) is applicable here: the role of ICT in the routinization loop is to automate, while in the capability loop it is to informate, which in fact captures the essence of support offered by ICT in each case. At the strategic loop, selection criteria are being set for the appropriate technologies that support organizational capabilities.

In contrast with Andreu and Ciborra, we consider technology not only as a resource but also as a capability; in fact, we propose that technology becomes a capability when knowledge (as an organizational resource) can be 'managed,' partially with the support of (appropriate) technology. To substantiate this claim, both our theoretical and our empirical research on learning enactment are directed towards *the study of the impact made on organizations by technological propositions for 'knowledge management'* (i.e., the effects of introducing knowledge management systems in organizations).

Knowledge management applications, the result of convergence of document management and workflow systems augmented with web interfaces, arguably still target organizational 'knowledge' resources in a very functional and objectivist fashion. The main concern of such applications is the knowledge-oriented categorization of information resources (through links to actors and activities) and the distribution of these resources over digital channels to organizational actors. Even within this narrow realm, a host of research challenges emerges with the organizational adoption of such applications. As Rosenberg (1994) states, "the technology itself and the set of understandings that define its applicability and use are incomplete and unstable."

Learning being a social process, one challenge is to understand whether, how and why such systems contribute to learning enactment. For the purposes of this research we approach learning enactment through the dialectic relationship between work practices and learning as proposed by Andreu and Ciborra. Therefore, our study is concerned with how individual and organizational knowledge is 'translated' into firms' routines and competences, job descriptions, plans, strategies and cultures.

Technological propositions for knowledge management could potentially be of strategic importance for organizations provided that they perceptibly contribute to the organizational capability of exploiting knowledge as an organizational asset.

Should such systems become feasible, they would most probably need to traverse all loops in Andreu and Ciborra's learning ladder by creating knowledge resources from the routinization loop, contributing to the redefinition of organizational routines in the capabilities development loop, and by enabling the exploration of new or combinative (Kogurt and Zander, 1992) organizational capabilities in the strategic learning loop.

EMPIRICAL WORK

Overview

Our research approach follows the interpretivist paradigm (Walsham, 1993). We seek to apply our theoretical constructs into organizational settings with the primary goal of eliciting a deeper understanding on the phenomena surrounding learning enactment and draw findings that could inform the design and implementation of appropriate organizational learning approaches. Our unit of analysis is that of an organizational group, and the nature of our research output comprises ultimately organizationally feasible and systemically desirable (Checkland, 1981) proposals for organizational learning support.

Empirical research presented below comprises a single site (organization), longitudinal case study. It is a three-year-long study in its second year of development. We work with multiple informants within this business organization all of whom have an expressed stake in encouraging and supporting learning enactment in their firm. Our involvement with this organizational setting is intense and multifaceted. More specifically:

(i)   We are responsible for the design and delivery of a knowledge management application within an organizational unit whose work brief is deemed as critical for the sustainable development of the organization as a whole. The design of the system reflects the organization of work practices around business processes as discussed earlier.

(ii)   We have undertaken the commitment to engage in appropriate action to support this organization in the process of adopting in a meaningful manner the technological proposition (i.e., the system) that is being developed. The process of embedding this system into organizational work routines (in essence an organizational intervention) is framed as a capability development endeavor informed by the learning ladder framework.

(iii)   We are complementing work done in (i) and (ii) with inquiry into learning enactment and its relation to work practices within this organizational setting. In other words, we adopt a critical view on the learning ladder framework in terms of its contribution to learning enactment.

Evidence is being collected primarily through interviews, brainstorming and issue resolution meetings (concerning the knowledge management system and its adoption), and participant observation of organizational activity (pl. refer to the following section).

In brief, we study the evolution of an organizational intervention comprising knowledge management technology and its potential for supporting learning anchored on work practices. Technology in this research is viewed as (i) an enabler for capabilities development and (ii) a new type of organizational capability in itself. The particulars of the technical system design are not being presented in this chapter. For more information on this front, the reader may refer to www.model2learn.org.

The Case Setting

The organization under study is a medium to small (by EU standards) retail bank. The bank is ranked fourth in size at a national level; it employs around 4,000 people and has a network of 200 branches all deployed in a single EU country (Greece). The focal organizational unit for our study is the e-banking department, created in the January 2000. Preparatory work on the development and procurement of the necessary infrastructure to deliver electronic banking services had started in the bank approximately one year before that date. The bank launched its first 'bouquet' of e-banking services to the public in March 2000 with an extensive and intensive marketing campaign. It should be noted that at that time, the bank was the first to offer such an extensive range of electronic banking services in the local market.

The bank's "digital strategy" (their own term) comprised a number of banking services that its customers could access through "digital channels." Under digital channels, the bank grouped all types of transactions that a customer could perform over ATMs, Internet, phone (call center), mobile phone (based on SMS and WAP), while it also plans to develop services for interactive digital television.

At its inception, the e-banking department comprised groups responsible for marketing and sales, Internet activities, electronic commerce, call center services, ATM operations and mobile phone banking services. A few months' later, call center operations were consolidated as a separate (subsidiary) business organization.

E-banking operations were supported within the bank by a network of people, identified as "e-banking agents," located in each branch of the bank network. Initially, the role of the e-banking agent was assigned to the people that were responsible for the technical maintenance of the transaction systems in each branch ("the platform officers"). Very soon it was realized that these people lacked the necessary customer communications skills needed to promote the new services to the bank's large, disparate and unaccustomed-to-technology customer base. Subsequently, e-banking agent responsibilities were redistributed among branch staff already experienced with customer service (e.g., loan and investments consultants). The assignment of the e-banking agent role to specific employees and the training of these people were undertaken by the Human Resource Development department.

The brief of the e-banking department was "the management of the banking products and services offered through digital channels" (their own words). Management refers to the design and support of the banking products and services. The e-banking agents are the human interfaces of the e-banking department with the bank's customers. Their role, at least in the beginning, is to promote e-banking services and products to external and internal customers. To facilitate the promotion of e-banking services, agents were periodically subjected to face-to-face training regarding product and services characteristics, development of communication and marketing skills, and trouble-shooting.

At the time of the e-banking department establishment, a number of relevant initiatives were taking place in the bank. Of particular interest is the "competences mapping project" handled by the Human Resource Development department. The scope of this project, still currently under way, is to re-conceptualize the organization of work practices across all bank operations by placing emphasis of the skills required to meet the requirements in each operational front, rather than on job descriptions anchored on the detailed specification of tasks. This project, along with other re-organisation initiatives, is the result of a top-level decision to reshape all major operations "from inward-looking functional silos, to customer-oriented service provision by all bank employees" (their own words). The competences mapping project is hailed by the bank as the groundwork required to inform human resource development strategy, particularly in terms of re-deploying personnel around new and restructured operations, and in terms of managing training initiatives.

A second significant development was the provision of computer-based training services over the bank's intranet. These services, also launched at the beginning of 2000, were meant as complementary to traditional classroom-based training. Computer-based training courses were delivered organization-wide over the bank's intranet/extranet infrastructure packaged in what the bank termed as "a first version of our learning portal." Instructional content developed to date in this portal targets primarily sales and customer communications techniques.

Last but not least, at the time that our study set-off, the bank's main transaction systems had undergone extensive revamping "to exhibit a more customer-centric philosophy" (own words). In essence, the revamping comprised the integration of separate systems into a singe platform, the redevelopment of all major user interfaces to operational systems and the deployment of more management reporting tools. As a result, PC use penetration among the bank's employees more than doubled within the course of a year. An extensive personnel training effort on new systems functionalities is still under way across the bank.

The case of the bank for the research described in this chapter is not simply an organizational context we draw data from. Our involvement with the case setting is much more active and includes the following:

(i)   The development of a knowledge management application tailored to the needs of the e-banking department both in terms of providing knowledge-oriented support for their internal work arrangements, and in terms of providing learning opportunities both to them and to e-banking agents located in the branches, particularly through knowledge sharing and collaboration.

(ii)   Appropriate facilitation and support throughout the scooping, specification and (most importantly) deployment of (i), with special emphasis given to work context-sensitive adoption guidance and on alignment of this effort with related projects such as the competences mapping project, and the development of the learning portal.

Our partners and informants in this study include major stakeholders in the evolution of the e-banking department and the related developments within its environment (the bank). In fact, the group of people we are working with share, among them, most of the decision-making responsibility for the development and redefinition of the bank's operations. The informant group includes one of the two vice presidents of the bank responsible for IT, organizational development and new products. We are also in contact with the Human Resource Development director, who is responsible for the "competence mapping" project and the formulation of the training strategy. Regarding the e-banking department, the main stakeholders we work with are its director and the marketing manager. The former is responsible for e-banking strategy in terms of digital services and products offered, while the latter manages their promotion and the development of marketing skills to e-banking agents.

Stakeholder Perceptions: An Interpretation

At the executive level (according to the VP responsible), the move towards electronic banking services is regarded as a business imperative. Change in the bank's business environment is seen to call upon the redefinition of value propositions, highlighting the importance of knowledge and its exploitation, and the establishment of new organizational forms. At the moment, the bank is in a transitional period, in which the above issues are being discussed within the general debate regarding the shape and form of the bank's future as a virtual financial services institution. The new requirements affect several work fronts, which are contributing to the strategic reconfiguration of the traditional bank.

Special emphasis is given by our stakeholders to the exploitation of organizational and individual knowledge, along with the establishment of a knowledge-sharing and continuous learning culture that would set the groundwork of new strategic formulations. They perceive knowledge as the resource that would ensure the longevity and sustainable competitiveness of their organisation in the emergent digital business landscape, and therefore our stakeholders believe that knowledge should be accumulated systematically and most importantly incorporated within the design of electronic banking services and products. Traditional and hence physical paradigms of conducting banking operations are not viewed as useless though; they are being valued for the cumulative experiences they convey from traditional work practices derived from the daily interaction of employees with customers. It is believed that this knowledge, which is tacit most of the time, not only should be exploited by the people who are still engaged in traditional functions but also should be supplied to those who are building and transforming traditional banking services and products to electronic artifacts.

An important observation here is that in our case setting work practices are increasingly being perceived throughout the bank from a business process perspective. This point is exemplified by the emphasis placed on the 'customer orientation' of all operations and the integration of systems supporting day-to-day work (with its significant 'side-effect' of creating a central pool of information resources). Further to that, work practices in the newly established e-banking department have a definitive business process rather than functional orientation, as the manner in which this department operates is crossing traditional functional hierarchies and creating virtual work teams (collaboration with the e-banking agents).

Setting Priorities for Knowledge Enactment

When confronted with the issue of developing and exploiting knowledge resources, our respondents have articulated three areas of concern: (i) capturing customer knowledge and responses, and communicating them to top management (strategic learning implications); (ii) facilitating the design of new products and services (capability-learning implications); and (iii) improving existing business processes related with the promotion and support of electronic banking (routinization learning implications).

The customer and the knowledge related to him are of primary concern to the bank. The expressed requirements of our respondents (stakeholders) are the capturing and exploitation of this 'knowledge' "strategically," i.e., in terms that directly affect the enhancement and expansion of the spectrum of electronic services and products offered. To this end, they expect a supporting information system that will be deployed to facilitate the relevant 'knowledge processes' of the organization.

Our inquiry in the case setting thus far, but also our planned intervention through the system and the organizational support that we will provide, need to target the sources and carriers of knowledge. Knowledge assets can be generally assigned to two categories. The first category is 'knowledge of the customer' and the other is individual and organizational knowledge. Both types of knowledge are closely interrelated. Through the technological and organizational support envisaged, we actually seek to develop within the e-banking processes the capability to 'manage' both types of knowledge and ultimately help the organization to incorporate them in its organizational routines (i.e., knowledge enactment).

Learning processes emphasize the avoidance of passive absorption of information and target the development of tacit knowledge, in our case anchored on work practices. To this end, our intervention (system and organizational support) needs to involve the users in a learning process, where personal knowledge exploration and exploitation is taking placing. Exploration contributes to learning by using the system and learning by doing, while exploitation refers to finding efficient ways of working, understanding and interpreting existing work practices.

Priorities in Capabilities Development

The short life of the e-banking department has not permitted them yet to consolidate their understanding on the constituents of their capability base. It is reasonable to expect capabilities to spawn from the newly established work processes in due course. The technological intervention we propose is envisaged to support the capabilities-development process either by capitalizing on certain aspects of routinization of work practices (still quite volatile in this department) or by encouraging capability development by providing information that will challenge actors to adopt new ways of work. Moreover, our initial inquiry activities have urged the e-banking department to "contemplate on the way we work" (in their own words). In many cases, work practices documented in our study were considered for adoption as the norm.

Driven by concepts in the framework of Andreu and Ciborra, our inquiry has revealed three capabilities that the e-banking department wishes to develop. The first capability refers to "mastering of the processes of the electronic banking department." These processes entail, for our respondents, the acquisition of the knowledge needed for promoting effectively products and services and more specifically, the tasks involved in this (business) process, the resolution of problems in the flow of work and the efficient use of relevant systems (e.g., intranet, learning portal). Situations such as encountering an unusual problem or working with a new system may urge members of the department to adopt new ways of performing the process that in turn create new challenges for system support and work performance.

The second capability targeted affects more organisational entities than the e-banking department. It refers to "mastering of the individuals' skills and competences." In other words, based on our respondents' feedback, we suggest that management in the bank wishes to 'know better what its employees are capable of doing.' Moreover, an expressed requirement is to reorganize work around meaningful clusters of such capabilities. Our respondents expressed the wish to have systems that provide customized support for the execution of work tasks. Customization should follow capability profiles.

The third capability targeted is reflecting a need of top-level management, namely "the creation of a shared mental model among the bank's customers: that the specific bank is synonymous with the notion of electronic banking in Greece." The development of this capability exceeds the potential offering of any technology, but using appropriate technology can definitely support customer orientation of work practices and thus lead to more efficient customer service.

CONCLUSIONS AND FURTHER RESEARCH

Our inquiry thus far delivered findings that are closely associated with propositions in Andreu and Ciborra's framework. In our case setting, as suggested by these authors, learning requirements set off with the need for routinization. The development of electronic banking capabilities is anchored on existing resources and work practices. In our study we place faith in Andreu and Ciborra's assertion that technology can play a crucial role in the enactment of the routinization learning process. Therefore, we are about to deliver a system that attempts to exploit this notion. Moving up the learning ladder, capabilities acquire strategic significance by advising the organization for the *how* and *why* of the work processes. Technology enables the realization of capabilities, and capabilities reconfigure the way technology is being used. The system we are about to supply the bank with allows the users "grow" as well as share resources associated with their capabilities.

The interpretation of the organizational situation described in this chapter is evolving in parallel with the actual deployment of the knowledge management initiative in which we are actively involved. The outcome of this process will provide useful indications of how the firm can approach knowledge enactment and how it should evolve to cope with the knowledge requirements of its organizational routines and vice versa. Knowledge as a resource is difficult to grasp; this research aims at revealing the methods that can be deployed to best utilize this resource within the business processes of the organization regardless of their level — functional, tactical or strategic. It is in the intentions of the research to identify the relevance of ICT in the development of capabilities and define the terms under which this is happening. Moreover, we have to distinguish and discuss further the different types of learning enactment we encounter, look into how they are induced by the introduction of a technology in the management of knowledge and possibly revisit the learning ladder framework.

The contemporary knowledge environment of firms and the characteristics of its evolution comprise the drivers for describing the arrangements taking place in the work context. We propose a technological intervention, and we are primarily guided by this to explain the need and thereupon the phenomena, meaning the conditions and factors related to the organizational adoption of the knowledge-oriented ICT offerings. The research will approach the need of a work-related knowledge management system from a social, organizational and certainly technological perspective.

To this aim, we tried to investigate the implications of Andreu and Ciborra's learning model on technology deployment with regards to the empirical setting this research refers to. The need to manage knowledge across people and processes imposes certain imperatives for the development, introduction, adoption and use of any information technology. To this end, we use Andreu and Ciborra's model to guide the technological intervention in its integration with existing work practices and its evolution in an organizational capability.

The current research goes through its exploratory phase, trying to investigate the organizational environment that will be the subject of an innovative technological intervention. The aforementioned theories will be used to map the knowledge and learning processes, in order to assist the deployment of a technological capability, with the aim of an information system and accompanying organizational action. Further actions suggest the filtering of the theoretical streams towards a selective usage of constructs and the strengthening of the stream that is related to the social and organizational construction of technology. The final contribution of this research would probably be a framework describing the characteristics and processes that constitute the technological capability of knowledge-intensive organizations.

ACKNOWLEDGEMENT

Work presented in this chapter has been partially financially supported by the European Commission Information Society and Technologies programme through the MODEL project: Multimedia for Open and Dynamic Executives Learning (Project No. IST-1999-12181). The authors wish to acknowledge the Commission for their support. We also wish to acknowledge our gratitude and appreciation to all the MODEL project partners for their contribution during the development of various ideas and concepts presented in this chapter. More information on the MODEL project can be found at www.model2learn.org.

REFERENCES

Andreu, R. and Ciborra, C. (1996). Organizational learning and core capabilities: The role of IT. *Journal of Strategic Information Systems*, 5, 111-127.

Blumentritt, R. and Johnston, R. (1999). Towards a strategy for knowledge management. *Technology Analysis and Strategic Management*, *11*(3).

Boisot, H. M. (1998). *Knowledge Assets–Securing Competitive Advantage in the Information Economy*. Oxford: Oxford University Press.

Checkland, P. (1981). *Systems Thinking, Systems Practice*. New York: John Wiley & Sons.

Coombs, R. and Richards, A. (1991). Technologies, products and firms' strategies. Part 1 – A framework for analysis. *Technology Analysis and Strategic Management*, *3*(1), 77-85.

Davenport, T. H. (1993). *Process Innovation. Re-Engineering Work Through Information Technology*. Boston, MA: Harvard Business School Press.

Drucker, P. (1988). The coming of the new organization. *Harvard Business Review*, (January-February), 45-53.

Galliers, R.D. (1987). An approach to information needs analysis. In Galliers, R. D. (Ed.), *Information Analysis*. Reading, MA: Addison-Wesley.

Grant, R. M. (1996). A knowledge-based theory of inter-firm collaboration. *Organization Science*, 7, 375-387.

Kogurt, B. and Zander, U. (1992). Knowledge in the firm, combinative capabilities, and the replication of technology. *Organization Science*, *3*, 383-397.

Kim, D. H. (1993). The link between individual and organizational learning. *Sloan Management Review*, *35*(1), 37-50.

Laudon, K. and Starbuck, H. (1996). *Organizational Information and Knowledge*, 4. London: Routledge/Thompson Business Press.

Leonard-Barton, D. (1995). *Wellsprings of Knowledge*. Boston, MA: Harvard Business School Press.

Lundvall, B. and Johnson, B. (1994). The learning economy. *Journal of Industry Studies*, *1*(2).

Nanda, A. (1996). *Resources, Capabilities, and Competencies*. In Moingeon and Edmondson (Eds.), *Organizational Learning and Competitive Advantage*. London: Sage Publications.

Nonaka, I. (1994). A dynamic theory of organisational knowledge creation. *Organisation Science*, *5*(1).

Nonaka, I., Toyama and Nagata (2000). A firm as a knowledge-creating entity: A new perspective on the theory of the firm. *Journal of Industrial and Corporate Change*, *9*(1), 1-20.

Pfeffer, J. (1994). *Competitive Advantage Through People*. Boston, MA: Harvard Business Press.

Orlikowski, W. (1996). Improvising organizational transformation over time: A situated change perspective. *Information Systems Research*, 7(1).

Penrose, E. T. (1959). *The Theory of the Growth of the Firm*. Oxford: Basil Blackwell.

Polanyi, M. (1966). *The Tacit Dimension*. Magnolia, MA: Peter Smith.

Rosenberg, N. (1994). *Exploring the Black Box: Technology and Economics*. Cambridge, UK: Cambridge University Press.

Scott Morton, M. S. (1991). Introduction. In Scott Morton, M. S. (Ed.), *The Corporation of the 1990s*. New York: Oxford University Press.

Schumpeter, J. A. (1942). *Capitalism, Socialism, and Democracy*. New York: McGraw-Hill.

Senker, J. (1993). The contribution of tacit knowledge to innovation. *AI & Society*, 7, 208-224. London: Spinger-Verlag.

Starbuck, W. H. (1992). Learning by knowledge-intensive firms. *Journal of Management Studies*, 29(6), 713-740.

Sveiby, K. E. (1992). The knowledge company: Strategy formulation in knowledge-intensive industries. In Hussey, D. E. (Ed.), *International Review of Strategic Management*, 3. New York: John Wiley & Sons.

Teece, D. (1982). Towards an economic theory of the multi-product firm. *Journal of Economic Behavior and Organisation*, *3*, 39-63.

Teece, D. (1984). Economic analysis and strategic management. *California Management Review*, 26(3), 87-110.

Teece, D., Pisano, G. and Shuen, A. (1997). Dynamic capabilities and strategic management. *Strategic Management Journal, 18*(7), 509-533.

Walsham, G. (1993). *Interpreting Information Systems in Organizations*. New York: John Wiley & Sons.

Zuboff, S. (1988). *In the Age of the Smart Machine*. New York: Basic Books.

Chapter VIII

Bridging the Gap from the General to the Specific by Linking Knowledge Management to Business Processes

John S. Edwards and John B. Kidd
Aston University, UK

ABSTRACT

A phenomenon common to almost all fields is that there is a gap between theory and practical implementation. However, this is a particular problem in knowledge management, where much of the literature consists of general principles written in the context of a 'knowledge world' that has few, if any, references to how to carry out knowledge management in organisations. In this chapter, we put forward the view that the best way to bridge this gap between general principles and the specific issues facing a given organisation is to link knowledge management to the organisation's business processes.

After briefly reviewing, and rejecting alternative ways in which this gap might be bridged, the chapter goes on to explain the justification for, and the potential benefits and snags of, linking knowledge management to business processes. Successful and unsuccessful examples are presented. We concentrate especially on the issues of establishing what knowledge is relevant to an organisation at present, the need for organisational learning to cope with the inevitable change, and the additional problems posed by the growing internationalisation of operations.

We conclude that linking knowledge management in terms of business processes is the best route for organisations to follow, but that it is not the answer to all knowledge management problems, especially where different cultures and/or cultural change are involved.

INTRODUCTION

The main topic of this chapter is the implementation or the application of knowledge management. By this, we mean how the ideas and theories of knowledge management can be made applicable in an organisation. Too often we hear or read the rhetoric of knowledge management without there being any route mentioned to turn these ideas into practical applications. As Americans might say, what happens when "the rubber meets the road?"

We begin by explaining why we believe the application of knowledge management in a specific organisation is problematic. We then propose that the concept of business processes is the most suitable way to help resolve this problem, and go on to review some of the consequences (actual and potential) of rooting knowledge management in an organisation's business processes. We believe that this is the most appropriate way to make the theories of knowledge management applicable. However, the approach is not without its difficulties.

We discuss both the justification and some of the potential snags in the main body of this chapter, with a special emphasis on problems of internationalisation. Our conclusions, however, given the current state of knowledge about knowledge management, are as much in the way of a question as an answer. However, it is clear that while a process orientation may be necessary for successful knowledge management in an organisation, it is not sufficient on its own. For example, an appreciation of cultures and cultural distance is also essential, given that we now live and work in a "global village."

CAN KNOWLEDGE BE MANAGED?

Baseline Definitions

Despite the surge of interest in knowledge management over the past few years, there is no general agreement as to whether knowledge can be "managed" in any meaningful sense. Three views on this topic are apparent to us (others may suggest more):

1. Meaningful knowledge resides only in people's heads, and therefore managing organisational knowledge is an oxymoron (Weick & Westley, 1996).
2. All knowledge can be managed; the principal challenge is to "extract" it from its current location, whether that is a human mind or somewhere else.
3. The statement that "knowledge resides in people's heads" is literally true, but there are knowledge processes in organisations (and elsewhere), and these processes can be managed, even if it is not possible to manage the knowledge itself directly.

View number 1 implies that not only this chapter, but indeed the entire book is a waste of time, and thus need not be discussed further here. Many software vendors may be found advocating view number 2, which has its ancestry, at least in part, in the more mechanistic aspects of the expert/knowledge-based systems field. In our view, the history of that field demonstrates that this view is unlikely to be valid in most domains of knowledge (see for example Gill, 1995). Even the oft-cited Huber has modified his thoughts over a 10-year period to accept that knowledge can be "sticky" and thus difficult to "extract" even from a willing donor (Huber, 1991, 2000).

Most of the literature specifically on knowledge management, not surprisingly, adopts view number 3. This literature often refers to "knowledge processes" or "knowledge management processes." However, the meaning of these phrases is usually only weakly specified, if at all. It is implicitly assumed that "something to do with knowledge" is taking place in organisations.

TOWARDS THE IMPLEMENTATION OF KNOWLEDGE MANAGEMENT

In this section, we consider four routes to the implementation of knowledge management in an organisation. We identify these as follows:

*   The "knowledge world" route
*   The IT-driven route
*   The functional route
*   The business processes route

The "Knowledge World" Route

The discussion of the knowledge processes mentioned under view 3 in the previous section is most often considered at the level of the whole organisation, or in a "world of knowledge" that is not specifically linked to the activities that a particular organisation carries out. These features may be seen in the most commonly cited generic model of knowledge processes, that of Nonaka and

Takeuchi (1995), as shown in Figure 1. We should make it clear at this point that Nonaka and Takeuchi do go on to consider the practical realities of managing and encouraging these knowledge processes in organisations. However, many of those who cite Nonaka and Takeuchi's models seem to have lost the practical implementation aspects somewhere.

On an abstract level such discussion of knowledge management can be extremely valuable. However, in order for knowledge management to be implemented in an organisation, we believe that such a model has to be "attached" somehow to what the organisation actually does. It is necessary not only to understand how individuals learn, but also how they learn in a given organisation. In other words, we have to understand the processes by which individuals learn to "use their tools, to do what, why and with whom" — and how the organisational systems may help or hinder the individual's learning process. The same issue applies even more forcefully to group learning, since the organisation provides a crucial element of the group's context, whether that group is formal or informal, entirely internal or partly external.

We emphasise these points further in Figure 2. The figure is intended to indicate that a new individual in a firm will initially understand little of his/her new firm and its mores — but we trust he/she has some potential to learn.

Figure 1: Nonaka and Takeuchi's (1995) model of knowledge transfer processes

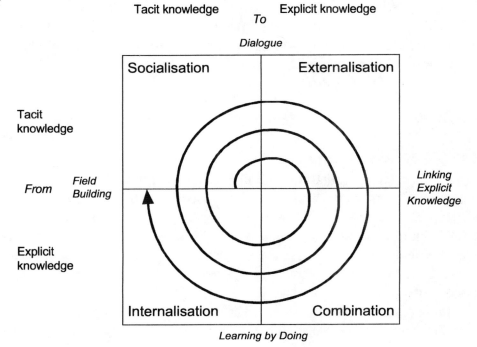

Figure 2: The 4-knows of individual/group learning

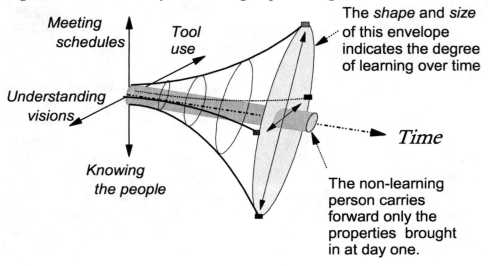

As time progresses, they will learn to use the best tools for the job (these might be a telephone or the ubiquitous PC). They will learn that management has provided the best tools possible so they can meet the schedules demanded by the managers, and imposed by customers. They will learn to integrate with the CEO's visions so that all 'do their part and pull together.' Lastly they will learn to commune with others over many business issues. Figure 2 is in part an echo of the schema presented by Nonaka and Takeuchi, though here the focus is on what the individual is doing, whereas Figure 1 focuses on what is happening to the knowledge.

However, none of these ideas, however expressed, provides a specific connection from the abstract ideas about knowledge to what the organisation actually does, or could do, or should do. Something more concrete is needed.

The IT-Driven Route

One possible route that has been adopted by some organisations is a natural progression from "view 2" on whether knowledge can be managed, as set out earlier. This route assumes that the fundamental requirement is for extraction and codification of as much knowledge as possible. For an organisation of any size, such a task evidently requires IT support, and the thrust of this route is that once the "correct" form of IT support for managing knowledge has been chosen, it is simply a matter of a great deal of hard work.

In our opinion, this technology-driven route is unlikely to work well, and may not achieve any improvement in knowledge management at all. One example of this from our own experience is of a heavy manufacturing firm. Knowledge management in this organisation was seen solely as an information systems issue; the knowledge management group was part of the information systems department. The "solution" was seen in terms of the implementation of a knowledge-sharing system based on Lotus Notes. However, there was no real consideration as to who would share what knowledge or for what specific purpose. Matters were not helped by the absence of a prior culture of knowledge sharing in the organisation. Consequently, the eventual use of the installed IT was poor; the only really successful use was by the knowledge management project team itself, where the "who, what and why" questions had been properly addressed!

The Functional Route

An alternative route to the implementation of knowledge management that at least has the potential to address the "who, what and why" questions is to organise the implementation around the existing organisational structure. The most commonly found structural elements intended to facilitate learning and knowledge sharing in organisations are departmental groupings based on functions. These have clear advantages in terms of what we might term professional development and allegiance. Davenport and Prusak (1998) report examples of successful knowledge transfer between groups of surgeons, and groups of tunnelling engineers, among others. However, this functional route also has the disadvantage that it encourages the compartmentalisation of knowledge. This problem can only worsen over time, as specialisations multiply and sub-divide. In addition, the professional divisions can actively prevent sharing of knowledge. It has, for example, taken decades for hospital doctors in the UK National Health Service to allow other professionals such as pharmacists and physiotherapists to participate in decision making about treatment of individual patients on an equal footing. On a wider scale, modern Western medical science has come to separate "diet" and "drugs," at least until the very recent past, in a way that Chinese medicine, for example, never has done.

We believe, therefore, that although the functional route to implementation will allow some management of knowledge to take place, progress may be limited, and in the worst cases this route may be counter-productive.

The Business Processes Route

It is clear that the managers in an organisation have to translate the goals of any strategic programme or initiative — whether on knowledge management or something else — into practical, implementable reality; in other words, to connect with "what the organisation does." Various management thinkers have presented models of this, for example:

- Porter's (1985) value chain;
- Earl's (1994) view of core processes, the ones that are done directly for external customers;
- Beer's "System Ones" (1985), the systems that make the organisation what it is,
- core competences/competencies as espoused by Hamel and Prahalad (1994).

There are some significant differences in detail between these perspectives. For example, Beer and Porter have substantially different views as to what constitute the primary activities of an organisation. In Beer's view, the primary activities are those that distinguish this organisation from one in a different line of business. Porter, by contrast, sees the activities of all organisations as fundamentally similar. Nevertheless, what these views have in common is that all of their definitions are consistent with looking at the organisation in terms of what it does, rather than how it is structured. From our perspective, this means looking at knowledge learning and exchange in terms of its underlying business processes. Note that we use the term *business* processes throughout this chapter, but such processes exist equally in not-for-profit organisations, and we believe the concepts discussed here are equally applicable in that context.

Defining 'Business Processes'

There are many definitions of a business process. We prefer that of Davenport: "A structured, measured set of activities designed to produce a specified output for a particular customer or market." (Davenport, 1993, p.5)

Among the characteristics of business processes that in our opinion justify their use as a foundation for knowledge management in organisations are the following.

1. Business processes have identifiable customers, whether internal or external. *Knowledge is of little relevance unless put to use for a customer of some kind.*
2. Business processes cut across organisational boundaries. *Knowledge does not need to, and does not obey the artificial boundaries within an organisation.*
3. Business processes consist of a structured set of activities. *Choosing the appropriate way to structure activities is an important part of the knowledge.*
4. Business processes need to be measured. *Without some form of measurement as a comparison, knowledge cannot be validated.*
5. While the parts of a business process are important, the overriding requirement is that the overall process works. *True knowledge of the organisation must take a holistic view.*

An additional argument, presented by Braganza (2001), is that viewing knowledge management in terms of an organisation's processes gives a much-needed *supply-side* view of knowledge. This is complementary to the demand-side view of knowledge that stems, for example, from considerations 'of data leading to information leading to knowledge.' Again, this links with our earlier argument; Beer and Earl particularly concentrate on this supply-side perspective. Beer indeed goes even further, to include the informal processes and activities of the organisation as well as the more formalised ones.

A further though indirect justification for the use of business processes in this role is that they are now becoming part of the mainstream of management thought. The new version of the ISO9000 family of standards for Quality Management Systems, including ISO9001: 2000, is constructed on the basis of a "process approach." The ISO9000 term *realisation process* is equivalent to Earl's core process or Beer's primary activity.

Completing our argument, the knowledge that an organisation requires must, logically, be related not just to what that organisation does, but also to how it does it. Thus we must think about this knowledge, and how to manage it, by reference to that organisation's business processes. But should we be focusing on the current processes, or future, changed processes? Clearly good knowledge management must include both, but this does raise difficulties.

CHANGE AND THE NEED FOR FLEXIBILITY
Types of Change
In looking at how the organisation moves from the present into the future, it is possible to distinguish three fundamentally different sets of circumstances:
- Continuing *status quo* operation.
- Incremental change or improvement (also called evolutionary change or continuous improvement).
- Radical change or improvement (also called revolutionary, discontinuous or step change).

Note the use of "improvement" as synonymous with "change" here. We do recognise the possibility that change occurs which worsens a particular situation, but in this chapter we take the optimistic view that in a competent organisation such reverses will be only temporary.

Each of these circumstances has different implications for the knowledge the organisation needs, but conversely knowledge drift is itself one of the key drivers for change. One of the main reasons for process change cited in the business process re-engineering (BPR) literature (Hammer, 1990; Hammer & Champy, 1993), is that: "the old ways no longer seem to be effective." In our terms, if old ways are ineffective, this must mean that the knowledge needed to accomplish the activity has changed. Work on knowledge management from an organisational behaviour perspective confirms this view of knowledge as being dynamic. Scarbrough et al. (1999), for example, describe knowledge as *relatively transient*, in other words changing at different times, even in the same organisation.

The Organisation as a Learning Entity

The requirements for organisational learning are similarly affected by whatever changes the organisation is undergoing. These effects may well permeate through all the human resource management activities of the organisation, right down to recruitment. Elsewhere we have discussed how top-down knowledge management and bottom-up organisational learning must be complementary to each other — changing together to meet the changing circumstances in which the organisation finds itself (Kidd & Edwards, 2000). Again, as most learning relates to the *how* of the organisation's activities rather than the *what*, a focus on business processes will be helpful, if not essential.

Knowledge management, organisational learning and business processes are all inextricably linked. Together they require an appropriate combination of human, organisational and IT support. We now go on to consider the issue of change in more detail.

CHANGE AND KNOWLEDGE MANAGEMENT

In considering knowledge, learning and change, we start from the perspective that all those who work in an organisation are thinking beings, capable of reflecting on what they are doing. The principal implication of this is that the "obvious" three-category view of change in the future, as presented in the previous section, is in fact misleading. It may be a valid depiction of change, but it is not the most useful way to consider future needs for knowledge and knowledge management.

In our opinion, there are three scenarios of change to be distinguished:
1.   Status quo/continuous improvement: the same processes with perhaps minor changes to the activities.
2.   Radical change to one process, with the customers and the organisational boundaries remaining the same.
3.   Radical change across the whole organisation, where anything may change, even the nature of the organisation itself. Indeed, as we shall see later, such change may extend well beyond a single organisation, to a sector, region or country.

We argue that the requirements of continuing status quo operation and incremental improvement are effectively the same in terms of knowledge management and organisational learning. It is hard to conceive of a status quo that is enforced so solidly that no improvement ever takes place at all. We will admit that we are aware of some organisations — or at least parts of them — where the type of thinking mentioned at the start of this section is not encouraged, or even positively discouraged. Brief examples are given below.

Examples Within Scenario 1

In the first of these scenarios, we suggest that any learning that takes place must be related to the current process, and will probably be done in the first instance by the actors currently involved in carrying out that process. Thus the management of learning and/or knowledge also involves only incremental change. This does not necessarily mean that it is easy.

We have experience of a situation where even transferring knowledge from workers on one shift to workers on the same equipment on another shift presented serious obstacles. One shift team had developed a clearly superior operating practice, but the other two shifts working on the same production activities refused to adopt their proposed practices. Each shift had its own operational management, and the organisation's middle management were therefore the main communication channel between shift teams. However, this middle layer of managers tended to work "normal office hours," and so had very little involvement with the two of the three shift teams who worked "abnormal" hours. Partly as a consequence of this, the people concerned hardly ever met informally either. The official channels for communicating to and from the non-day shifts were therefore the only ones that could be used. As a result, nothing much happened. Only when a conscious effort was made to exchange management personnel between shifts did matters begin to improve. Changing this management process enabled knowledge sharing about the related business process to take place.

Even in an organisation where development is discouraged, like the archetypal 1930s-style production line environment satirised by Charlie Chaplin in the film *Modern Times*, change does still occur. Although there may be little scope for an individual to modify the way that they perform their current task while they are performing it, even these organisations would allow "offline" incremental improvement. In the 1950s production line, this might have taken place via work-study investigations, or (in more enlightened cases) a suggestion box scheme.

As a further example of discouraging development, we recall Fred Olsen, the boss of Digital (DEC), who banned conversations about PCs in the 1980s since he believed they were trivia that 'would go away.' As history shows, they did not go away — Olsen left, and eventually Digital was bought by successful PC manufacturer Compaq! Digital's business vision was based on the principle of tailoring the product to fit the customer's needs. This worked very successfully for their main mini-computer market in the 1980s. By the time Digital (after Olsen) began to produce PCs, their learning curve was at odds with that of their more successful competitors, who had realised that PCs were now commodity items that required being cheaply mass-produced.

Examples Within Scenarios 2 and 3

The remaining two scenarios differ in whether the radical re-engineering is of one process, or of the whole business. Note that it might well be possible to re-engineer most of the processes in a business one after another without really changing the nature of the business overall. There are several examples of organisations that have recently taken a process-based approach to knowledge management with the intention of improving the processes, but not radically changing the business: here we offer three examples — the Unisys Corporation, the Objective Corporation and General Electric.

Unisys (Wizdo, 2001) has embarked upon a company-wide knowledge management initiative, whose objectives include:

- accelerating the speed and scope of organisational learning,
- decreasing the time it takes to reach critical mass in new markets,
- uniting cross-boundary groups,
- increasing innovation in product and process.

Wizdo identifies three increasingly ambitious categories of "transformation" in business: efficiency, innovation and re-invention. The Unisys knowledge management program regards a focus on processes as essential in achieving the two 'higher' categories, although at present the emphasis is on innovation. From our perspective they are re-engineering one process at a time.

Objective Corporation (Fisher, 2001) has adopted a similar process orientation over the past five years. They have found that such an emphasis has not only improved knowledge management within the business, but has had significant impact on the performance of the business itself. Indeed we can refer the reader back to Figure 2 and its discussion. A coherent training programme, with an emphasis on understanding, would be likely to increase the overall organisational performance through the betterment of its constituent personnel.

Probably the largest process-based change initiative, which with the benefit of hindsight can be seen to have had substantial knowledge management aspects as well, is that which has taken place at General Electric (GE) over the last 20 years. Jack Welch, until recently the CEO, completely transformed the company through his strong leadership and by using the knowledge of all its employees — especially those on the shop floor (Lucier & Torsilieri, 2001). GE's "corporate university" at Crotonville has proven to be central to this approach, making the link between Welch's strategy from the top down and the employees' knowledge and learning from the bottom up. They all would seem to understand the rationale of "what, how, who…."

Two Cautionary Tales

It might be easy to conclude from these examples that a process focus always leads to success in knowledge management, or indeed business in general. Unfortunately, this is by no means always the case. Here we present two cautionary tales.

One of the original "success stories" in process re-engineering concerned the application process at Mutual Benefit Life Insurance (Hammer, 1990). The changes to that process were undoubtedly successful, with results such as a reduction in processing time from 5-25 days to 2-5 days. Flow of new business (and funds) in was greatly improved on the basis of an innovative programme including such features as IS professionals and line managers changing roles for a year. However, this did not stop Mutual Benefit Life from first having to file for protection against bankruptcy and then going into administration. They had re-engineered the wrong process; a key one, but not the one that was most problematic for their business. In parallel with all these beneficial changes, the (unchanged) process of investment in real estate and mortgages was making a series of imprudent choices that brought the company to its knees. This was a failure of knowledge management at the management level. Just possibly, company-wide implementation of the change programme would have averted this, but a process focus by itself did not.

Timing of knowledge availability can also be a problem. Robinson et al. (2001) report on the organising of unplanned maintenance (i.e., responding to equipment failures) in an automobile manufacturing facility. Although a process perspective has been taken, the facility being studied is a relatively new one, and therefore has not yet experienced the full range of unplanned maintenance issues. Clearly this gives rise to potential knowledge management problems: how can they know what to do in a situation that has not previously arisen? The transferability of knowledge from other, older, facilities is being investigated as a possible way to overcome the problems. In general, the half-life of knowledge is problematic; however, since there are no easily applicable rules as to what to discard, what data and learning will be unwanted in the new situation, and conversely what will still be valid.

A further potential problem with a process focus is that of over-formalisation, whether of the business processes themselves or the forms of knowledge management in use. There is a risk that too much formalisation will lose the benefits of such means of knowledge sharing and transfer as storytelling and informal communities of practice. A process route to implementing knowledge management will certainly not lessen these risks, and may even increase them compared to the functional route.

INTERNATIONALISATION

One of the most radical changes that an organisation can undertake is to move from a national market and operations to operate on an international scale. Initially, in order to derive cost-cutting benefits, an organisation might venture overseas to access lower cost raw materials or lower cost labour markets to assemble components which are brought back home to satisfy home customers who do not perceive any changes to the vendor's organisational boundaries. Internally the organisation may have grave difficulties in achieving effective learning within the new supply chain. A process view is, in our view, essential to have any chance of success in this, but it is not sufficient and of course the firm must eventually pass beyond these Scenario 1 changes (in our terminology). We now discuss these issues further.

The Concept of 'Distance' and its Effect Within Scenario 2

Space does not permit a deep theoretical development here, but we would argue that 'distance' is a pervasive concept reaching deep into our everyday life. We have our own feelings about "what should be," and when these are broken for whatever reason, we may react at any level—from being mildly puzzled to grossly affronted. Often however we are inconstant in our reactions, and this happens more often in situations where there are cross-cultural issues that leave us bewildered or where there are strong power brokers who distort our ability to cope and react, as is our habit, under normal circumstances.

Research proposes that internationalisation should also be studied as a process (Aharoni, 1966). In consequence a number of different models of the internationalisation process have been developed. One of the most commonly cited models is the "Uppsala model" based on the Nordic studies of Johanson and Wiedersheim-Paul (1975) and Johanson and Vahlne (1977). This suggests that organisations will internationalise in stages as they overcome "psychic distance" (factors which inhibit the flow of information between markets). Johanson and Wiedersheim-Paul (1975) also suggest that organisations will enter countries with successively higher psychic distance. While it is not validated for some industries and markets (Turnbull, 1987; Forsgren, 1989; Erramilli, 1990), the Uppsala model is still put forward as a likely description of the internationalisation process of small, internationally inexperienced organisations (Forsgren, 1989; Johanson and Vahlne, 1990; Buckley et al., 1988). This is important since we note that in all countries the vast majority of firms may be classified as SMEs (Small & Medium Enterprises). In the UK for instance, in 2000, 99% of firms were defined as 'small' although they created 38% of the nations' turnover (DTI Statistical News Release — P/2000/561— 7th August 2000). It follows that some of these firms will venture abroad, and probably will follow the Uppsala model.

Informal support for this 'thesis' was given by Efurth (2001) while discussing aspects of the work of Dzever et al. (2001). The gist of the argument was that the Swedes offer a view of human resource management and entrepreneurship that is clearly distinguished from the Anglo-U.S. or the Asian models. This would correspondingly affect the requirements for knowledge management. Such confirmation is important as process models similar to those above are surfacing in research: such as Brouthers and Brouthers (2001) who review again the cultural distance paradox in joint ventures and mode of entry to another country by single or multi-national organisations; by Larsson et al. (1998) who propose a matrix framework to categorise the issues that 'joint' venture organisations may encounter; and by Kumar and Nti (1998) who note the discrepancies between processes and outcomes. Thus within organisational cultures we may suggest that training be given to help make the intangible more clear in the eyes (and concepts) of the other — and once more we may refer to the subtlety of concepts carried through the learning cycle in Figures 1 and 2. Yet we know from work in knowledge-based systems that knowledge domains have to be well defined and quite restricted, and that *effective* knowledge management systems need to include links to human knowledge that continues to remain tacit. Thus if the cultural distance (a measure akin to the 'psychic distance') between the parties is too large (Kogut & Singh, 1988), the partners will not achieve (even) a slight congruency.

Although we can envisage organisations moving from Scenario 1 change into Scenario 2 change, and perhaps finally Scenario 3 change, most of this work refers essentially to Scenario 2, that of radical change to one process, with the customers and the organisational boundaries remaining the same. A development of the Larsson matrix by Edwards and Kidd (2001) implies that when a willingness to 'work with the other' goes wrong, there is potential to descend into anomic states rather than cooperate or at least work in a cooperative mode. Equally, when an organisation ventures into a region grossly culturally different (e.g., Anglo-Americans in Asia) they may see the local host organisations employing staff using 'rules' derived from what they see as cronyism, nepotism or simple favouritism, and using working practices they see as somewhat corrupt (Kidd & Li, 2001). Here an understanding of the processes will not be sufficient on its own. The enjoining of radically different cultures may prove too great a threat to the morale of the merging organisation's work force as they fight to retain knowledge. This may mean, for example, that they will not cooperate in any way with those whom they view as 'the enemy.'

It must be conceded that this may be seen to be quite correct historically, at least on some occasions. Entering organisations have taken-over and dissolved indigenous industries; the cotton trade in Manchester, UK, or the UK motorcycle industry after the Japanese 'invasion' are just two cases. Not all foreign direct investment (FDI) is good FDI — Cantwell and Janne (1999), and Driffield and Munday (2000) show that there are benefits accruing from investments which stimulate indigenous organisations; but all is not rosy — they also suggest that local adverse effects can occur, namely that inefficient organisations may be bankrupted under the new competition. The knowledge needed to be successful will have changed, but the organisations do not know about it until too late.

The Problematic Scenario 3

Taking this further, especially in this era of globalisation, brings us back to Scenario 3: radical change across the whole organisation, where anything may change, even the nature of the organisation itself.

Looking back at our five reasons for "thinking of process" in knowledge management, all of them may become problematic.

1.   The customer may change in subtle ways, even for the same product or service in a different country.
2.   Existing knowledge applied overseas may not be sufficient.
3.   Organisational structures — real or virtual — will differ in different countries. Actual and perceived boundaries will multiply when alliances are involved, yet from the point of view of knowledge, all remain artificial.
4.   Even transparent measurement can be problematic, especially if the two partners in a joint venture have radically different objectives (perhaps technology transfer for one partner, and access to a new market for the other).
5.   Finally, even holism may be interpreted differently in different cultures, although further discussion is beyond our scope here.

We close this section by offering an increasingly important example from international human resources management — the consideration of demographic and economic migrants. Ronås and Ramaurthy (2001) present a powerful description of international labour migration linked to globalisation. Often (they say) there is contract migration when a migrant's sojourn is linked to a specific job and for a specific time. However, there are also many instances where there is an escalator of people from poor countries moving to relatively better developed countries, while that nation's people move onwards to even better developed nations. Sometimes, as in the case of Japan (and soon in Italy), there will be the need to import labour to maintain the local economy. Ronås and Ramaurthy also cite the case of Germany, where even they, over the period from 2000 through 2005, anticipate a need to allow 6,000 migrants annually per million inhabitants simply to maintain the size of the working population. Under these circumstances there may be great cultural distances observed even within one organisation, notwithstanding errors in perception by staff from country A of the workforce of an alliance firm in country B who may in fact be employing many workers from country C.

Radical changes will therefore need to take place across the whole organisation, as nothing in the knowledge exchange and learning systems may be taken for granted. For example, working practices due to local legislation or religious tolerance will have to be observed and absorbed. To overcome some of this effect, we may suggest that the continuing development of and greater familiarity with Information and Communications Technology will facilitate outsourcing and/or teleworking, thereby reducing the need for migration. But this demands earlier infrastructure investment at a national level that just has not taken place in most newly developing regions. This mode will still demand human tolerance, compromise and understanding of "the other" in order to make the processes work well.

CONCLUSIONS

We have explained why we believe that considering knowledge management in terms of business processes is the best route for organisations to follow. We have cited some good examples, but also some indications that a process focus is not the answer to all knowledge management problems, especially where different cultures and/or cultural change are involved.

We conclude with an unanswered question concerning change and knowledge management. In terms of organisational performance, greater potential benefit comes from greater change. But when great change occurs, some of the organisation's existing knowledge, whether it be in stories or systems (or even people) will be less valid in that new context. How does the organisation know, before the change occurs, which of the knowledge that will be?

Returning to the Digital example: in today's purchasing climate, some customers look deeply into an organisation's supply chain to ascertain the ethical and ecological properties of the product's origin, even questioning the origins of its components (Dzever et al., 2001). Thus, ironically enough, Digital, 20 years on, might have been able to retain its marketplace and its original stakeholders' confidence through a continued use of its U.S. design and production chain, and by being perceived to not unethically milk the labour market of developing countries. But hindsight is a wonderful thing!

The key medium- and long-term knowledge challenge is thus "what to keep, and what to throw away." We believe that relating the knowledge to business processes will help, but there will always be an element of, yes, luck, in such matters. Greater change does, after all, involve greater risk. Innovation implies change; change implies lessening the dependence on history as a predictor of the future. Except, that is, in finding those who are adaptable and receptive to change. But will they be forever thus? Who can tell? In the end, as is appropriate, knowledge management is a "people thing" — manageable with care!

REFERENCES

Aharoni, Y. (1966). *The Foreign Investment Decision Process*. Boston, MA: Harvard University Press.

Argyris, C. and Schön, D. (1978). *Organizational Learning: A Theory of Action Perspective*. Reading, MA: Addison-Wesley.

Beer, S. (1985). *Diagnosing the System for Organisations*. Chichester: John Wiley & Sons.

Braganza, A. (2001). Knowledge (mis)management... and how to avoid it. Presented at *Information Management 2001*, Olympia, London, 1-2 November.

Brouthers, K. D. and Brouthers, L. E. (2001) Explaining the national cultural paradox. *Journal of International Business Studies*, *32*(1), 177-189.

Buckley, P. J., Newbould, G. D. and Thurwell, J. (1988). *Foreign Direct Investment by Smaller UK Firms*. London: Macmillan.

Cantwell, J. A. and Janne, O. (1999). Technological globalisation and innovative centres: The role of corporate technological leadership and location hierarchy. *Research Policy*, *28*, 119-144.

Davenport, T. H. (1993). *Process Innovation: Reengineering Work Through Information Technology*. Boston, MA: Harvard Business School Press.

Davenport, T. H. and Prusak, L. (1998). *Working Knowledge: How Organizations Manage What They Know*. Boston, MA: Harvard Business School Press.

Driffield, N. L. and Munday, M. C. (2000). Industrial performance, agglomeration, and foreign investment in the UK. *Journal of International Business Studies*, *31*(1), 21-37.

Dzever, S., Quester, P. G. and Chetty, S. (2001). Country-of-origin effects on industrial buyer's product perception in the Asia-Pacific region: A comparative study of Australia, New Zealand, Thailand and Cambodia. In *Proceedings of the 18th EAMSA Annual Conference*, Berlin, 31 Oct-2 Nov: (2) 221-243.

Earl, M. J. (1994). The new and the old of business process redesign. *The Journal of Strategic Information Systems*, *3*(1), 5-22.

Edwards, J. S. and Kidd, J. B. (2001). Knowledge management when 'the times they are a-changin.' In Remenyi, D. (Ed.), *Proceedings of the Second European Conference on Knowledge Management*, 171-183. Bled, Slovenia, November 8-9.

Efurth, C. (2001). Private communication at the *18th EAMSA Annual Conference*, Berlin, 31 Oct–2 Nov.

Erramilli, M. K. (1990). Entry mode choice in service industries. *International Marketing Review*, *7*(5), 50-61.

Fisher, G. (2001). A framework for deploying knowledge management in an

EDRM environment. Presented at *Information Management 2001*, Olympia, London, 1-2 November.

Forsgren, M. (1989). *Managing the Internationalisation Process: The Swedish Case*. London: Routledge.

Gill, T. G. (1995). Early expert systems: Where are they now? *MIS Quarterly*, *19*(1), 51-81.

Hamel, G. and Prahalad, C. K. (1994). *Competing for the Future*. Boston, MA: Harvard Business School Press.

Hammer, M. (1990). Re-engineering work–don't automate, obliterate. *Harvard Business Review*, (July-August), 104-122.

Hammer, M. and Champy, J. (1993). *Re-Engineering the Corporation–A Manifesto for Business Revolution*. London: Nicholas Brealey Publishing.

Huber, G. P. (1991). Organisational learning: The contributing processes and the literatures. *Organizational Science*, *3*(3), 383-397.

Huber, G. P. (2000). Transferring sticky knowledge: Suggested solutions and needed studies. In Edwards, J. S. and Kidd, J. B. (Eds.), *Knowledge Management Beyond the Hype: Looking Towards the New Millennium. Proceedings of KMAC 2000*, Aston Business School, 17-18 July: 12-22.

Johanson, J. and Vahlne, J.-E. (1977). The internationalisation of the firm: A model of knowledge development and increasing foreign market commitments. *Journal of International Business Studies*, *8*(1), 23-32.

Johanson, J. and Vahlne, J.-E. (1990). The mechanism of internationalisation. *International Marketing Review*, *7*(4), 11-24.

Johanson, J. and Wiedersheim-Paul, F. (1975). The internationalisation of the firm– Four Swedish cases. *Journal of Management Studies*, (October), 305-322.

Kidd, J. B. and Edwards J. S. (2000). Fast-moving global supply chains: How organisational learning may offer bridges in crossing cultures. In Remenyi, D. (Ed.), *Proceedings of the First European Conference on Knowledge Management*, 49-59. Bled, Slovenia. 26-27 October.

Kidd, J. B. and Li, X. (2001). Leaders and transparency: Problems of cronyism in Asia. *Proceedings of the 18th EAMSA Annual Conference*, 37-59. Berlin, 31 Oct–2 Nov: (1).

Kogut, B. and Singh, H. (1988). The effect of national culture on choice of entry mode. *Journal of International Business Studies*, *19*(3), 411-432.

Kumar, R. and Nti, K. O. (1998) Differential learning and interaction in alliance dynamics: A process and outcome discrepancy model. *Organizational Science*, *9*(3), 356-367

Larsson, R., Bengtsson, L., Henricksson, K. and Sparks, J. (1998). The interorganizational learning dilemma: Collective knowledge development in strategic alliances. *Organizational Science*, *9*(3), 285-306.

Lucier, C. E. and Torsilieri, J. D. (2001). Can knowledge management deliver bottom-line results? In Nonaka, I. and Teece, D. J. (Eds.), *Managing Industrial Knowledge: Creation, Transfer and Utilization*, 231-243. London: Sage Publications.

Nonaka, I. and Takeuchi, H. (1995). *The Knowledge-Creating Company*. Oxford: Oxford University Press.

Porter, M. E. (1985). *Competitive Advantage: Creating and Sustaining Superior Performance*. New York: Collier Macmillan.

Robinson, S., Alifantis, A., Edwards, J. S., Hurrion, R. D., Ladbrook, J. and Waller, T. (2001). Modelling and improving human decision making with simulation. In Peters, B. A., Smith, J. S., Medeiros, D. J. and Rohrer, M. W. (Eds.), *Winter Simulation Conference 2001*. San Diego, CA: The Society for Computer Simulation.

Ronås, P. and Ramaurthy, B. (2001). International labour migration and globalisation. *Nordic Newsletter of Asian Studies*, 3(October), 3-6.

Scarbrough, H., Swan, J. and Preston, J. (1999). *Knowledge Management and the Learning Organisation: A Review of the Literature*. London: Institute of Personnel and Development.

Turnbull, P.W. (1987). A challenge to the stages theory of the internationalisation process. In Rosson, P. J. and Reid, S. D. (Eds.), *Managing Export Entry and Expansion*. New York: Praeger.

Weick, K. E. and Westley, F. (1996). Organisational learning: Affirming the oxymoron. In Clegg, S. R., Hardey, C. and Nord, W. R. (Eds.), *Handbook of Organisation Studies*, 440-458. London: Sage Publications.

Wizdo, L. (2001). Organisational models for enterprise knowledge management. In Remenyi, D. (Ed.), *Proceedings of the Second European Conference on Knowledge Management*, 755-766. Bled, Slovenia, 8-9 November.

Chapter IX

Designing Organisational Memory in Knowledge-Intensive Companies: A Case Study

Dee Alwis, Vlatka Hlupic and George Rzevski
Brunel University, UK

ABSTRACT

Organisational memory refers to the storage of a company's collective expertise and experience that is cultivated through human and technological networks for improving organisational performance. A knowledge-sharing environment gives employees access to the most innovative and creative ideas that exist within the company and translates into significant business opportunities for the organisation. In this chapter, the issues related to designing organisational memory in knowledge-intensive companies are investigated using a case study example. Key findings of the case study are outlined, and a framework is proposed to assist knowledge-intensive organisations in implementing and managing a corporate knowledge base.

INTRODUCTION

It is now widely recognised that knowledge is more relevant to sustained business than the traditional factors of production — land, labour and capital (Drucker, 1993). Companies are using information technology to be globally competitive in the emerging knowledge economy. But it is the application of human intellect — the capacity for understanding, reflecting and reasoning — that adds greatest value to organisational activities and create differentiation in the market place (Quinn, 1992). Knowledge-intensive companies are best placed to take advantage of the explosive growth of the knowledge economy. We define knowledge-intensive companies as *those organisations that create new knowledge by means of collaborative efforts of their staff and incorporate this knowledge into their products and services*. They can include corporations, small businesses, universities and colleges, hospitals and government agencies, working in sectors as diverse as management consulting, financial and legal, teaching, specialist medical care or marine biology. Sveiby (1997) describes the product of the knowledge-intensive organisations as solving customer problems that are unique and therefore hard to solve in a standardised manner.

In this chapter, the issues related to designing organisational memory in knowledge-intensive companies are investigated using a case study example. The current knowledge management practices employed by the knowledge-intensive company are explored, and both social and technological processes that the company needs to put in place when designing an organisational knowledge base are reviewed. An overview of some of the premises underlying the practices of knowledge management is provided, and these premises are related to the concept of organisational memory. The key findings of the case study carried out are outlined. These are then linked to the framework proposed, within which the company can harness their organisational knowledge.

KNOWLEDGE MANAGEMENT AND ORGANISATIONAL MEMORY

Knowledge management is the explicit and systematic management of vital knowledge and its associated processes of creation, organisation, diffusion, use and exploitation (Skyrme, 1997). In order to manage knowledge as a resource, it is first necessary to understand the characteristics of knowledge. Among the many knowledge schemata presented in the KM literature, the dichotomy between tacit and explicit knowledge (Nonaka, 1994) has advanced our understanding of organisational knowledge flow and transfer. Polanyi (1966) used the phrase "we can know more than we can tell" to describe tacit knowledge. Tacit knowledge refers to personal knowledge, which is internalised in people's minds, acquired through experience and shared in a direct way (Nonaka, 1994). Explicit knowledge on the other hand is knowledge that we can easily articulate and share, and is transmittable in formal and systematic languages. When knowledge is explicitly captured, it is then learned and absorbed by others in the organisation, which in turn creates tacit knowledge.

Organisational memory refers to the storage of a company's collective expertise and experience that is cultivated through human and technological networks for improving organisational performance (Brooking, 1999). Knowledge in the minds of organisational members is increasingly recognised as the most valuable resource (Stewart, 1997). Another kind of potential knowledge that is equally important is the information people use in their work that is currently scattered in various databases that cannot talk to one another — handbooks, filing cabinets and emails. The ability to tap and re-use this knowledge is what will differentiate a company from its competitors. Organisational memory enables companies 'know what they know' by helping companies to gain insight and understanding from its own experience, and prevents them from repeating the mistakes made elsewhere in the company by drawing lessons from similar situations in the past (O'Dell, 1998).

The concept of organisational memory is complex. The skill, expertise and experience embedded in people's brains cannot be effectively captured, by merely tracking the shared knowledge. It is important to recognise the value of tacit knowledge, which is learned only by experience and communicated only indirectly. Where tacit knowledge can be made explicit, however, by codifying it as a computer program, a recipe, a formula or even a product specification, then personal knowledge becomes organisational knowledge. This can then be shared and stored, so that it will not be lost when the individual eventually leaves the organisation. When tacit knowledge cannot be made explicit, the organisation can only hold on to it by encouraging holders to pass on their knowledge by apprenticing others and making sure that it is held by several people (Nonaka and Takeuchi, 1995). But people will not pass on their tacit knowledge if it means losing their bargaining power and control of their work, or if they believe it will endanger their own job security. People exchange their insights and know-how in a culture based on trust or if they gain some personal benefit from doing so (Dixon, 2000). "That personal benefit may be no more than having others acknowledge their expertise, the smile they get in return or seeing the sigh of relief on the recipient's face."

KNOWLEDGE MANAGEMENT IN KNOWLEDGE-INTENSIVE ORGANISATIONS: A CASE STUDY

This single site case study was an exploratory study in which the authors were trying to investigate the knowledge underlying the company's business and how that knowledge is used, rather than establishing or testing specific hypotheses. The study examined the current practices that are in place to create, capture and share knowledge and their effectiveness in terms of achieving business goals. A case study approach was selected as the most appropriate way to gather empirical data in order to (a) cover contextual conditions and not just the phenomenon of study and (b) utilise multiple sources of evidence (Yin, 1994). Yin further suggests that this approach is useful in understanding complex social phenomena.

The findings of the study are based on authors' observations, interviews and informal discussions over a period of two years. A semi-structured questionnaire was used to evaluate how key employees feel about knowledge sharing. Further informal interviews and company documents were used to get a more in-depth perspective and to distill the basic information. The questionnaire consisted of two parts. Part I focused on seeking the employees' perceptions of current information exchange, and how the informal knowledge is captured. Part II attempted to elicit the employees' perceived effectiveness of the present knowledge management attempts in place and the possible future scenarios with regard to the knowledge management efforts. The authors have drawn on the existing literature to guide the fieldwork carried out and to provide ways of synthesising the results. Results derived from the study were used to develop a framework for designing organisational memory, essentially focusing on formalising the knowledge-creating process within the company.

Company Profile

The case study company, Technology Innovations Limited (TI), is a research and development enterprise based in the UK. Through the use of innovation and intellectual property, it generates technology solutions in the areas of optics, communications, multimedia, sensors and digital signal processing. Its employees work with customers to develop new products and technologies based on these innovations. The company founds this work on a 70-year-old tradition of landmark technological innovations. TI's customers are mainly blue chip enterprises throughout the world, the government departments such as the Ministry of Defence (MOD) and the European Community (EC). It has nearly 100 scientists and engineers who are organised into four formal technical groups based on their expertise. The qualities that these employees possess are a critical success factor for TI's survival and growth in a very competitive marketplace.

TI has set up several communication links for the exchange of information within the company. The knowledge-sharing applications currently in use include the PC and LAN network that links all employees in the company, e-mail that is designed to facilitate both the formal and informal exchange of messages, and the shared network drives that are allocated to specified groups of people. Several databases are in place for employees to record and share information. However, these individual databases are not linked to each other in a way that would facilitate ease of search. For example, if an engineer wants to find out how many European Community projects were undertaken by the company during the past five years, or the technological areas each project belonged to, s/he has to search for this information in several files. These files are scattered throughout the company, in both manual and computerised form. Although this information will be meticulously documented, it will be isolated in individual project files.

TI has employed significant initiatives to encourage dissemination of knowledge throughout the company. They also underscore the importance of teams, relationships and networks as the basis for effective knowledge transfer. The techniques used to encourage mutual learning and collaboration comprise of the following: inter-departmental meetings; company-wide presentations by the senior management; various informal discussions between departments to allow a free flow of ideas; "lunchtime" technical conferences on selected themes, where company experts give talks on their areas of expertise and describe their experiences; the monthly newsletter in which employees are encouraged to present their suggestions and views; and off site meetings for brain storming and team building. These knowledge-dissemination techniques do not as yet involve any information technology capabilities to capture, retain and re-use its collective knowledge.

The company operates an annual performance-related bonus scheme where the bonus is calculated for each technical group, based on formulae that are determined in advance of each year. These formulae measure the groups' performance against specific targets, principally relating to sales and net profits. The bonus is shared between the members of the group, according to the individual contributions to the projects. The company does not currently have any formal incentive schemes that reward contribution to knowledge sharing. The performance appraisal process does not cover knowledge sharing or participation in inter-group forums. The reward systems and promotion patterns unwittingly encourage a high level of internal competitiveness and therefore reduce the likelihood that pertinent information will be shared. For example, customer or technical information gained by one employee may create a competitive advantage in internal promotions.

Interpretation of the Case Study Results

Appendix A presents a summary of the responses to the questionnaire. The responses obtained in this case study confirm that there is a high level of awareness of the need for managing knowledge and the value it can bring to the business. Therefore they rarely need to make a business case for the concept.

The responses show that employees receive various types of information on a regular basis, the bulk of the reports being in the form of e-mail attachments. The company's attempt to share information, by pushing it at people, has resulted in employees being overwhelmed by information. There is no corporate information infrastructure in place, where everyone within the company can access knowledge and expertise on an as-needed basis. Employees struggle to extract timely, accurate and relevant information from growing sets of data. This tremendous amount of information hinders rather than helps productivity.

It is evident that the company uses meetings, forums and discussions extensively to create knowledge through the processes of social interaction and collaboration. Our observations show, however, that effort is lacking to record and disseminate the deliberations of these groups of people, and make the content and outcomes readily accessible to a wider circle of employees.

The responses relating to the methods used to record the project-experiences show that the project managers currently record the same information in several unconnected databases. There is no central facility to capture and leverage technical experiences in terms of lessons learned that relate to projects undertaken. This information is currently available in individual files, a considerable proportion in paper form or in the heads of a few employees. As a result, knowledge for building on previous experiences is not always readily accessible to people external to the project. There was evidence that people sometimes repeated the processes or worked with limited information, in the absence of the benefit of the related expertise that is available in other parts of the company.

Most respondents reported that their time spent on non-productive work is relatively small. This is in contrast to the statistics extracted from the project time sheets, which reflect higher percentages of time spent on non-billable administrative work. There was initially little realisation by the individuals of the extent of time spent on handling repetitive tasks. Our observations show that vital information and centralised systems that would significantly reduce the daily processes, freeing up employees to address more business critical problems, are not often available or readily accessible.

Over 85% of TI's employees are involved in the creative process. As with any other company employing knowledge workers, TI has a high staff turnover. The learning process that people undergo once they enter this company all too often leaves with them. Often, when people leave, they take an entire storehouse of knowledge about their job with them. If the company could somehow capture a part of that person's experience, then the reciprocal benefit would be effected when the person leaves or is placed on another project. Approximately 40% of the employee base joined the company within the past two years. This means a lot of new technical staff and a lot of company-specific experience needs to be gained quickly in order to improve the quality of work. This makes knowledge sharing essential.

TI's attitude to innovation has been one of great creativity, but with a certain lack of structure. The company actively encourages regular meetings and informal discussions between departments, and these meetings, informal discussions and the use of email provide an informal environment for employees to pose questions and swap ideas. However, there are no formal mechanisms in place to record these events for future use, and opportunities for leveraging functional expertise and judgment are largely untapped.

There are issues relating to the organisation's culture and human resource policies that are supportive of knowledge creation and transfer. There is scope for collaboration to be enhanced through an appraisal and reward scheme, which recognises the extent and nature of an individual's contribution to the company's knowledge base. The types of incentive schemes currently in operation reward group performance, but they also indirectly and unwittingly encourage competition between members in a group, and discourage sharing of knowledge across technological groups. It is for example unlikely that employees will voluntarily share the hard-earned insights and expertise that make them valuable.

The responses show that satisifaction and fulfillment is the best way to instill a sharing attitude in knowledge professionals. However, knowledge workers will only share knowledge with the company once a basis of trust has been established. Appreciating the dynamics of information politics is essential when planning a collaborative culture.

TI's employees are currently exposed to a lot of information. Information and knowledge, however, are two distinct entities. What adds value to information is the application of intelligence through experience, interpretation and reflection. A knowledge management programme will provide the means to capture and leverage the knowledge derived from the mass of diversified information. The responses indicate that the knowledge management techniques currently in use within the company are mainly unstructured and do not involve the use of any advanced information technology capabilities to organise its collective knowledge. For instance, there is no information systems support in place to track the information and experiences into knowledge bases, where the information can be regularly reused for business advantage. As a result, some vital know-how may only be available in isolated pockets of the organisation, trapped in individual minds and local venues.

The study shows that there is considerable interest and potential for implementing a system to manage the corporate memory. The company has a vast treasure house of knowledge, know-how and practices that they can leverage more effectively. If tapped and mapped, this information could yield considerable gains in customer satisfaction and organisational competence. A programme that captures the company's collective know-how to determine such things as best practices, leverage tacit knowledge of individuals and identify field experts would have a significant impact on the company and enhance the effectiveness of knowledge-intensive work processes.

TOWARDS A FRAMEWORK FOR DESIGNING ORGANISATIONAL MEMORY

The proposed framework for the design of organisational memory is based on an extensive literature search to clarify fundamental concepts and theories of knowledge management, and on insight gained in conducting a rich case study in a knowledge-intensive company (described in the previous sections). The focus has

Figure 1: Five main elements of the framework

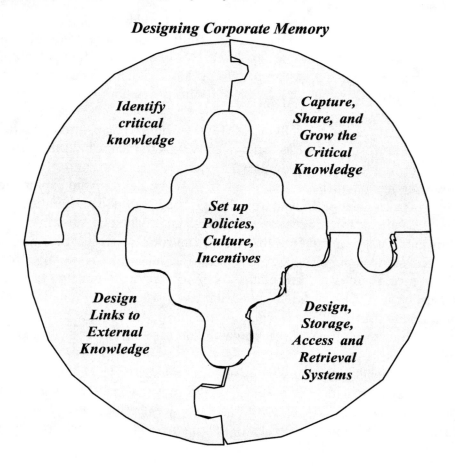

been to help the company to share the knowledge of individuals as a means of improving the competency and efficiency, rather than attempt to automate the knowledge-intensive work. Although the framework has been designed in the context of TI, many components of this framework could be relevant for other (particularly those which are knowledge intensive) organisations.

The approach we have developed for designing organisational memory consists of the following five steps:

1. Identify the type of knowledge that is critical for improving the company performance. The types of knowledge in this context are:

   a. knowledge about customers — the ability to grow the business through long term relationships with satisfied customers

   b. knowledge about competitors — the ability to stay ahead of competitors

   c. knowledge about business partners — the ability to form mutually beneficial relationships with business partners

   d. knowledge about company's products and services — the capability to deliver superior value through products and services

   e. knowledge about company's internal resources such as people, processes and intellectual property assets

   - the ability to attract and retain employees with critical expertise and skills
   - the ability to carry out efficient and cost-effective processes
   - the ability to generate and exploit patents and know-how

2. Set up organisational policies, culture, incentives and similar drivers that will ensure knowledge workers gain by sharing the critical knowledge identified in step 1 with others.

3. Develop methods to capture, share and grow the critical knowledge identified in step 1 and obtained as a result of step 2.

4. Design effective storage, access and retrieval systems to enable knowledge workers gain from knowledge accumulated in organisational memory as a result of step 3.

5. Provide knowledge workers with communication and collaborative links to external environment such as customers, suppliers and business partners and to external knowledge bases to bring new insight into the organisation.

Although the term "steps" infers a linear sequential order, these steps can be carried out in parallel. The framework uses a holistic approach focusing on content, culture, processes and technology. The five pieces fit together like a jigsaw puzzle, forming a process for developing wealth-creating knowledge. Each element by itself does not create organisational memory, but taken as a whole, these elements can contribute to the development of organisational capabilities through the identification and replication of dispersed and hidden knowledge.

Identifying the Critical Knowledge

In an increasingly complex world, organisations have to react to intensifying competition. Such competitiveness is dependent on harnessing the critical knowledge that guides the criteria that the company must fulfill in order to succeed. For the company that we studied, the critical knowledge was the knowledge about company's products and services and about internal resources, particularly about the skills of their knowledge workers.

The assessment to identify critical knowledge includes the following steps:

- Analysing *existing knowledge assets* that could be leveraged and document their existence
- Asking diagnostic questions to *assess their importance*:
  - Is the company making the best use of this knowledge?
  - Can the competition imitate this asset?
  - Can this knowledge "walk out of the door"?
- Identifying the *benefits* that could be gained if the company improves its way of sharing this knowledge.
- *Rating* these knowledge assets in terms of relevance to company's strategic advantage.

The completed assessment should enable the company to identify areas of high tacit content of knowledge in relation to the amount that has been captured and explicated.

Culture and Incentives

Cultural barriers can represent the biggest hindrance to gaining the real value from a knowledge base. The case study shows that TI already has a collaborative team-based corporate culture. Therefore, it is important for the company to support and stimulate the existing knowledge-creating activities and to provide the appropriate environment to allow knowledge to flow seamlessly. These involve:

- Having a working environment that *encourages ideas and experiences to flow* smoothly through formal and informal networks within the business.
- Supporting the existing work environment that encourages *initiative and innovation*.
- Creating a culture of *trust and learning* that makes employees feel comfortable sharing knowledge.
- Identifying and utilising a *diverse set of skills and expertise*.
- Creating a culture that *empowers employees*.
- Introducing a *reward system* for sharing knowledge including *recognition*.

A recurring problem in knowledge transfer appears to be one of motivation. Not everyone in the company is motivated to share their know-how and to use information provided by others. Furthermore it is not easy for people to 'write down' what they know or to realise that someone else would be interested in the knowledge they have. Since the process of getting down everything a knowledge worker knows would be futile, richest tacit knowledge can only be transferred by encouraging people to interact.

Employees need various forms of encouragement to stimulate them to share knowledge and derive value from knowledge that lies throughout the organisation. Companies need to cultivate a culture encouraged by a reward system that encourages knowledge workers to both share what they know and to pass on their success stories as well as failures in the way of lessons learned. The transfer is more effective when it is part of an environment that values sharing. Embedding knowledge development and transfer in the employees' career development will be more effective than providing financial incentives to promote and reward sharing. Additionally, investing in staff development and training helps a company to alter the behaviour and attitudes of individuals who in the past have been used to hoarding knowledge, since trust and cooperation are critical factors in the integration of a knowledge base into the company's employee base.

Capturing Sharing and Growing Knowledge

A corporate knowledge base is a tool that aids companies in capturing their accumulated know-how and other intellectual assets and make them available to achieve accelerated business benefit. A common approach to designing organisational memory is to capture procedural knowledge about the business in an explicit form and enter it into *electronic knowledge repositories*. Collecting existing knowledge and best practices from project reports, white papers and other documents enable a company to asses and catalogue its existing intellectual assets. Knowledge repositories, however, typically capture only a very small percentage of an organisation's core knowledge since much of this knowledge is personal. Therefore other approaches should be used to make it easier for employees to access minds of experts.

A starting point would be to create a profile of experts often called *corporate yellow pages* that lists who knows what throughout the organisation. Here, users facing a technical problem can search by category of skill to locate subject experts. Another approach would be to transfer individuals' tacit knowledge, that which is gained through experience, context specific and hard to formalise, into a corporate knowledge base by supporting *community based electronic discussion*. Designing organisational memory, however, extends beyond building repositories. The intricacies of the design process should also incorporate support for sharing and transfer of knowledge through informal processes to create new knowledge.

The transfer of tacit knowledge can be facilitated through *reflective conversation and structured dialogue among employees*. Experts should be encouraged to give talks on their areas of expertise and describe their experiences. These sessions can be audio or video recorded for distribution and training, enabling employees to apply what they learn to critical processes.

Identification and transfer of internal best practices and lessons learned across the entire organisation form a key component of knowledge creation. This process helps spread the experiences of teams around the organisation. The process also involves helping the recipients adapt and apply those practices to new situations to create new knowledge. Failed efforts and decisions provide equally useful insights into what did not work to avoid repeating past mistakes, duplicating the efforts and starting each project from scratch.

Supporting collaborative work between teams to enable application of distributed skills that exist in an organisation is an essential part of designing organisational memory. Collaborative relationships enable tacit knowledge to be shared among people with a shared goal, allowing greater use of the valuable technical expertise.

The development of communities of practice, where tips are exchanged and ideas are generated as part of a social activity, provides another way of exchanging tacit knowledge. When people work together in tightly knit groups, knowledge is created and held collectively.

The key to enhancing organisational memory is to capture ongoing experiences using techniques such as *learning histories* and *post-project reviews*.

Designing Access and Retrieval Systems

Management and utilisation of knowledge within an organisation creates the need to capture and store the collective knowledge and learning gained in a form in which it can be searched, retrieved and shared with other people. The massive growth in the capability of electronic systems has made it possible to capture and store large volumes of digital information in a form that can be accessed quickly and easily, regardless of time and place. It is important to have a standardised company-wide architecture to enable this effort. A knowledge base consists of several sub-components. These include *repositories* that hold explicit knowledge and the associated rules to capture, refine and distribute content; *collaboration platforms* that support distributed work and incorporate pointers, skills databases and informal discussion forums; and *networks* that support communication and conversation such as leased lines, shared spaces, industry forums and trade nets.

Since knowledge captured in an explicit format can lose its context, insight and experience, the content of a repository should be enriched with an element of tacit knowledge:

Table 1: Knowledge processes and the associated technologies

Process	Type of Knowledge	Technology
Find knowledge	Tacit and explicit	Search engines and browsers that scan both formal and informal sources of knowledge, skill databases.
Acquire new knowledge	Tacit and explicit	Collaborative decision-making tools, rational capture tools, distributed tools such as Lotus Notes databases and intranets.
Package and assemble knowledge	Explicit	Information-refinery tools, intelligent agents, push technology.
Reuse and apply knowledge	Explicit	Customer support, best practice and project record databases, decision support systems.
Transfer of real-time contextual knowledge	Tacit and explicit	Video conferencing and groupware to record and detail group deliberations.
Create socio-technical networks	Tacit and explicit	Discussion databases, electronic forums and project work teams.

- Contextual information—how the information is used, what factors should be considered when using it and where is it applicable or not applicable.
- Pointers to originators—contact details of originators and links to related experts.
- Discussion forums — places where dialogue can continue.
- Addition of multimedia material—video recordings of training courses and presentations.

By systematically capturing its intellectual assets—internal company structures and processes, customer relations and the expert profiles of people—in the corporate knowledge base, the company can make the knowledge available to all employees simultaneously. The most difficult challenge however is to keep the knowledge base up to date with current activities, since without appropriate culture and incentives, people will not be stimulated to contribute to the knowledge base and use this knowledge.

The processes to capture an organisation's individual and group knowledge and the technologies that can be deployed to enable these processes are listed in Table 1 below.

Facilitating Access to External Knowledge

Many breakthroughs in scientific discovery have been serendipitous, influenced by the freedom of intellectual pursuit and ready access to people and knowledge bases with a variety of backgrounds. Stimulation provided by external sources such as joint venture partners, consultants, academic institutions and external knowledge databases is invaluable in bringing new knowledge into the organisation. Thus external access and distribution has become a priority for knowledge workers. Access to environment scanning and market intelligent systems to gather knowledge enables employees to gain new insights into a whole range of external factors such as technological, political, economic and regulatory developments. While extranets allow companies to collaboratively tap into knowledge-based resources of partners and those of ally firms, the Internet makes it possible to invisibly tap into external electronic information on competitive intelligence. The global reach of the Internet also enables it to connect users anywhere, anytime, as long as they have access to the Web. New knowledge can be created through these interactions, in order to continue the growth of the organisation and its knowledge base.

BUSINESS VALUE OF CORPORATE MEMORY

Knowledge and the intellectual capital it creates are difficult to measure accurately and hard to value. The main reason is because it is hard to measure such an intangible concept. However, research has shown that companies can generate tremendous value for its employees, customers and shareholders by harnessing the collective knowledge. An effective corporate memory will:

- Help an organisation to 'know what they know.'
- Eliminate duplicate and redundant business practices—not reinventing the wheel.
- Facilitate better capturing and sharing of best practices.
- Leverage knowledge and intellectual capital to improve service delivery.
- Improve time-to-market time scales.
- Help employees avoid repeating mistakes when working on similar projects.
- Help identify "knowledge communities" that don't appear on the corporate organisation charts.
- Achieve reduction in employee training time.
- Reduce the cost of creating and distributing corporate data.
- Decrease the cycle time for distributing information throughout the organisation.
- Provide greater interaction and improved information flow between customers and suppliers.

For a knowledge coordination programme to succeed, the company must clarify the end result in terms of the business value to be achieved. The extent of the benefits to be derived will depend on how the company strikes the right balance between people, processes, content and technology.

SUMMARY AND CONCLUSIONS

The focus of the case study described in this chapter was to explore the means of capturing, storing and providing access to the knowledge assets of TI. The study identifies a number of problems that have not been addressed by the company in its current knowledge management efforts. The authors have drawn on the existing literature to guide the fieldwork carried out and to provide ways of synthesising the results. The value of this synthesis stems from facilitating the analysis of how the company collects and leverages its experience, and the limitations imposed by the current system. The main contribution of this study is the development of a framework for designing organisational memory, essentially focusing on leveraging the pockets of expertise that exist within the company and formalising the knowledge-creating process.

The focus of the framework is on supporting the connectivity of knowledge workers through social and technological networks, providing them the opportunity to collaborate in order to develop greater insight. The authors stress the importance of soft and qualitative elements of knowledge transfer, recognising the importance of tacit knowledge and viewing the organisation as a living and evolving organism. The framework provides a core set of factors which will apply to most businesses that employ knowledge workers. However, since every company is unique, with their own culture, processes and problems, practitioners must develop a knowledge transfer strategy in the context of their own organisation.

The next step in the development of this framework would be to empirically assess its applicability in TI and also in other organisational settings.

Every company can benefit from managing knowledge better. Knowledge management is about understanding human and other intellectual assets, and its critical role lies in its ability to support thinking and collaboration. Organisational memory allows companies to learn from past decisions, both good and bad, and to apply the lessons learned to complex choices and future decisions. When the design of the system supports the productive relationships between colleagues, instead of between people and information, the company is likely to tap new and previously unknown talents and competencies.

REFERENCES

Brooking, A. (1999). *Corporate Memory: Strategies for Knowledge Management*. International Thomson Publishing.

Dixon, N. M. (2000). *Common Knowledge: How Companies Thrive by Sharing What They Know*. Boston, MA: Harvard Business School Press.

Drucker, P. F. (1993). *Post Capitalist Society*. Butterworth Heinemann.

Nanaka, I. (1994). A dynamic theory of organisational knowledge creation. *Organisation Science*, 5(1).

Nonaka, I. and Takeuchi, H. (1995). *The Knowledge-Creating Company*. Oxford: Oxford University Press, Inc.

O'Dell, C. and Grayson, C. J. (1998). *If Only We Knew What We Know*. New York: The Free Press.

Polanyi, M. (1966). *The Tacit Dimension*. Magnolia, MA: Peter Smith.

Quinn, J. B. (1992). *Intelligent Enterprise*. New York: The Free Press.

Skyrme, D. J. (1997). *Knowledge Management: Making Sense of an Oxymoron*. Available: http://www.skyrme.com/insights.

Stewart, T. A. (1997). *Intellectual Capital: The New Wealth of Organisations*. Nicholas Brealey Publishing Limited.

Sveiby, K. E. (1997). *The New Organizational Wealth: Managing and Measuring Knowledge-Based Assets*. San Francisco, CA: Berrett Koehler Publishing.

Yin, R. K. (1994). *Case Study Research: Design and Methods* (second edition). Thousand Oaks, CA: Sage Publications.

APPENDIX

A summary of responses obtained from a questionnaire

Question	Response	Percentage of respondents
Part I: On Sharing Information and Transfer of Knowledge		
1. How frequently do you share critical information between the technical groups within the company?	Weekly Monthly Rarely	70% 10% 20%
2. What mechanisms do you use to share information?	E-mail One-to one discussions Meetings	100% 100% 100%
3. What methods do you currently use to record project experiences such as success stories, problems encountered and solutions found?	Individual project files Customer database Quality workbench database Shared network drives Central project office files	100% 60% 60% 60% 40%
4. What methods do you use to capture and store the informal knowledge that is generated during discussions, brainstorming sessions and other meetings?	Visit (to customer) reports Meeting log books Personal log books Formal minutes of meetings Customer files Project files Patent query requests lodged with Patents department	100% 100% 100% 100% 70% 50% 20%
5. How much of your work is spent on activities that provide low value to customers?	Less than a quarter of the time More than a quarter of the time	60% 40%
Part II: On Managing Knowledge in the Company		
6. Do you have any KM processes or tools within the company at present?	Yes No Don't know	70% 20% 10%
7. What types of knowledge are critical to your company's competitiveness?	Knowledge about customers Knowledge about competitors Best practices/processes Emerging technologies Knowledge about suppliers Regulations and legislation	90% 80% 80% 50% 50% 50%
8. Are there any technology tools you would like implemented, in order to enhance your company's knowledge base?	Knowledge repository Directory of in-house experts Decision support tools Groupware	80% 80% 60% 50%
9. What benefits do you believe your company could gain from more active management of its knowledge?	Efficiency Flexibility Increased responsiveness Improved decision making Improved quality	90% 90% 90% 70% 70%
10. Do you have a reward scheme for sharing knowledge?	Yes No	70% 30%
If yes, please describe.	Group sales commissions Group performance bonuses Bursary scheme for patent query requests lodged Recognition Negative rewards (informal penalty reflected in pay awards)	50% 100% 10% 50% 10%

Chapter X

Opportunities for Data Mining and Customer Knowledge Management for Shopping Centers

Charles Dennis, David Marsland and Tony Cockett
Brunel University, UK

ABSTRACT

Shopping centers are an important part of the UK economy and have been the subject of considerable research. Relying on complex interdependencies between shoppers, retailers and owners, shopping centers are ideal for knowledge management study. Nevertheless, although retailers have been in the forefront of data mining, little has been written on customer knowledge management for shopping centers. In this chapter, the authors aim to demonstrate the possibilities and draw attention to the possible implications of improving customer satisfaction. Aspects of customer knowledge management for shopping centers are considered using analogies drawn from an exploratory questionnaire survey. The objectives of a customer knowledge management system could include increasing rental incomes and bringing new life back into shopping centers and towns.

INTRODUCTION

Shopping centers are an interesting topic for knowledge management — relying on interdependency between owner, retailers and shoppers. Why are shopping centers important? Firstly, planned shopping centers comprise a substantial part of the UK economy, employing over three-quarters of a million people and playing a 'key role in the investments of pension funds' (Davies et al., 1993; OXIRM, 1999). Shopping centers are therefore important not just to customers, but also employees and indeed to many others because of the investments of their pensions. Secondly, retail and shopping centers form the heart of UK towns and create a focus for the community. Shoppers tend to follow the provision of attractive shopping areas. Improving shopper satisfaction can lead to changes in population, expenditure, residence patterns and bring new life to run-down areas (Dennis et al., forthcoming 2002b). The findings of the research could be applicable to traditional high streets and towns as they are to purpose-built shopping malls — if there is in place some form of central administration such as Town Center Managers. This chapter considers the possibilities for shopping centers to make their offer more attractive using techniques of data mining and customer knowledge management.

DATA MINING AND CUSTOMER KNOWLEDGE MANAGEMENT IN THE RETAIL CONTEXT

Data mining has been defined as:

"The process of exploration and analysis, by automatic or semi-automatic means, of large quantities of data in order to discover meaningful patterns and rules."

(Berry and Linoff, 1997)

Berry and Linoff (2000) list six data mining activities: (1) classification; (2) estimation; (3) prediction; (4) affinity grouping or association rules; (5) clustering; and (6) description and visualization. Retail studies have included many other techniques (e.g., sequence-based analysis; fuzzy logic; neural networks; fractal-based algorithms (Rao, 2000; Rensselaer Polytechnic Institute, 1999). Nevertheless, Berry and Linoff's six categories serve our purposes here.

Data mining has many uses, but the aspect of most concern here is what is usually known as 'Customer Relationship Management' (CRM). Good CRM means: (1) presenting a single image of the organisation; (2) understanding who customers are and their likes and dislikes; (3) anticipating customer needs and addressing them proactively; and (4) recognizing when customers are dissatisfied and taking corrective action (Berry and Linoff, 2000).

Some UK retailers recognize the potential of data mining in discovering customer knowledge. For example, Halfords and Sainsbury's uses Brann Viper software, Tesco and John Lewis Dunn Humby (*Computer Weekly,* 16 January and 29 May 1997). Most, though, jealously guard their customer knowledge capital. The authors argue that dissemination of this knowledge to a shopping center owner could result in meeting shopper requirements better.

Since the mid-1980s, there has been an increasing recognition that "knowledge is a fundamental factor behind an enterprise's success" (Wiij, 1994) — a statement that applies in the retail industry as in others. This chapter will consider shopping center customer knowledge management from Wiij's (1998) third, broadest focus: "all knowledge activities affecting success ... using knowledge assets to realize their value." The specific concern is with customer knowledge management — the management and exploitation of customer knowledge. There are two aspects of this knowledge: (1) knowledge about customers; and (2) knowledge possessed by customers (Rowley, 2001). The empirical study reported here concerns the first aspect, but we will conclude with a recommendation for further research on the second.

Richards et al. (1998) argued that the marketing success of an enterprise is founded on "a continuous dialogue with users, leading to a real understanding ... the more mundane the category [shopping centers?], the more dependent on knowledge." In the early 1980s, data warehousing transformed operational data into knowledge for decision-making. As retail IT systems company NCR put it: "For retailers the key ... is to establish data warehouses to improve and manage customer relationships" (Teresko, 1999).

Data mining can use programming methods to identify patterns among data objects — for example between products in a shopping basket. The well-known early example is the 'diapers-beer' link on Friday evenings spotted by Wal-Mart in the U.S. By placing the two side by side, more fathers took home extra beer when they went to buy the diapers after work. Woolworths (UK) have installed a system costing UK£2 million, claimed to have boosted sales in women's toiletries alone by more than UK£5 million per year (Bird, 1996). The authors contend that incorporating data mining and customer database aspects within a framework of knowledge management can help increase knowledge value.

The main focus of this chapter concerns the opportunities for data mining and customer knowledge management for shopping centers. Data mining normally refers to large quantities of data, so our survey of 287 respondents must be near the smaller end of the scope. Nevertheless, the dataset has been useful in illustrating the utility of aspects of data mining and customer knowledge management that may be suitable for larger-scale use. Further, the exercise has demonstrated that a full data warehouse is not essential. Rather, effective data mining techniques can be applied to a smaller sample drawn from a large database. Another aspect for discussion (not the main focus of this chapter, though) concerns the possibilities of extending customer knowledge management to the sharing of information between shopping center managers and potentially competing retailers. The case for such sharing is not clear-cut. Howard (1995) pointed out that shopping center landlord/tenant relationships are characterized by bargaining and outright conflict. Most UK shopping centers are not customer-orientated (according to Howard). This statement may be arguable, but we concur to the extent that more customer knowledge could help shopping centers to make their offers more attractive. Howard is on safer ground in pointing out that more marketing success could be achieved by a utilizing a partnership approach for collecting, sharing and using information. Howard (1997) cited a store manager at the successful Lakeside (UK) center as claiming that CSC (the owner of Lakeside) is different and has a more open relationship between retailers and center management. The information-sharing approach (Howard implied) has contributed substantially to CSC's success.

Some retailers, notably the UK market leaders Tesco (supermarkets) and Boots (drugstores), have exploited customer knowledge by means of loyalty schemes. Such schemes have been successful for retailers but are unlikely to pay for themselves by increased loyalty (Field, 1997). Rather, the benefits arise from their function of facilitating the flow of information and rewards between suppliers and consumers (Worthington, 1999), i.e., as part of a customer knowledge management system. Some UK towns and shopping centers have experimented with loyalty schemes, but as far as the authors are aware, the potential knowledge benefits have not been fully explored. In the Cobham (small town in Surrey, UK) and Lakeside (regional out-of-town shopping center in Essex, UK) schemes, data from customer receipts had to be entered by hand. For the town or center management, the method provided access to customer transaction information, without needing the explicit agreement of individual retailers to data sharing. There is, of course, a privacy issue concerning the use of customer data in this way. The shopping centers may well have taken the view that the transaction data belonged to the individual shoppers—who gave written consent for the data use when they requested the loyalty card. Certain large retailer tenant(s), though, are understood to have considered that they owned the data concerning their shoppers' transactions, and to have objected to the use of that data by the shopping center landlord's loyalty scheme. Some schemes including Lakeside and Cobham have been dropped under the burden of paperwork or lack of support from retailers (Hallsworth, 2000). Lakeside replaced the loyalty card with an 'affinity' credit card —the administrative load was transferred to banks, but customer data were lost to Lakeside. Nevertheless, the authors contend that loyalty schemes can be successful. The essential aspect is to design them from the start for customer knowledge management.

In the interests of providing a preliminary illustration, this chapter reports exploratory mall interview surveys at UK shopping centers. In a full-scale application, data mining for customer knowledge management would be applied to a customer database, but such a dataset was not available to the researchers. As an alternative, data mining techniques such as cluster analysis and predictive modeling have been applied to the findings of a questionnaire survey. The standard SPSS program has been used for the analysis, being less expensive and more applicable to this scale of project than would be a custom data warehouse. The authors have explored the differences in behaviour between shoppers and drawn attention to differences between exemplar segments as to which attributes are critical in shopping center choice.

EXPLORATORY STUDY

The results are from a survey of 287 respondents at six shopping centers varying in size from small in-town sub-regional to large regional out-of-town. A 'regional' center is defined as having a gross retail area of greater than 50,000 m^2 and a 'sub-regional' one 20,000-50,000 m^2 (based on Guy, 1994a, b; Marjenen, 1993; Reynolds, 1993). The objective was to determine which specific attributes of shopping centers were most associated with spending for various subgroups of shoppers. If it can be demonstrated that customer knowledge management can enhance the attractiveness of shopping centers and lead to increased store sales, there will be an incentive for retailers to 'buy in' to the idea of sharing customer data.

The study evaluated shoppers' comparative ratings of two shopping centers, one of them being the center where the interview took place. The alternative center was the one where they shopped most (or next most after the interview center) for non-food shopping. The questionnaire instrument was based on the 'attributes of image' elements employed by McGoldrick and Thompson (1992a; b), together with additional constructs derived from analyses of preliminary unstructured interviews. Respondents stated their perceptions of the 'importance' of each of 38 attributes, including those identified by Guy (1994a; b) as figuring in consumers' choices of shopping destination, for example, 'quality of stores,' 'cleanliness' and 'availability of rest rooms,' following a similar procedure to that used by Hackett and Foxall (1994). Each attribute was also 'rated' for both the center studied and the alternative center. Respondents estimated perceived travel distance and time to both centers, and supplied details such as age, location of residence and occupation of the main earner in the household. Examination of the characteristics of the sample indicated the distribution of socio-economic groups, age and sex reasonably representative of that anticipated at UK shopping centers. The number classified in the higher socio-economic groups of managerial, administrative, professional, supervisory or clerical (ABC1 on the UK JICTAR scale) was 59%. This compared, for example, with a figure of 63% for the Lakeside (UK) out-of-town regional center (owner's proprietary survey of 2,000 respondents over two years) and 55% for the Treaty Centre, in-town, sub-regional (Hounslow, UK—from the center 'Education pack' citing 'street surveys'). The proportion in the younger age groups 16 to 44 years was 65% in our sample compared with 73% at Lakeside and 67% at the Treaty Centre. Our sample was 69% females compared with 60% at Lakeside and 59% at the Treaty Centre.

Further questions concerned typical perceived monthly spending at each of the two centers. As McGoldrick and Thompson (1992b) pointed out, much of the variation in shoppers' expenditure relates to factors such as income or socio-economic groups, rather than travel distance or attributes of the shopping center. Following this approach, the main dependent variable was the 'individual relative spend.' A value of 100 indicated all expenditure at the center studied and none at the alternative center. A value of 50 indicated half of the expenditure at each center. The same approach was used to scale perceived travel distance and time producing the variables 'individual relative travel distance' and 'time.'

The view of 'attractiveness' taken by the authors is that any product (such as a shopping center) "can be seen as a bundle of expected costs and rewards" which East (1997, page 131) found was 'upheld by research.' East drew support from Westbrook's (1980) finding that an overall measure of retail satisfaction correlated well with a simple addition of the satisfactions. In the authors' procedure, the measures of satisfaction and dissatisfaction have been taken from the respondents' ratings of the shopping center compared to their main alternative center (on five-point semantic differential-type scales). These satisfactions for the individual attributes were weighted, firstly by the 'importance' of the attribute to the respondent (also on a five-point scale) and secondly by the degree of association with the stated relative spending. Once weighted, satisfactions were added, giving an overall 'attractiveness' measured value. The next stage was to combine the attractiveness measurements with the relative travel time or distance variables, to derive (statistically significant) models of individuals' relative spending. More detailed derivations of the attributes and models have been reported elsewhere (Dennis et al., 1999; 2000a).

Attribute evaluations have been considered as interval rather than ordinal data (following the approach of Oppewal and Timmermans, 1999). Ordinary least squares regression analysis has been used to investigate associations between shopping center attributes and shoppers' spending at the center studied compared to a competing center. For example, 'cleanliness' was the attribute most associated with the spending of female shoppers, $R^2 = 0.075$. Individual regressions were performed for each variable; multiple regression was less appropriate on account of multicollinearity (Dennis et al., 1999). Attribute ratings have been summed and combined with travel distance to allow comparisons between the subgroups of the fit of each model. R^2 values were between 0.09 and 0.40 — i.e. 'modest.'

In the analysis of the results, we have firstly used conventional demographics to group shoppers, eliciting the most significant shopping center attributes separately, for example, for females and males. A further stage concerned the identification of attributes for various motivation clusters. Retail data mining schemes have aimed to identify subgroups that share similar shopping motivations. Researchers (Boedeker, 1995; Boedeker and Marjenen, 1993; Jarrett, 1996) have identified shopping center motivation clusters. Targeted marketing mixes satisfy these more appropriately, increasing satisfaction, sales and profits. These researchers identified two subgroups (among others) that could be described as 'shopping' and 'service' motivations. It is hypothesized that members of these two groups can be identified as individuals for marketing communications purposes. Those primarily motivated to shop by attributes such as quality of the stores and selection of merchandise can be contrasted with those more interested in service and experience aspects such as the availability of good rest rooms and cleanliness. Accordingly, our study has also included a cluster analysis approach aimed at identifying the attributes critical for shoppers motivated by the importance of 'shops' *vs.* 'service.'

RESULTS

Table 1 lists the 'top six' attributes associated with individual relative spending for the subgroups. This table is designed to be read horizontally with comparative groups (e.g., females *vs.* males) side by side. The R^2 columns indicate the coefficients of determination of the specific attributes from linear regression with relative spending. Thus, these R^2 values are used here as a parameter to indicate the strength of the association between the attributes for the particular groups and shopper spending. Below the 'females *vs.* males' comparison follows a comparison of higher *vs.* lower socio-economic groups. 'ABC1' refers to the (UK, JICTAR) classifications of managerial, administrative, professional, supervisory and clerical. 'C2DE' categories include manual workers, senior citizens and unwaged. Comparisons of higher vs. lower income and age then travel by auto vs. public transport follow. The final comparison is of the shopper clusters that we have termed 'service importance' vs. 'shops importance' motivation.

Table 1: The 'top six' significant attributes for each segment, ranked in order of the coefficient of determination, R^2, associated with individual relative spending

	R^2	
FEMALES (199 respondents: UK£68 per month)		MALES (88 respondents: UK£58 per month)
Cleanliness *	0.075	General layout
Nice place to spend time	0.063	Nice place to spend time
Availability good rest rooms	0.056	Lighting *
Friendly atmosphere	0.053	Sheltered access *
Selection of merchandise	0.051	Helpfulness of staff
Eating and drinking	0.048	No undesirable characters *
ABC1 (168: UK£73)		C2DE (113: UK£53)
Nice place to spend time	0.156	Nice place to spend time
Lighting *	0.118	Cleanliness
Access by road *	0.113	Good for children
Friendly atmosphere	0.101	Quality of stores
General layout	0.101	General layout
Cleanliness	0.092	Availability good rest rooms
INCOME UK£20000 + (101: UK£89)		INCOME UP TO UK£20000 (81: UK£59)
Nice place to spend time	0.077	Lively or exciting *
General layout	0.069	General layout
Cleanliness	0.062	Covered shopping *
Availability good rest rooms	0.046	Cleanliness
Selection of merchandise	0.045	Selection of merchandise
Quality of the stores	0.043	Nice place to spend time
AGE UP TO 44 YEARS (186: UK£65)		AGE 45 YEARS + (100: UK£65)
General layout	0.070	Nice place to spend time
Availability good rest rooms	0.069	Cleanliness
Selection of merchandise	0.039	General layout
Nice place to spend time	0.038	Availability good rest rooms
Lighting	0.035	Friendly atmosphere
Value for money	0.034	Eating and drinking
TRAVEL BY AUTO (149: UK£81)		PUBLIC TRANSPORT (57: UK£60)
Nice place to spend time	0.079	Selection of merchandise
Covered shopping	0.072	Quality of the stores
General layout	0.069	Shoppers nice people *
Selection of merchandise	0.044	Availability of seats *
Choice of major stores	0.039	Big shopping center *
Eating and drinking	0.038	Value for money *
SERVICE IMPORTANCE (74: UK£82)		SHOPS IMPORTANCE (213: UK£59)

All listed attributes were significantly associated with individual relative spending at p = 0.05.
The number of respondents and the average monthly spending for each subgroup is indicated in parentheses.
* Segments significantly different at p = 0.05 with respect to the association with spending of these attributes (combination of Monte Carlo and t-test, Dennis et al., 1999b).

Conventional Demographics

Females vs. males: The attributes significant for females were clearly different to those for males, with 'cleanliness' top for females, significantly different with respect to the association with spending compared to males. Only one of the 'top six' attributes for females ('nice place to spend time') was significant for males. Conversely, three out of the 'top six' attributes were significantly more associated with spending for males than for females ('lighting', 'sheltered access' and 'no undesirable characters'). Space limitations preclude a full discussion, but for females, two separate factors have been elicited (maximum likelihood extraction and varimax rotation—Kinnear and Gray, 1997). We have named these factors **shopping** (including, for example 'selection of merchandise') and **experience** (exemplified by 'friendly atmosphere'). On the other hand, for males the concerns were with the **center** ('lighting' and 'sheltered access'—the factor analysis did not produce separate factors for males). The interviewers reported that many males were in the center mainly to accompany females. Our interpretation of these results is that females, who were enjoying the trip, were naturally concerned with 'shopping' and 'experience.' Conversely, males who were simply 'there' were more evaluative of the 'center.'

Upper vs. lower socio-economic groups: For managerial, administrative, professional, supervisory and clerical (ABC1s), 'lighting' and 'access by road' were significantly more associated. For manual workers, senior citizens and unwaged (groups C2DE), 'good for children' and 'quality of the stores' were among the most significant. The differences are to some extent understandable in light of our observation that upmarket shoppers are more likely to travel by auto, whereas those from the lower socio-economic groups are more likely to bring children on shopping trips.

Higher vs. lower income groups: 'Lively or exciting' and 'Covered shopping' were significantly more associated for the lower income respondents. The authors speculate that lower income (and lower socio-economic group) shoppers might tend to live nearby, patronizing as alternatives small, unexciting local centers. Therefore, they might tend to appreciate the benefits of lively covered shopping centers more than do the more upmarket customers who may take these benefits for granted.

Older vs. younger shoppers: 'Eating and drinking' was in the 'top six' for the older shoppers who we expect might shop at a slower pace than younger ones and take more refreshment breaks.

Shoppers travelling by auto vs. public transport: 'General layout,' 'choice of major stores' and 'eating and drinking' were in the 'top six' for shoppers travelling by auto, but not significant for public transport. Four of the 'top six' were significantly more associated for 'public transport': 'Shoppers nice people,' 'availability of seats,' 'big shopping center' and 'value for money.' The authors consider that most of these attribute differences are related to differences in spending power. For example, shoppers travelling by public transport are more likely to appreciate (free) seats, compared to the more affluent auto travelers who choose to relax in a restaurant, bar or café.

Cluster Analysis: Shoppers Motivated by the 'Importance' of 'Shops' vs. 'Service'

An alternative to the conventional demographics approach was the search for clusters of buyers who shared needs or wants for particular benefits. A cluster analysis (SPSS 'K-means,' minimizing the squared distances of each value from its cluster center, (Kinnear and Gray, 1997) based on 'importance' scores has identified distinct subgroups of shoppers classified by 'importance motivation.' The main attributes that distinguished the clusters (with the average 'importance' scores on the 1 to 5 scale, where 1 was 'no relevance' and 5 was 'extremely important') are listed in Table 2. These segments were described as 'shops importance motivation' (abbreviated to 'shops'), Table 2 (a), and 'service importance motivation' ('service'), Table 2 (b). The two 'importance motivation' clusters were strikingly different in attributes significantly related to relative spending (the final section of Table 1). As hypothesized, 'quality of the stores' and 'selection of merchandise' were both in the 'top six' for the 'shops' group, with 'quality of the stores' being significantly more associated with spending for the 'shops'

Table 2(a): Shops importance motivation cluster

	Final cluster center 'Importance' sc(
Variety of the stores	3.49
Quality of the stores *	**3.41**
Covered shopping	3.30
Access by public transport **	**3.14**

Table 2(b): Service importance motivation cluster

	Final cluster center 'Importance' sc(
Parking facilities **	**4.47**
Access by auto **	**4.29**
Cleanliness **	**4.22**
Availability of good rest rooms **	**4.01**
Value for money **	**3.99**
Helpfulness of the staff **	**3.96**

Differences between clusters 'Importance' scores significant at: * p = 0.05   ** p = 0.001. 'Importance' scores are on the 1 to 5 scale, where 1 is 'no relevance' and 5 is 'extremely important.' Only attributes above the scale mid-point (3.00) are listed, and each attribute is listed once only, in the cluster where most dominant.

group than for 'service.' For the 'service' shoppers, 'availability of good rest rooms' and 'cleanliness' were among the most significant. Not so expected, 'other shoppers nice people' and 'lively or exciting' were significantly more associated with spending for 'shops' than 'service' shoppers. One possible interpretation might be that consumers motivated by 'shops' are evaluating not just the tangible merchandise but also the shopping experience. Our term 'shops' encompasses not just the physical environment of the shops but also the wider systemic shopping environment.

Compared to 'shops,' the 'service' shoppers were slightly higher socio-economic group (63% ABC1s vs. 59%), income (60% UK£20000 per year + vs. 53%) and age (42% 45 + vs. 33%) than the 'shops' group. They predominantly traveled by car (90% vs. 52% — see Figure 1).

MODELS OF RELATIVE SPENDING

The regression models for the various groups are reported in Table 3. These are introduced in the same order as in the reporting of the critical attributes for these groups in the 'Results' section above and in Table 1. The models describe the relationships observed between relative spending for the groups vs. the attractiveness of the centers and the distance shoppers travel. The first column is the group for which the model applies (the numbers of respondents in each group were indicated in Table 1). The second column is the constant from the regression

Figure 1: Characteristics of the 'service' and 'shops' clusters

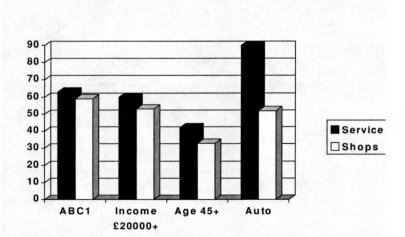

Table 3: Models for shopper segments

	Constant	Attractiveness Coefficient	Distance Coefficient	R^2	Significance p
Females	28.3	0.63	-0.24	0.19	<0.0001
Males	21.1	0.49	0	0.09	<0.01
ABC1	19.0	0.72	-0.19	0.20	<0.01
C2DE	34.4	0.50	-0.24	0.13	<0.01
Income UK£20000+	28.6	0.62	-0.24	0.17	<0.01
Income up to UK£19000	27.0	0.58	-0.19	0.18	<0.05
Age up to 44	29.3	0.58	-0.23	0.16	<0.0001
Age 45 +	18.0	0.61	0	0.14	0.0001
Auto	32.8	0.53	-0.20	0.15	<0.01
Public transport	31.8	0.58	-0.22	0.19	<0.05
'Shops motivation'	19.4	0.70	-0.21	0.17	0.0001
'Service motivation'	39.6	0.54	-0.28	0.22	<0.01
All respondents	26.0	0.62	-0.20	0.16	0.0001

equation, representing the amount of relative spend not associated with the variations in attractiveness and distance. The third and fourth columns are the regression coefficients for attractiveness and distance respectively. The fifth column is the coefficient of determination, R^2 of the regression equation, and the sixth the degree of significance (p-value). These two columns indicate modest correlations. All of the models would be normally be described as 'significant.' All except model numbers 6 (lower income) and 10 (travel by public transport) would actually be considered 'highly significant.' The final column is simply the identification number allocated to each model to facilitate discussion.

For example, for the 'shops' group:

(11) **Spending = 19.4 + 0.70 X Attractiveness - 0.21 X Distance**

Whereas for the 'service' shoppers:

(12) **Spending = 39.6 + 0.54 X Attractiveness - 0.28 X Distance**

These models mean that we can be confident (at normal test levels) that an increase in the attractiveness of a center would result in an increase in spending at that center. For example, for the 'shops' group (11), the increase in spending for a given improvement in attractiveness would be greater than for the 'service' group (12). By going back to the weighting that each attribute carried in the attractiveness model, it is possible to predict by how much spending would be likely to increase for any given improvement in any attribute. The models also mean that spend was inversely related to the distance that shoppers traveled to the center.

Figure 2: Estimated sales of shopping centers vs. the Brunel Attractiveness Index — Polynomial plot forced through the origin

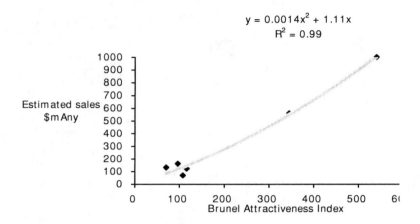

In the 'Exploratory study' section earlier, the procedure for calculating respondents' weighted satisfactions was outlined. The satisfactions for all attributes were summed to give each respondent's total satisfaction score for the center studied. The average of the respondents' satisfaction scores represented a measured attractiveness score for each center, the 'Brunel Attractiveness Index.' This index has been described more fully elsewhere (Dennis et al., 2002a forthcoming, 2002b). Stated briefly, the Brunel Attractiveness Index is an empirically derived measure of shoppers' evaluations of the attractiveness of shopping centers.

The utility of the models has been investigated by examining the relationship between the empirically measured attractiveness and the estimated sales turnover. Figure 2 illustrates the relationship between our measured attractiveness, the Brunel Attractiveness Index and the estimated sales turnover for the six centers. The sales value scale has been changed by an arithmetical factor in order to disguise commercially sensitive data. The sales turnover values are necessarily estimates based on the questionnaire responses plus footfall data of unknown reliability supplied by the center managements. The estimates, though, were made before the models were designed — and were not used in the development of the index. From an inspection of Figure 2, it would appear that the modeling procedure has been effective in measuring attractiveness in a manner relevant to sales turnover.

The models are useful in estimating changes in spending that could result from improving aspects of a shopping center. For the high spending 'service' shoppers (model 12 in Table 3), a 25% improvement in the ratings for cleanliness and rest rooms could be associated with an increase in spending for those shoppers of 10%, equivalent to an increase in the total center sales turnover of over 3%. One measure of the validity of the subgroups is the improvement in 'fit' of the models. 'Service' vs. 'shops' had the best fit, with R^2 increased to an average of 0.195 for the two subgroups. Apart from 'income' (average R^2 0.175), the models from the other pairs of groups did not improve the fit above the overall level of 0.16. 'Service' vs. 'shops' discriminated well between high and low customer spend, with the 'service' segment's average stated monthly spend UK£82, compared with the overall average of UK£65.

DISCUSSION AND CONCLUSIONS

Information from a customer database can be used to identify needs of different groups of customers. This knowledge can help shopping centers to improve marketing communications and customer satisfaction. Cluster analysis has identified a group of customers that shopping centers and retailers will want to target: high-spending 'service' shoppers. How can they be identified, given the high costs of a data warehouse? Firstly, this experimental study has demonstrated that a full data-mining system is not essential. Analysis, identification of target segments and assessment of cost-effectiveness can be carried out on a small sample, with only simple processing needed on a complete database. As in this experiment, the SPSS program can be used — saving the costs of custom software. For future, larger-scale projects, though, the authors recommend the use of a multi-agent system. Such systems can handle text alongside quantitative data and furnish individual shoppers with a 'personal agent.' This represents customized marketing segmentation — a software 'personal shopper' for every participating consumer. So far in this chapter, we have considered the knowledge **about** customers aspect of customer knowledge management. The personal agent system could address the knowledge **possessed by** customers aspect. It could be argued that such a system might not work in the UK cultural context. For the customers, though, this would be a small step from the well-established loyalty card. The customer might only be aware of the difference when presenting a 'smart card' to obtain benefits or information. Customers having a personal agent could receive communications specifically targeted to their needs and wants. There are a number of ways that this could be achieved, but one of the simplest would be for customers to present their card for reading at an information kiosk in order to receive personalized vouchers and information sheets.

In the 'models of relative spending' section above, it was pointed out that a (probably achievable) improvement of 25% in the ratings for 'cleanliness' and 'rest rooms' could be associated with an increase in spending by the service shoppers of 10%. The 10% increase for this group would add 3% to the total center sales turnover. A regional shopping center would gain tens of millions of dollars sales, with retailers seeing a seven-figure increase in gross profits. In the medium term, rental incomes follow sales: shopping center owners could expect US$2 million in increased rents.

Customer knowledge management systems could be based on data sourced from loyalty schemes. Worthington (1999) reviewed the typology of local loyalty cards in the UK. Integrated chips (e.g., Nottingham), and magnetic stripe payment (Hereford; Lakeside) or non-payment (Chester; Meadowhall) are applicable and cost-effective for cities and regional shopping centers. The main distinguishing feature of the higher-spending 'service' shopper cluster was the preponderance of auto as the means of travel—90% of the group (illustrated in Figure 1). Therefore, for smaller centers, a scheme could be based on parking. For in-town centers that charge for parking, our solution is the '**parking lot membership scheme.**' Shoppers would buy a '*carnet*' of tickets at a discount and fill in a detailed 'lifestyle' questionnaire including the information needed for the database. Parking lot schemes are already in use in Australia (Worthington and Hallsworth, 1999). For centers that offer free parking, the suggestion is to recruit shoppers at a kiosk in the parking lot, offering incentives such as a prize drawing.

The results presented in this chapter have demonstrated what can be achieved using some of the typical data mining activities applied to a simple dataset of survey data. In terms of Berry and Linoff's six activities, we have (1) 'classified' using, for example, standard socio-economic groupings, evaluating critical attributes for those segments; have (2) 'estimated' potential increases in sales arising from changes to these critical attributes using (3) 'predictive' modeling. We did not use (4) 'association rules' in the usual basket analysis context. Rather our 'affinity grouping' was achieved using (5) 'cluster' analysis — the most effective classification technique of our modeling exercise. Finally, we contend that our analysis and modeling process has assisted the (6) 'description and visualization' of shopper behavior.

In terms of Berry and Linoff's four components of CRM, we have outlined an effective procedure for measuring the (1) 'image' of a shopping center. Evaluating the image of the different customer groups has led us to (2) a greater 'understanding of who the customers are and their likes and dislikes.' Although the methodology does not (3) 'anticipate' customer needs, the survey approach does at least allow needs and wants to be 'identified and addressed proactively.' Similarly, using survey data in the database has identified a number of instances of (4) 'customer dissatisfaction,' leading to recommendations for 'corrective action.' CRM is normally implemented by a system of personalized communications (e.g., welcome letter, satisfaction questionnaire, special offers and so on). The details are beyond the scope of this chapter, but an applicable strategy should be facilitated by the installation of a simple data mining and customer knowledge management system. Shopping center managers could obtain a similar level of data to ours from (for example) a membership questionnaire, and could use a similar analysis process to that described here. Such activities would have to comply with data protection principles, but in the UK at least, many shoppers are willing to part with personal and transaction information in exchange for benefits — the principle behind the success of the Tesco and Boots loyalty cards.

Adding real sales transaction information would enrich the possibilities (although this raises the possibility of conflict with retailers over ownership of the data). Shoppers might be grouped according to spending on fashion/designer styles rather than bargains? A knowledge management network between retailers and the center would be a further stage — allowing wider access to graphs, patterns and associations in the data. There is a parallel in systems that multiple grocery retailers operate with suppliers. It is understood that supermarkets such as Tesco allow suppliers direct, real-time access to individual store sales and stock data via the Internet. In this model, a retailer and (potentially competing) suppliers share data in a knowledge network managed by the retailer. Bearing in mind the relationships of conflict rather than cooperation (mentioned in the earlier part of this chapter) that, according to Howard (1997), dominate shopping center landlord/tenant relationships, cooperation in a knowledge management network might seem unlikely. Nevertheless, Howard did identify one UK shopping center owner (CSC) that was the exception. On the basis of the limited empirical results reported here, little further analysis of this issue is possible, but we contend that further research into retailer/shopping center networks could be worthwhile for the more enlightened centers and retailers.

Dennis et al. (2002a forthcoming, 2000b) have argued that the most successful shopping centers are those where 'active marketing' and 'pro-active management' feature. Bennett and Gabriel (1999) contended that market orientation is central to the rapid introduction of knowledge management in UK companies, pre-supposing and spreading customer information. Change-friendly enterprises are more likely to have extensive knowledge management systems than others are. The authors predict that a rapid uptake of knowledge management is likely for the most successful, marketing-orientated shopping centers. There are substantial benefits to be gained from the customer knowledge database.

Finally, the authors accept that there have been many limitations in this small exploratory study. A true data mining system would be expected to work on a much larger dataset. The benefits predicted from a customer knowledge management system are purely speculative at this stage. Therefore, a more extensive pilot and research program is recommended. This could take the form of (1) a further questionnaire survey with more respondents and shopping centers, (2) a pilot scheme based on exchange of customer information for parking discount benefits (at a paid-for parking lot), and (3) a pilot 'personal agent' trial based on a smart card. This trial could run on shopper data at a single shopping center gathered by, for example, a parking lot membership scheme as outlined above. If this pilot were to achieve no more success than confirming the effects of cleanliness and rest rooms found in our exploratory survey (which was carried out at nominal cost), the center could expect a medium-term increase in rental income alone of US$2m. In our view, there is a clear case for the cost-effectiveness of further research in this area.

REFERENCES

Bennett, R. and Gabriel, H. (1999). Organizational factors and knowledge management within large marketing departments: An empirical study. *Journal of Knowledge Management, 3*(3), 212-225.

Berry, M. J. A. and Linoff, G. S. (1997). *Data Mining Techniques for Marketing, Sales and Customer Support*. Chichester: John Wiley & Sons.

Berry, M. J. A. and Linoff, G. S. (2000). *Mastering Data Mining*. Chichester: John Wiley & Sons.

Boedeker, M. (1995). New type and traditional shoppers: A comparison of two major consumer groups. *International Journal of Retail and Distribution Management, 23*(3), 17-26.

Boedeker, M. and Marjanen, H. (1993). Choice orientation types and their shopping trips: An empirical study of shopping trips to the city center vs. to an edge-of-town retail park. *Seventh International Conference on Research in the Distributive Trades,* Stirling, University of Stirling, Institute for Retail Studies.

Bird, J. (1996). Data in knowledge out. *Management Today*, September, 70-72.

Davies. R., Howard, E. and Reynolds, J. (1993). *The Shopping Centre Industry 1993: Thirty Years of Growth*. Oxford: Oxford Institute of Retail Management/British Council of Shopping Centres.

Dennis, C. E., Marsland, D. and Cockett, W. A. (1999). Why do people shop where they do? *Recent Advances in Retailing and Services Science, 6th International Conference*. Organizer: The European Institute of Retailing and Services Studies, Eindhoven, The Netherlands. Location: Puerto Rico, July 7-10.

Dennis, C. E., Marsland, D. and Cockett, W. A. (2000a). Objects of desire:

Attraction and distance in shopping centre choice. *International Journal of New Product Development and Innovation Management*, 2(2), 43-60.

Dennis, C. E., Marsland, D. and Cockett, W. A. (2000b). Can a shopping centre be a brand? *Proceedings of the 11th International EARCD Conference on Retail Innovation,* (CD-ROM) ESADE, Barcelona, July 13-14.

Dennis, C. E., Murphy, J., Marsland, D., Cockett, W. and Patel, T. (2002a, forthcoming). Measuring image: Shopping centre case studies. *International Review of Retail, Distribution and Consumer Research*, 12(4).

Dennis, C. E., Marsland, D. and Cockett, W. (2002b, forthcoming). Central place practice: Shopping centre attractiveness measures, hinterland boundaries and the UK retail hierarchy. *Journal of Retailing and Consumer Services*, 9(4), 185-199.

East, R. (1997). *Consumer Behaviour*. Englewood Cliffs, NJ: Prentice Hall.

Field, C. (1997). Data goes to market. *Computer Weekly*, (January 16), 44-45.

Guy, C. M. (1994a). *The Retail Development Process: Location, Property and Planning*. London: Routledge.

Guy, C. M. (1994b). Whatever happened to regional shopping centres? *Geography*, 79(4) 293-312.

Hackett, P. M. W. and Foxall, G. R. (1994). A factor analytic study of consumers' location specific values: A traditional high street and a modern shopping mall. *Journal of Marketing Management*, 10, 163-178.

Hallsworth, A. (2000). Britain's loyalty cards — An unmanageable retail innovation? *International Journal of New Product Development and Innovation Management*, 2(2), 133-144.

Howard, E. (1995). *Partnerships in Shopping Centres*. Oxford: Oxford Institute of Retail Management.

Howard, E. (1997). The management of shopping centres: Conflict or collaboration? *The International Review of Retail, Distribution and Consumer Research*, 7(3), 261-286.

Jarratt, D. E. (1996). A shopper typology for retail strategy development. *The International Review of Retail Distribution and Consumer Research*, 6(2), 196-215.

Kinnear, P. R. and Gray, C. D. (1997). *SPSS for Windows*. Hove: Psychology.

McGoldrick, P. J. and Thompson, M. G. (1992a). The role of image in the attraction of the out-of-town centre. *The International Review of Retail, Distribution and Consumer Research*, 2(1), 81-98.

McGoldrick, P. J. and Thompson, M. G. (1992b). *Regional Shopping Centres: Out-of-Town Versus In-Town*. Aldershot: Avebury.

Marjanen, H. (1993). *Store Location Analysis and the Mystery of Consumer Spatial Behaviour: Competition Between Downtown Shopping Areas and Out-of-Town Shopping Centres as a Special Case.* Turku (Finland), Turku School of Economics and Business Administration.

Oppewal, H. and Timmermans, H. (1999). Modeling consumer perception of public space in shopping centers. *Environment and Behaviour, 31*(1), 45.

OXIRM. (1999). *The Shopping Centre Industry: Its Importance to the UK Economy.* Oxford: Oxford Institute of Retail Management/MCB.

Rao, B. P. (2000). Improving retail effectiveness through technology: A survey of analytical tools for physical and on-line retailers. *Technology in Society, 22*, 111-122.

Rensselaer Polytechnic Institute. (1999). *Data Mining.* http://www.rpi.edu/~arunmk/dml.html.

Reynolds, J. (1993). The proliferation of the planned shopping centre. In Bromley, D. F. and Thomas, C. J. (Eds.), *Retail Change Contemporary Issues.* London: UCL.

Richards, I., Foster, D. and Morgan, R. (1998). Brand knowledge management: growing brand equity. *Journal of Knowledge Management, 2*(1), 47-54.

Rowley, J. (2001). Eight questions for customer knowledge management in e-business. *Proceedings of the e-Business Workshop,* IBM/de Montfort University.

Teresko, J. (1999). Information rich, knowledge poor? *Industry Week, 248*(3), 19.

Westbrook, R. A. (1980). Intrapersonal affective influences upon consumer satisfaction. *Journal of Consumer Research, 7*(June), 49-54.

Wiij, K. M. (1994). *Knowledge Management: The Central Management Focus for Intelligent-Acting Organisations.* Arlington, VA: Schema.

Wiij, K. M. (1998). Knowledge management: An introduction and perspective. *Journal of Knowledge Management, 1*(1), 6-14.

Worthington, S. (1999). A classic example of a misnomer: The loyalty card. *Journal of Targeting, Measurement and Analysis for Marketing, 8*(3), 222-234.

Worthington, S. and Hallsworth, A. (1999). Cards in context—The comparative development of local loyalty schemes. *International Journal of Retail and Distribution Management, 27*(10), 420-428.

Section III

People and Technology: Current Trends in Knowledge and Business Process Management

Chapter XI

Managing Knowledge in a Collaborative Context: How May Intellectual Resources Be Harnessed Towards Joint Effect?

Sajda Qureshi
Erasmus University Rotterdam, The Netherlands

Vlatka Hlupic
Brunel University, UK

Gert-Jan de Vreede
Delft University of Technology, The Netherlands

Robert O. Briggs
GroupSystems.com, USA and
Delfth University of Technology, The Netherlands

Jay Nunamaker
University of Arizona-Tucson, USA

ABSTRACT

The value of electronic collaboration has arisen as successful organisations recognize that they need to convert their intellectual resources into customized services. The shift from personal computing to interpersonal or collaborative computing has given rise to ways of working that may bring about better and more effective use of intellectual resources. Current efforts in managing knowledge have concentrated on producing, sharing and storing knowledge while business problems require the combined use of these intellectual resources to enable organisations to provide innovative and customized services. In this chapter the collaborative context is developed using a model for electronic collaboration through the use of which organisations may mobiles collaborative technologies and intellectual resources towards achieving joint effect.

INTRODUCTION

For modern organisations, knowledge is increasingly being seen as a strategic resource that needs to be created and harnessed effectively in order for the organisation to survive and achieve competitive advantage. It is believed that managing this strategic resource can enable an organisation to achieve particular benefits such as minimisation of costs, innovation of products, product development procedures, improved quality, flexibility in a dynamic market and improved customer service. For organisations to be successful, they must be capable of continuously acquiring, assimilating, disseminating, sharing and using knowledge (Senge et al., 1994; Huber, 1991). Alavi and Leidner (1999) identify an emerging line of information systems referred to as knowledge management systems (KMSs) that target professional and managerial activities by focussing on creating, gathering, organising and disseminating an organisation's "knowledge" as opposed to "information" or "data." Hibbard and Carrillo (1998) believe information technology, which supports knowledge management, such as data mining, groupware, document management, and search and retrieval applications, are widely available and already exist in many companies.

Efforts in organisations attempting to manage knowledge have concentrated on codifying or explicating knowledge and propose infrastructures for storing knowledge as well as refining, managing and distributing it (such as described in Zack, 1999, Hansen et al., 1999). While these efforts are valuable in themselves, practical considerations such as motivating employees to add to such databases and use them in their "knowledge work" have thwarted the success of such codification strategies. It has been suggested that problems which stem from traditional business environments that hoard knowledge is an obstacle which is preventing knowledge management efforts from being a complete success (Hibbard and Carrillo, 1998). In addition, Vance (1997) suggests that the reason information and knowledge may not be easily transferred from the holder to the person needing it may be because it is inarticulable in the mind of the holder.

Despite these problems with knowledge management efforts, Quinn (1992) suggests that most successful enterprises today can be considered "intelligent enterprises" as they convert intellectual resources into a chain of services in a form most useful for certain customers by selling the skills and intellects of key professionals. The effective performance and growth of knowledge-intensive organisations requires integrating and sharing knowledge that is often highly distributed (Zack, 1999). Distributed knowledge is often personalised and resides in the pockets and communities within and outside of the organisation. According to Polanyi (1966) tacit knowledge is personal, context specific and therefore hard to formalise. Personalised knowledge is subjective, experiential and lies in mental models containing cognitive elements such as paradigms, perspectives and beliefs that help individuals perceive and define their world, and lies in mental models containing technical elements such as skills and expertise. This knowledge is also seen to form the core competence or intellectual capital of the intelligent enterprise and has to be supported if the intelligent organisation is to remain competitive (Nunamaker et al., 2002; Quinn, 1992). If this is true, then why are organisations still grappling with their intellectual resources?

This chapter begins by elucidating the context of collaboration and the forms of collaborative effort enhanced through the use of collaborative technologies. It proposes a model describing four conditions necessary for successful collaboration: shared spaces and collaborative culture enable collaboration, whereas goal congruence and resource constraints are required for collaboration to take place. This model provides the structure of this chapter. The third section describes how collaborative technologies have created shared spaces for more efficient and effective collaborative work. Knowledge management activities constraining collaborative culture are then discussed, and the creation of goal congruence and overcoming resource constraints are seen to be brought about through the creative use of electronic collaboration and simulation technologies. Examples of collaborative contexts in which personalised knowledge is managed are provided, and finally, the chapter concludes with implications and guidelines for managing knowledge in collaborative contexts.

THE COLLABORATIVE CONTEXT

Collaboration is the degree to which people in an organization can combine their mental efforts so as to achieve common goals (Nunamaker et al., 2001). The act of collaboration is the act of shared creation and/or discovery in which two or more individuals with complementary skills interact to create shared understanding that none had previously possessed or could have come to on their own (Schrage, 1990, p.40). Schrage adds that collaborative technologies have changed the contexts of interaction completely. Many conversations can take place at the same time. Ideas generated by different people on a shared screen for all to see inspire conversations within the group. Ideas are both external and manipulable. People can create icons to represent ideas and concepts, which others can modify or manipulate until they become both community property and a visual part of the conversation.

Electronic collaboration is the use of networking and collaborative technologies to support groups in the creation of shared understanding. Electronic collaboration fosters new kinds of collective work made possible with advanced collaboration technologies. The use of collaborative technologies enables conversations with new kinds of properties — these shift from being fixed to being externalised and negotiated (Schrage, 1990). In addition, Nunamaker et al. (2001) suggest that there are three levels of collaborative effort that may be made more effective through the use of collaborative technologies:

1.   With *collective effort*, people work on their own. Group productivity is simply the sum of individual efforts. Technologies such as shared network directories, word processors and spreadsheets may be used effectively to support collective efforts.

2.   With *coordinated effort*, people make individual efforts, but they have critical hand-off points. Productivity depends on the level of individual effort and on the coordination among those efforts. E-mail, team databases and workflow automation may support coordinated efforts.

3.   With *concerted effort* all members must make their effort in synchrony with other members. The performance of any member directly affects the performance of the other members. There are no individual efforts. Collaborative reasoning tools may be used to enhance the value created by concerted efforts. Examples of collaborative reasoning tools include electronic brainstorming tools, group outlining tools and idea categorizers.

Electronic collaboration has made it possible to harness intellectual resources across space and time. It has given the concept of work a new meaning: anytime, anywhere, in real space or cyberspace (Cascio, 1999). For many employers the virtual workplace, in which employees operate remotely from each other and from managers, is a reality now, and indications are that it will become even more prevalent in the future. Venkatraman and Henderson (1998) suggest *"information technology now enables knowledge and expertise to become drivers of value creation and organisational effectiveness."* This suggests that harnessing the intellectual capital of an organisation to create value cannot be achieved without the assistance of information technologies.

Technology alone cannot enable this value creation. Effective collaboration has to take place in order for intellectual capital to be effectively used to create value. The conditions necessary for successful collaboration in electronic environments are described by authors such as Qureshi et al. (2000, 2002), Byrne (1993), Mowshowitz (1997), Nunamaker et al. (2001), Schrage (1990), Vreede and Bruijn (1999) to be the following:

1.   There must be a shared space where different perspectives may be shared and shared understandings generated.

2.   There must exist one or more congruent purposes (such as to solve a problem, create or discover something) or goal-oriented virtually organised activities that have to be managed.

3.   It must occur within constraints including limits of expertise, time, money, competition and cultural considerations, and there must be a need to share these resources.

4.   Collaboration must be seen as a legitimate way of working and must be part of the organisation's accepted work practice.

   These conditions are illustrated in Figure 1. Congruent goals and resource constraints are required for collaboration to be effective. If these two conditions are absent, then electronic collaborative technologies may be of little use or even have an adverse effect on the organisation. If goals do converge and there are resources that need to be overcome through collaboration, then the use of electronic collaboration can add value — even bring about significant gains. Once the need for collaboration is clear, then shared spaces where different perspectives may come together in physical face-to-face or virtual environments will enable collaboration to take place. A collaborative culture also enables electronic collaboration to be effective.

Figure 1: Conditions for successful collaboration (Qureshi et al., 2002)

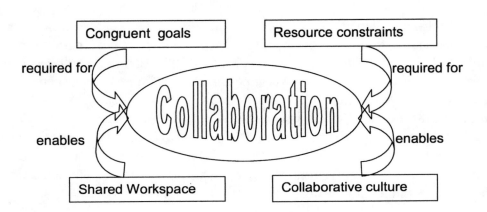

First the enabling conditions for successful collaboration are discussed in the light of what we know about current knowledge management efforts. As described later on, shared spaces provided by collaborative technologies have changed the contexts for collaboration significantly. The following section explains how knowledge management activities are still restricting the emergence of a collaborative culture in organisations and thus holding back the development of collaborative efforts in managing knowledge. In the light of this paradox, the creation of goal congruence and overcoming resource constraints are also discussed.

COLLABORATIVE TECHNOLOGIES FOR CREATING SHARED SPACES

Collaborative technologies for the creation of shared spaces include message systems, computer conferencing systems, procedure processing systems, calendar systems, shared filing systems, co-authoring systems, screen sharing systems, Group Support Systems (GDSS), advanced meeting rooms, and finally team development and management tools. Together these technologies are often included in the umbrella term "groupware" (Coleman and Khanna, 1995). Groupware can be defined as to represent "computer-based systems that support groups of people engaged in a common task (or goal) and that provide an interface to a shared environment" (Ellis et al., 1991).

Group Support Systems (GSS) represent a subset of groupware. A GSS is a socio-technical system consisting of software, hardware, meeting procedures, facilitation support and a group of meeting participants engaged in intellectual collaborative work (Eden, 1995; Jessup and Valacich, 1993). GSS are employed to focus and structure group deliberation, while reducing cognitive costs of communication and information access among teams working collaboratively towards a goal (Davison and Briggs, 2000).

There are various commercially available GSS. The most widely used GSS is GroupSystems, originally developed at the University of Arizona and commercialised by GroupSystems.com. GroupSystems consists of different modules, each of which supports one or more group activities such as generating, organising and evaluating ideas (see Table 1).

Many different ideas can be generated in parallel and recorded instantaneously. As this process is not hindered by factors such as dominance of boisterous orators, turn yielding cues and pressure to conform, key information items that would have otherwise been lost can be highlighted and further developed. An example of the categorizer module in action is depicted in Figure 2.

Table 1: Modules in GroupSystems

Module	Supports Groups...
Categorizer	Making lists of ideas with underlying comments. Lists can be organised in definable categories.
Group Outliner	Establishing hierarchical order in a list of ideas with underlying comments.
Electronic Brainstorming	During divergent brainstorming activities by automatically rotating electronic cards with ideas.
Topic Commenter	Commenting on a number of definable topics.
Vote	Evaluating ideas using various voting techniques, such as Yes/No; 4; 5; and 10-pt scales; allocation; and multiple selection.
Alternative Analyzer	Evaluating ideas using a number of definable criteria with varying weights.
Survey	Designing and executing (stand-alone) questionnaires.

Figure 2: GroupSystems categorizer module

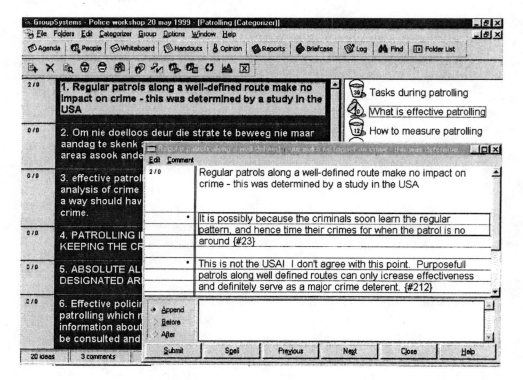

GSS are often used in meeting room environments, as they have become a very popular means of running efficient and effective meetings. In particular, GSS have been gaining much attention among researchers and practitioners for their ability to enhance decision making by making the management of knowledge more effective. GSS technology has been deployed in meeting rooms in the U.S. Navy, Air Force and Pentagon (Briggs et al., 1998). Examples of these are illustrated in Figure 3.

GSS have also been used in international organisations such as the United Nations and the Commonwealth Secretariat to support negotiation processes in policy making. Various businesses have deployed GSS for the productivity gains that have been achieved in terms of the reduction in meeting time, increase in return on investment and increased satisfaction, e.g., IBM (Nunamaker et al., 1989), Boeing (Post, 1993), and the Nationale-Nederlanden Insurance in The Netherlands (Vreede, 2001).

Universities have employed GSS in their education and research programmes. The use of GSS in education (in schools and universities) has brought about a shift in the role of the instructors and their relationships with their students (Vreede et al., 1999). This shift in the role of the instructor can be paraphrased as "from the sage on the stage to the guide by the side" (Briggs and Brown, 1997). Together with these changes in mode of instruction, the technology has moved to being multi-locational. This means that instead of bringing groups together in an electronic meeting room, the electronic meeting facility can move to places where groups traditionally meet.

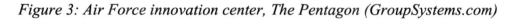

Figure 3: Air Force innovation center, The Pentagon (GroupSystems.com)

This type of electronic collaboration has become a powerful means of capturing, exchanging and managing personalised organisational knowledge. In this way, electronic collaboration becomes instrumental in capitalising on an organisation's intellectual capital. Nunamaker et al. (2001) and Qureshi et al. (2002) suggest that an organisation's potential to create value through the use of its intellectual capital is affected by the extent to which collaborative activities can take place. For optimum collaborative knowledge management activities, organisations must seek collaborative support that extends the electronic meeting room into an electronic meeting space, enabling any time any place collaboration.

Nunamaker et al. (2001) suggest that *"we are moving towards an age of any time any place collaboration."* Fuelled by the exponential growth of the Internet, the World Wide Web and local area networks, there are various communication technologies that enable this flexible form of collaboration. These include combinations of electronic mail, real-time conferencing, and multicast audio and video used to support, for example, Internet-based concerts and presentations (Sproull and Kiesler, 1991; Grudin and Palen, 1995). An example of multi-point videoconferencing is provided in Figure 4.

Any time any place collaboration can also be achieved through information sharing technologies such as digital whiteboards, computer bulletin boards and threaded discussion groups (netnews, etc.), document management systems that provide for the creation and reuse of documents as well as the control of access, concurrency and versioning (Ellis et al., 1991; Whitaker, 1996). Such a suite of

Figure 4: Video-conferencing for communication and coordination

Figure 5: Erasmus University's electronic meeting room

collaborative technologies is for example included in the Electronic Meeting Room of Erasmus University's Faculty of Management in The Netherlands. As illustrated in Figure 5, this room contains GSS as well as shared workspaces for distributed collaboration.

To provide an overview of this myriad of collaboration technologies, various authors have suggested taxonomies for the classification of groupware applications and products (see e.g., Johansen, 1991; Grudin and Poltrock, 1997; Ellis et al., 1991). However, the use of collaborative technologies has yet to be considered in terms of the type collaborative effort required. We present a taxonomy below based on the three levels of collaborative effort previously discussed, and the three key requirements for group productivity: communication, thinking and information availability (Briggs and Nunamaker, 1994). Communication is required for a group to accomplish its goals. Groups also need structured methods to guide their fundamental thinking process. Such methods are also referred to as problem-solving processes or decision-making processes. Finally, groups cannot be productive if they do not have the appropriate information for the task at hand available.

Combining these levels of collaboration and group productivity requirements results in the taxonomy presented in Table 2. Such taxonomy is useful in making sense of the plethora of collaborative technologies and software currently available. For each cell the type of supporting technology is listed. This provides an overview of the functionalities that support the type of collaborative work defined above. As

Table 2: The Groupware Grid — A taxonomy for collaborative technologies

	Communication support	Thinking support	Information availability
Collected effort	Multimedia presentations	Spreadsheet	Database systems
Coordinated effort	Email Workflow management	Project management tool Team scheduling tool	Multi-user database Notice boards
Concerted effort	Video-conferencing Computer conferencing	Group decision support	Screen sharing system

Table 3: Examples of collaborative technologies mapped to the Groupware Grid

	Communication support	Thinking support	Information availability
Collected effort	Microsoft PowerPoint Visio Professional	Microsoft Excel SPSS	Microsoft Access Windows Explorer
Coordinated effort	E-Room Lotus Notes	E-Room Microsoft Project	E-Room Lotus Notes
Concerted effort	GroupSystems NetMeeting	GroupSystems DecisionExplorer	GroupSystems GroupIntelligence

different types of technologies may support the functionalities described in Table 2, some examples of such technologies are given in Table 3.

From the above it follows that the value of using certain collaborative technologies depends on the collaborative task at hand and the group productivity requirements. Support for coordination among individuals carrying out a collaborative work process requires a different combination of technologies than do concerted collaboration efforts. In addition to the shared spaces provided by these technologies, a collaborative culture is also needed to enable collaboration if value is to be created from the intellectual capital of an organisation. In the following section, the cultural constraints imposed by traditional knowledge management activities are described. The reasons why organisations are still grappling with trying to create value from their intellectual resources are discussed.

KNOWLEDGE MANAGEMENT ACTIVITIES CONSTRAINING COLLABORATIVE CULTURE

Courtney et al. (1997) suggest that in order to support communication, it is necessary not only to have proper media with which to communicate, but also a social network or "community of minds" whose members know one another and speak the same language. This means that a culture of communication enables effective collaborative effort. In addition, Holsapple and Whinston (1987) add that as organisations will be increasingly regarded as joint human-computer knowledge processing systems, they will be viewed as societies of knowledge workers who are interconnected by computerised infrastructures. This suggests that knowledge management activities will be most effective when conducted collaboratively.

However, the concept of managing knowledge is still in its formative stages and very much an "individualised" concept. Sveiby (1997) attempts to explain the concept of knowledge management by analysing research publications in this field. He claims that the people involved in knowledge management can be divided into two categories. The first one is where people come from a background, which is computer, and/or information science oriented who perceive knowledge to be an object and knowledge management refers to 'Management of Information.' This is very much conducive towards a culture of managing information as inventory through which information, often referred to as knowledge, is packaged and stored or distributed to relevant individuals in a sequential manner. Different authors define even knowledge management activities with the same name differently. For example, according to Angus and Patel (1998) knowledge gathering refers to the bringing in of information and data, organising related to ensuring that the knowledge is easily accessible by giving it context through linking items to subject, refining relates to adding value to knowledge using various means including identifying relationships, abstracting synthesis and sharing, whilst knowledge dissemination is associated with ensuring that the right people have access to this knowledge. Kramer (1998) describes gathering knowledge as the process of collecting knowledge, organising it involves classifying knowledge with the aim of giving it meaning so that it can be located with ease by those searching for it, distribution refers to dispersing the knowledge. These knowledge management activities provide little room for collaboration, since collaboration entails the collective use and combined development of knowledge.

Although the volume of literature on knowledge management is in general increasing, especially with regard to its "soft" (human and organisational) aspects (e.g., Gupta and Govindarajan, 2000; Hansen and Oetinger, 2001), there is less information available about technical aspects or software tools for knowledge management (Hlupic et al., 2002). Examples of publications offering some insight into KM tools include Borghoff and Pareschi (1998), Gamble and Blackwell (2001), Quinn et al. (1997), and Skyrme (1999). In essence, if knowledge

Table 4: Knowledge management activities identified in KM literature

AUTHORS	KNOWLEDGE MANAGEMENT ACTIVITIES				
Ruggles (1997)	Generation	Codification	Transfer		
Angus and Patel (1998)	Gathering	Organising	Refining	Disseminating	
Kramer (1998)	Gathering	Organising	Distributing	Collaboration	
Ferran-Urdaneta (1999)	Creation	Legitimisation	Sharing		
Jackson (1999)	Gathering	Synthesis	Storage	Communication	Dissemination
Macintosh (1999)	Developing	Preserving	Using	Sharing	

management tools support knowledge management activities within organisations, they should capture the complexity of content and the richness of knowledge (Duffy, 2001). The literature, however, does not offer consensuses as to what these activities are, which is illustrated in Table 4.

Sveiby's (1997) second category of knowledge management consists of writers from a philosophy, psychology, sociology or business/management who consider knowledge to be related to processes and knowledge management to be the 'Management of People.' This management of people has taken the form of urging employees to share their knowledge with each other. Various performance appraisal mechanisms have been put in place to ensure that key knowledge and expertise is shared, transferred or codified. These strategies have not been very successful as 1) experiential knowledge is very difficult to communicate and thus share with colleagues, 2) employees often equate sharing key knowledge or information with losing their competitive advantage and 3) entering project information into company databases is seen as a waste of time.

Knowledge management tools have also restricted the management of personal knowledge. Ruggles (1997) defines knowledge management tools as technologies that enhance and enable knowledge generation, codification and transfer. Knowledge generation relates to the creation of new ideas, the recognition of new patterns, the synthesis of separate disciplines or to the development of new processes. Knowledge codification refers to organising and classifying the knowledge obtained through knowledge generation, while knowledge transfer relates to knowledge dissemination. Knowledge transfer is often hindered by barriers such as *temporal distance* (if knowledge is exchanged in a conversation between two people and not captured, nobody else could make use of such knowledge); *spatial distance* (physical distance involved within organisations and between customer suppliers); and *social distance* (barriers related to hierarchical, functional and cultural differences between people involved in communication). These barriers have made it difficult for a collaborative culture to emerge in organisations.

CREATION OF SHARED UNDERSTANDING AND GOAL CONGRUENCE

While collaborative work can potentially enhance the gains to be made from managing personalised knowledge, it can also hinder the process of using knowledge to joint effect. The main obstacle lies in traditional notions of knowledge management that focus on the inventorisation of knowledge and those that force employees to share or codify knowledge that cannot be imparted in any coherent form. As previously stated, effective collaboration for the management of personalised knowledge also requires goal congruence and the need to overcome resource constraints. Goal congruence is the degree to which the private goals of individuals are compatible with the declared goals of a collaborating group. Goal congruence does not necessarily mean goal sharing. Consider, for example, the case of a rock and roll band. The guitar player might seek artistic expression, while the drummer might seek wealth and fame. Their private goals are not shared, but they are congruent with the declared goal of cutting an album.

Simulation models have been used to align perceptions of stakeholders and arrive at goal congruence in many ways. The extent to which members collectively increase an organisation's ability to acquire new areas of expertise largely depends on the ability of the individuals to communicate and share information. The structure of the organisation must be conducive to information sharing and its dissemination. Senge et al. (1994) propose learning laboratories or 'microworlds' that are microcosms of real business settings that allow managers to play roles within a simulated organisational environment. The idea is to enhance the mental models of managers as they collectively learn how and in what ways their strategies affect the organisation at large. In this respect, it is the transformation and impact of information that brings about an increase in the extent to which learning takes place in an organisation.

In addition, simulation modelling forces assumptions about a work situation to be made explicit and often measurable. This means that resource constraints can often be better understood and the use of collaborative technologies can enable these resource constraints to be collectively overcome. Simulation models may be used to generate new insight about business processes through "what if" analysis. The process of simulation model development usually involves an extensive collection of data that needs to be analysed, and this often results in generation of new understanding. There are business simulation games (such as Tango KM Business Simulation Game supported by Sveiby Knowledge Management) specifically designed for managing organisational knowledge, and simulation models can be developed to evaluate various knowledge management strategies.

When Robinson and Pidd (1998) investigated factors that play a key role in the success of a simulation project, they discovered that communication and interaction between stakeholders (e.g., clients, simulation consultants, and people working with processes being modeled) involved in simulation model development are crucial. This suggests that the role of GSS in communicating stakeholder perceptions is an important one. Studies of GSS, together with various modeling techniques, confirm this and have provided valuable understanding into the power and pitfalls of combining two very powerful ways of supporting organisational processes (see e.g., Dean et al., 2001; Vreede, 1998; Vreede and Dickson, 2000; Appelman et al., 2002).

In their studies at the Criminal Investigations Department of the Amsterdam Police Force, Vreede and colleagues used GSS to elicit the perceptions of different stakeholders (Vreede, 1998; Vreede and Dickson, 2000). The results of the GSS sessions where used as input for a dynamic simulation modeling process that was conducted in close cooperation with the same stakeholders. Consecutive models were simulated to groups of stakeholders who then discussed their models using the GSS. The use of GSS together with dynamic simulation modeling enabled a powerful participative approach to be developed that enabled the collaborative design of organisational processes and the development of information system prototypes. In addition, Appelman et al. (2002) used GSS with the System Dynamics model building technique to support negotiations among a group of airlines and agents in an international process of negotiations. They found that GSS was useful in bringing together the conflicting political interests, yet did not offer direct support to match the elicited stakeholder views included in the group model building. They suggested that the negotiation process could have been more successful had the GSS been used more to manage the conflict and the group model building, and less to model the desired outcome.

IMPLICATIONS FOR MANAGING KNOWLEDGE IN COLLABORATIVE CONTEXTS

We have seen thus far that the shared spaces provided by collaborative technologies can enhance knowledge management efforts by providing support for communication, collective thinking and information availability. Personalised knowledge can be put to joint effect through collective, coordinated and concerted effort. Used effectively, electronic collaboration can become a powerful means of creating value by using an organisation's intellectual capital. In the following sections examples of various collaborative contexts in which knowledge has been managed are provided.

Communication and Thinking Support for Collective Knowledge Sharing

Knowledge sharing and communication in the context of simulation models is achieved through animation of model performance and graphical display of model results which could be viewed simultaneously by people distributed geographically through the use of Groupware applications. For example, Taylor (2000) provides an example of use of NetMeeting (groupware application supported by Microsoft) for communicating knowledge obtained from simulation models. NetMeeting successfully linked a simulation modelling application across three sites (two in

London, one in the USA). Since then, several companies that participated in this experiment have introduced NetMeeting for end user support and use it regularly. This demonstrates that groupware (net-conferencing), i.e., the form of knowledge management and simulation modelling, is a sensible combination.

Communication Support for Coordinated Knowledge

Qureshi and Zigurs (2001) describe how the Central and Eastern European node within Shell Europe Oil Products Retail Network had to be managed as a whole and investment plans had to be proposed for the entire Central and Eastern European node. Qureshi and Zigurs (2001) suggest that the use of collaborative technologies actually enable better face-to-face meetings. The decision-making process relied on a network of people from different geographical locations and expertise to work together. This network was composed of a core team for all retail activities established in Budapest, and an extended team of planners, engineers and other staff located throughout the node. As most of the team members had never met before, they received training in trust building, communication etiquette, agenda sharing and timely responses. The teams used NetMeeting for teleconferencing and that was seen as ideal for communicating management decisions to the rest of the team, sharing documents and above all not having to travel long distances to meet. Additional communication channels used were email, telephone and scheduling software (Schedule+). As the team members felt no need to see each other's faces, videoconferencing was not used at all and face-to-face contact was minimal.

Communication and Thinking Support for Coordinated Knowledge Management

Qureshi and Zigurs (2001) suggest that simple adaptable technologies enable more complex virtual collaboration. This is because collaborative technologies present opportunities for sharing knowledge and skill, for mobilizing resources towards joint effect, and for providing more innovative and customised products and services. Managing knowledge is viewed as key to enabling KPMG's consultants to provide customised services. Its knowledge management system, K-World, is an intranet in which electronic communication, workflow, resource planning, external newsfeeds and document sharing systems are available to consultants. It is seen as a knowledge repository that stores all information on employees and their expertise, projects and clients. K-World also makes available task-specific information related to tax treaties, fiscal regulations per country and audit techniques. The virtual spaces provided by K-World have yet to be used to form relationships among professionals from different functional areas, let alone within their own area. However, more recently KPMG has started using K-Client, a distributed collaboration system to manage contacts with international clients. As of June 2001, KPMG has over 6,000 members working in over 1,000 virtual spaces (eRooms) in seven countries with people accessing the facilities from 64 countries.

CONCLUSIONS

Managing knowledge in a collaborative context enables organisations to create value through the use of their intellectual capital. The use of the knowledge and expertise of an organisation's employees requires a careful understanding of the collaborative context, the type of knowledge required for the task to be accomplished, and an alignment of goals and resources required to complete the task. The vast arrays of collaborative technologies available for use in collaborative knowledge management efforts are poised to meet the challenges of growing globalisation of work environments and the need to manage geographically dispersed expertise. In bringing these perspectives together, and highlighting opportunities and pitfalls, this chapter provides a unique view of the ways in which knowledge may be managed through electronic collaboration.

The potential to create value by managing personalised knowledge through electronic collaboration is far reaching. But how can managers make use of this potential and avoid the pitfalls described in this chapter? The following guidelines provide managers with some key pointers as to how the gains from managing knowledge in a collaborative context may be maximised:

1. Make sure that there is a match between the type of collaborative effort — collective, coordinated and concerted; and the group productivity requirements — communication, thinking and information availability.
2. Ensure that the level of collaborative effort required and the type of knowledge management activities to be undertaken are well aligned. A cultural conflict between the collaborative creation of value and the inventorisation of information may be problematic.
3. Avoid inventorising information and imposing guidelines for knowledge sharing or codifying. Instead, emphasise the need to collectively build upon the available pool of knowledge and expertise in order to provide innovative products and services that meet customer needs.
4. Recognise that temporal, spatial and social distance exists when attempting to support the transfer of knowledge, information or data.
5. Adopt a strategy for enhancing learning mechanisms that continue to update the organisation's core competencies. Provide support for collective thinking and the creation of shared understanding through tools and techniques such as collaborative simulation modelling.

6. Ensure that there are sufficient facilitation and conflict management roles available to the organisation's knowledge management processes.

When implementing these guidelines it is important to recognise the collaborative context within which knowledge can be managed to create value varies. This means that the above guidelines should be implemented with sensitivity to the organisation's goals, structure and processes.

REFERENCES

Angus J. and Patel J. (1998). Knowledge management cosmology. *Informationweek,* (March 16), 59.

Alavi, M. and Leidner, D. (1999). Knowledge management systems: Emerging views and practices from the field. *Proceedings of the 32nd Hawaii International Conference on System Sciences.*

Appelman, J., Rouwette, E. and Qureshi, S. (2002). The dynamics of negotiation in a global inter-organizational network: Findings from the air transport and travel industry. *Group Decision & Negotiation*, in press.

Appelman, J. and Qureshi, S. (2001). The use of electronic group support and group model building to enable change in a distribution channel structure in the travel industry. In Sprague, R. and Nunamaker, J. (Eds.), *The 34th Hawaii International Conference in Systems Sciences*. IEEE Computer Society Press.

Borghoff, U. M. and Pareschi, R. (Eds.). (1998). *Information Technology for Knowledge Management*. Berlin: Springer.

Briggs, R. O., Adkins, M., Mittleman, D., Kruse, J., Miller, S. and Nunamaker Jr., J. F. (1998). A technology transition model derived from field investigation of GSS use. *Journal of Management Information Systems*, *15*(3), 151-195.

Briggs, R.O. and Brown, H. M. (1997). From the sage-on-the-stage to the guide-on-the-side: Re-engaging the disengaged learner with collaborative technology. *Working Paper*, University of Arizona.

Briggs, R. O. and de Vreede, G. J. (2001). From information technology to value creation technology. In Dickson, G. and DeSanctis, G. (Eds.), *Information Technology and the New Enterprise: New Models for Managers*. Englewood Cliffs, NJ: Prentice Hall.

Briggs, R. O. and Nunamaker Jr., J. F. (1994). Getting a grip on groupware. In Lloyd, P. (Ed.), *Groupware in the 21st Century*, 61-72. London: Adamantine Press Limited.

Byrne, J. A. (1993). The virtual corporation. *Business Week*, (February).

Cascio, W. F. (1999). Virtual workplaces: Implications for organizational behavior. In Cooper, C. L. and Rousseau, D. M. (Eds.), *The Virtual Organiza-*

tion. Trends in Organizational Behavior, 1-14. Chichester,UK: John Wiley & Sons.

Coleman D. and Khanna R. (Eds.). (1995). *Groupware: Technology and Applications.* Englewood Cliffs, NJ: Prentice Hall.

Courtney, J., Croasdell, D. and Paradice, D. (1997). Lockean inquiring organizations: Guiding principles and design guidelines for learning organizations. *Proceedings of the 1997 America's Conference on Information Systems.* http://hsb.baylor.edu/ramsower/ais.ac.97/papers/courtney.htm.

Davison, R. M. and Briggs, R. O. (2000). GSS for presentation support. *Communications of the ACM, 43*(9), 91-97.

Dean, D., Orwig, R. and Vogel, D. (2001). Facilitation methods for collaborative modeling tools. *Group Decision and Negotiation.*

Dennis, A. R. and Gallupe, R. B. (1993). A history of group support systems empirical research: Lessons learned and future directions. In Jessup, L. M. and Valacich, J. S. (Eds.), *Group Support Systems — New Perspectives.* New York: Macmillan Publishing Company.

Dennis, A. R., Haley, B. J. and Vandenberg, R. J. (1996). A meta-analysis of effectiveness, efficiency, and participant satisfaction in group support systems research. *Proceedings of the 17th International Conference on Information Systems,* Cleveland, Ohio.

Duffy, J. (2001). The tools and technologies needed for knowledge management. *Information Management Journal, 35*(1), 64-67.

Eden, C. (1995). On evaluating the performance of 'wide-band' GDSS's. *European Journal of Operational Research, 81,* 302-311.

Ellis, C. A., Gibbs, S. J. and Rein, G. L. (1991). Groupware: Some issues and experiences. *Communications of the ACM, 34*(1), 39-58.

Fjermestad, J. and Hiltz, S. R. (1998). An assessment of group support systems experimental research: Methodology and results. *Journal of Management Information Systems, 15*(3), 7-149.

Fjermestad, J. and Hiltz, S. R. (2000). A descriptive evaluation of group support systems case and field studies. *Journal of Management Information Systems, 17*(3).

Gamble, P. R. and Blackwell, J. (2001). *Knowledge Management: A State of the Art Guide.* Kogan Page.

Grudin, J. and Palen, L. (1995). Why Groupware succeeds: Discretion or mandate? *Proceedings of ECSCW '95,* 263-278. Kluwer.

Grudin, J. and Poltrock, S. E. (1997). Computer-supported cooperative work and groupware. *Advances in Computers, 45,* 269-320.

Gupta, A. K. and Govindarajan, V. (2000). Knowledge management's social dimension: Lessons from Nucor Steel. *Sloan Management Review, 42*(1), 71-80.

Hansen, M. T., Nohria, N. and Tierney, T. (1999). What's your strategy for managing knowledge? *Harvard Business Review*, (March-April).

Hansen, M. T. and von Oetinger, B. (2001). Introducing t-shaped managers: Knowledge management's next generation. *Harvard Business Review*, (March), 107-116.

Hibbard, J. and Carillo, K. M. (1998). Knowledge revolution — getting employees to share what they know is no longer a technology challenge–it's a corporate culture challenge. *Information Week*, 663.

Hlupic, V., Pouloudi, A. and Rzevski, G. (2002). Towards an integrated approach to knowledge management: 'Hard', 'soft' and 'abstract' issues. *Knowledge and Process Management, The Journal of Corporate Transformation*, *9*(0), 1-14.

Holsapple, C. W. and Whinston, A. B. (1987). Knowledge-based organizations. *Information Society*, 2, 77-89.

Huber, G. P. (1991). Organization leaning: An examination of the contributing processes and the literatures. *Organization Science*, *2*, 88-115.

Jessup, L. M. and Valacich, J. S. (Eds.). (1993). *Group Support Systems: New Perspectives*. New York: Macmillan.

Johansen, R. (1991). *Leading Business Teams*. Reading, MA: Addison-Wesley.

Kramer M. (1998). Knowledge management becomes catch phrase but eludes easy definition. *PC Week*, *7*(December), 95.

Mowshowitz, A. (1997). Virtual organisation. *Communications of the ACM*, *40*(9).

Nunamaker, J., Briggs, R. O., Mittleman, D., Vogel, D. and Balthazard, P. A. (1997). Lessons from a dozen years of group support systems research: A discussion of lab and field findings. *Journal of Management Information Systems*, *13*(3), 163-207.

Nunamaker Jr., J. F., Romano Jr., N. C. and Briggs, R. O. (2002). Increasing intellectual bandwidth: Generating value from intellectual capital with information technology. *Group Decision & Negotiation*, forthcoming.

Nunamaker Jr., J. F., Vogel, D. R., Heminger, A., Martz, B., Grohowski, R. and McGoff, C. (1989). Experiences at IBM with GSS. *Decision Support Systems*, *5*(2), 183-196.

Polanyi, M. (1996). *The Tacit Dimension*. London: Routledge and Kegan Paul.

Post, B. Q. (1993). A business case framework for group support technology. *Journal of MIS*, *9*(3), 7-26.

Quinn, J. B. (1992). *Intelligent Enterprise*. New York: The Free Press.

Quinn, J. B., Baruch, J. J. and Zien, K. A. (1997). *Innovation Explosion: Using Intellect and Software to Revolutionize Growth Strategies*. New York: The Free Press.

Qureshi, S., Bogenrieder, I. and Kumar, K. (2000). Managing participative diversity in virtual teams: Requirement for collaborative technology support. In Sprague, R. and Nunamaker, J. (Eds.), *The 33rd Hawaii International Conference in Systems Sciences*. IEEE Computer Society Press.

Qureshi, S., van der Vaart, A., Kaulingfreeks, G., de Vreede, Briggs, B. and Nunamaker, J. (2002). What does it mean for an organisation to be intelligent? Measuring intellectual bandwidth for value creation. *The 35th Hawaii International Conference in Systems Sciences*. Cocoa Beach, FL: IEEE Computer Society Press.

Qureshi, S. and Zigurs, I. (2001). Paradoxes and prepgatives in global virtual collaboration. *Communications of the ACM*.

Robinson, S. and Pidd, M. (1998). Provider and customer expectations of successful simulation projects. *Journal of the Operational Research Society*, *49*(3), 200-209.

Ruggles R. (1997). *Knowledge Tools: Using Technology to Manage Knowledge Better*. http://www.businessinnovation.ey.com/mko/html/toolsrr.html.

Senge P. M., Roberts C., Ross R. B., Smith B. J. and Kleiner A. (1994). *The Fifth Discipline Fieldbook: Strategies and Tools for Building a Learning Organisation*. Nicholas Brealey.

Schrage, M. (1990). *Shared Minds: The New Technologies of Collaboration*. New York: Random House.

Skyrme, D. J. (1999). *Knowledge Networking: Creating the Collaborative Enterprise*. Oxford: Butterworth Heinemann.

Sproull, L. and Kiesler, S. (1991). *Connections: New Ways of Working in the Networked Organization*. Cambridge, MA: The MIT Press.

Stein, E. and Zwass, V. (1995). Actualizing organizational memory with information systems. *Information Systems Research*, *6*(2), 85-117.

Sveiby, K. E. (1997). *The New Organizational Wealth: Managing and Measuring Knowledge-Based Assets*. San Francisco, CA: Berrett-Koehler Publishers.

Taylor, S. (2000). Groupware and the simulation consultant. In Joines, J. A., Barton, R. R., Kang, K. and Fishwick, P. (Eds.), *Proceedings of the WSC'2000 (Winter Simulation Conference 2000)*, Orlando, USA, December.

Vance, D. M. (1997). Information, knowledge and wisdom: The epistemic hierarchy and computer-based information system. *Proceedings of the 1997 America's Conference on Information Systems*. http://hsb.baylor.edu/ramswoer/ais.ac.97/papers/vance.htm.

Venkatraman, N. and Henderson, J. C. (1998). Real strategies for virtual organizing. *Sloan Management Review*, *34*(2), 73-87.

Vreede, G. J. de (2001). A field study into the organizational application of GSS. *Journal of Information Technology Cases & Applications*, *2*(4), 27-47.

Vreede, G. J. de (1998). Collaborative support for design: Animated electronic meetings. *Journal of Management Information Systems*, *14*(3),141-164.

Vreede, G. J. de, Briggs, R. O. and Santanen, E. (1999). Group support systems for innovative information science education. *Journal of Informatics Education and Research*, *1*(1), 1-11.

Vreede, G. J. de and Bruijn, H. de (1999). Exploring the boundaries of successful GSS application: Supporting inter-organizational policy networks. *DataBase*, *30*(3/4), 111-131.

Vreede, G. J. de and Dickson, G. W. (2000). Using GSS to support designing organizational processes and information systems: An action research study on collaborative business engineering. *Group Decision and Negotiation*, *9*(2), 161-183.

Whitaker, R. (1996). *Computer Supported Cooperative Work (CSCW) and Groupware: Overview, Definitions, and Distinctions*. www.informatik. umu.se/~rwhit/ CSCW.html. Accessed July 17, 2000.

Zack, M. (1999). Managing codified knowledge. *Sloan Management Review*, 45-58.

Chapter XII

Technical Aspects of Knowledge Management: A Methodology for Commercial Knowledge Management Tool Selection

Nayna Patel and Vlatka Hlupic
Brunel University, UK

ABSTRACT

One of the repercussions of the ever-rising popularity of knowledge management is a sudden increase in the number and range of knowledge management tools available on the software market. This can present a problem for organisations that are required to sift through the vast number of tools in the hope of finding one that meets their requirements. Moreover, guidelines describing how to go about selecting a commercial knowledge management tool do not currently exist. Therefore, the aim of this chapter is to present a set of guidelines to aid the evaluation and selection of a commercial knowledge management tool. In order to achieve this, a methodology is proposed that outlines factors and issues that could be taken into consideration during the selection of a knowledge management tool. Furthermore, an overview of criteria specific to knowledge management tools that can be used to evaluate and ascertain the features present in a knowledge management tool are also suggested.

INTRODUCTION

Knowledge management has attracted a great deal of interest in the past few years. However, this appears to have focused on the organisational and human aspects (Davenport, 1996). The technical aspect of knowledge management has been acknowledged, but few academic studies have ventured beyond this point. While research efforts have been centred on the organisational and human issues of knowledge management, software vendors have been busy bombarding the market with various knowledge management tools. Consequently, an overwhelming number of knowledge management tools exist on the software market (Angus et al., 1998; Davenport and Prusak, 1998; Silver, 2000). This is not immediately perceived as being problematic since the greater the choice, the more competitive and dynamic the market. However, the overwhelming alternatives can make it difficult for organisations to select a suitable knowledge management tool that adequately meets their requirements. This is further complicated by the fact that, while some of these tools have been designed specifically as knowledge management tools, others have been re-packaged, re-labelled and re-marketed as knowledge management tools (Angus et al., 1998). Other disciplines and even areas within information systems and computing have overcome this problem by creating a set of guidelines that aid the selection of suitable software tools. In light of this, it appears feasible to provide a similar facility for knowledge management tools.

Therefore, the motivation for this research stems from the lack of guidelines available for the selection of knowledge management tools. The purpose of this chapter is to demonstrate a methodology that has been designed to aid the selection of a commercial knowledge management tool. The chapter begins by demonstrating how knowledge management tools fit into the broader context of knowledge management. Following this is an illustration of the methodology and a description of how it was designed. A part of the methodology involves the evaluation of candidate knowledge management tools. Therefore, an evaluation framework that could be used to achieve this is also described. The chapter concludes by reflecting on the methodology and discussing further work in this area.

KNOWLEDGE MANAGEMENT TOOLS IN CONTEXT

The area of knowledge management has been subjected to a great deal of controversy with regards to the lack of a common definition or concept. However, there does appear to be some consistency in relation to the components and the activities, often referred to as processes, which constitute knowledge management.

This research can be classified under the 'Technology' component of knowledge management which is illustrated in Figure 1.

Figure 1 shows that knowledge management consists of two areas — knowledge management activities and knowledge management components. The former, knowledge management activities, is divided into the three areas of knowledge generation, knowledge organisation and knowledge sharing. These represent the primary activities that can take place, either in isolation or in various combinations, during a knowledge management deployment. The latter components of knowledge management consist of culture, business processes and *technology*. These reflect the aspects of an organisation that must be taken into consideration for a knowledge management effort to be successful. Unlike the activities, the components must not exist in isolation as part of a knowledge management exercise. In fact, all three components should receive equal, and combined, attention (Borghoff and Pareschi, 1997; Davenport, 1997; Davenport and Prusak, 1998; Milton et al., 1999; Trauth, 1999; Vaas, 1999, Duffy, 2001). Therefore, as mentioned in the previous section, the research specified within this chapter focuses on the technology component of knowledge management. However, prior to addressing knowledge management technology the remainder of this section describes the knowledge activities and components in more detail, in order to provide some background information and to clarify the context of this research.

Figure 1: Knowledge management activities and components

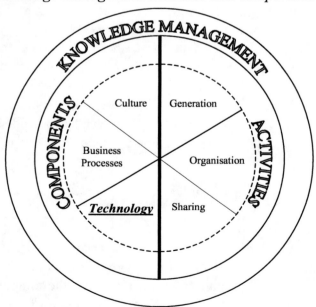

Knowledge Management Activities

Knowledge management activities refer to the phases that take place in order to achieve knowledge management. Table 1 describes the knowledge management activities specified by various authors. In general, knowledge management activities range from between three and five categories. Although the terms used are very similar, there appears to be some variance in the meanings. For instance, Angus and Patel (1998) claim that knowledge gathering refers to the bringing in of information and data. However, according to Kramer (1998) knowledge gathering entails the process of collecting knowledge. The subtle difference here is reference to what is being gathered. Angus and Patel (1998) are collating information and data whereas Kramer (1998) is gathering knowledge.

Essentially, it appears that the knowledge management activities involve obtaining knowledge in the first place, organising it so that it can be easily accessed at a later date and ensuring that the collated knowledge is exploited by sharing it with the people who require it. A number of authors have sub-divided each of the knowledge management activities further by associating various actions that refer to the way the activity is achieved. For example, Angus and Patel (1998) claim that knowledge can be gathered through pulling, searching, Optical Character Recognition (OCR) or voice input.

Knowledge Management Components

The other aspect of knowledge management that appears to contain some consistency is related to the areas that must be addressed during a knowledge management deployment. These include: culture, business processes and technology (Borghoff and Pareschi, 1997; Davenport, 1997; Davenport and Prusak, 1998; Milton et al., 1999; Trauth, 1999; Vaas, 1999, Duffy, 2001). The cultural aspect of knowledge management is often considered as one of the most difficult obstacles to overcome (Bicknell, 1999). This is attributed to traditional business practices of hoarding knowledge (Hibbard and Carillo, 1998). Previously, knowledge was perceived as an individual's power and secured their position, and in some cases led to promotion, within an organisation. However, the repercussions

Table 1: Knowledge management activities according to various authors

AUTHORS	KNOWLEDGE MANAGEMENT ACTIVITIES				
Ruggles (1997)	Generation	Codification	Transfer		
Angus and Patel (1998)	Gathering	Organising	Refining	Disseminating	
Kramer (1998)	Gathering	Organising	Distributing	Collaboration	
Ferran-Urdaneta (1999)	Creation	Legitimisation	Sharing		
Jackson (1999)	Gathering	Synthesis	Storage	Communication	Dissemination
Macintosh (1999)	Developing	Preserving	Using	Sharing	

of the knowledge age mean that in order to create a knowledge sharing environment, it is necessary for employees to change their way of thinking. Nevertheless, theory is very different from practice. Many suggestions have been made in order to improve the cultural environment, ranging from story telling (Reilly et al., 1999) to ensuring that employees feel confident that they will still be a valuable asset to the organisation if they share their knowledge (Angus et al., 1998; Hibbard and Carillo, 1998). Unfortunately, the cultural branch remains a major hindrance to the success of many knowledge management deployments.

A number of theorists believe that the key to creating a knowledge sharing environment is to re-design business processes (Angus and Patel, 1998; Hibbard and Carillo, 1998; Klamma and Schlaphof, 2000). This involves the radical re-design of business processes that exist within an organisation without allowing current practices to influence the resulting design (Davenport, 1993; Hammer and Champy, 1993; Robson and Ullah, 1996). Consequently, business processes are re-designed in order to accommodate a knowledge sharing environment. Furthermore, the resulting business processes should also consider, and support, the chosen knowledge management strategy. For instance, an organisation's strategy may consist of capturing information from consultants while they are working at a client site on a project. However, in order to achieve this, it is necessary for the consultants to keep a record of certain activities. This should be taken into consideration, and time to do this should be allocated within the re-designed business processes. Knowledge management strategies are a separate research area altogether and are out of the scope of this research and therefore are not covered in any detail.

According to Ruggles (1997) technology and culture are connected by the condition that technology is compromised if the appropriate knowledge sharing culture is not adopted. Technology, in the form of knowledge management tools, is used to facilitate the knowledge management activities. As described in the previous section (Knowledge Management Activities), these consist of knowledge generation, organisation and sharing (Ruggles, 1997; Angus and Patel, 1998; Davenport and Prusak, 1998; Kramer, 1998; Ferran-Urdaneta, 1999; Jackson, 1999; Macintosh, 1999). One example of a knowledge generation tool is software that creates user profiles according to the parts of a web site a user has navigated. The knowledge collated is exploited during the user's subsequent visits. For instance, if during the initial visit the user shows an interest in the sports sections of the web site, they would be presented with various links connected to sport on their next visit. If during this particular visit they only read the football articles, then the site would prioritise football articles. Each time the user visits the site, more knowledge is collected about them and, it is believed, the better their requirements are understood. Knowledge generation tools appear to vary quite considerably in where knowledge is obtained from and how it is generated. Some tools generate new knowledge by combining knowledge that already exists within an organisation. Others search the Internet to obtain the relevant knowledge.

Knowledge organisation tools are used to store and organise knowledge so that it is quick and easy to access by the people who need it. Although not immediately obvious, there are various ways that knowledge can be stored and organised. For instance, the method of cataloguing knowledge may be achieved automatically by the tool using a predefined set of criteria. Alternatively, it may be necessary for somebody, often referred to as a knowledge librarian, to organise the knowledge manually.

Davenport and Prusak (1998) claim that knowledge sharing tools are the most valuable of the three. The main aim of knowledge sharing tools is to disseminate knowledge to the relevant people efficiently and effectively. This may be achieved by using utilities such as conferencing, bulletin boards, messaging and file transfer. A conferencing facility would enable a group of people to work together although they may be located in a dispersed fashion. Tools of this calibre allow the use of features such as chat, whiteboard and application sharing so that all group members are able to see and understand what is being demonstrated. Furthermore, an item can be worked on collaboratively, with everyone present being able to view the same information. Table 2 displays a list of knowledge management tools and the functions associated with each. Furthermore, the relationship between the functions and knowledge management activities are also demonstrated.

This is only a small selection of the types of knowledge management tools available, and the list is constantly growing at a rapid pace. Furthermore, the lack of any formal techniques for knowledge management tool selection means that the process of choosing one is the responsibility of the purchasing organisation. This entails time, money and effort to be invested that could be utilised elsewhere, if some form of guidelines were available. It would be possible to use one of the numerous generic techniques that exist (Curry and Bonner, 1983; Martin and McClure, 1983; Lynch, 1985; Breslin, 1986; Klein and Beck, 1987; Anderson, 1990; Le Blanc and Jelassi, 1991; Sharland, 1991; Montazemi et al., 1996). However, these would need to be adapted to accommodate characteristics present in knowledge management tools. Furthermore, other disciplines including education (Berryman et al., 1994; Buckleitner, 1999), the health service (McDonald, 1996) and the military (Parnas et al., 1990; Dupuy and Leveson, 2000) can make use of such guidelines designed specifically for their areas. Therefore, a methodology that aids the selection of a commercial knowledge management tool has been designed and is presented in the following sections.

Table 2: Knowledge management tools

| KM TOOLS | KNOWLEDGE MANAGEMENT TOOLS | | | | | | |
| | GENERATION | | | ORGANISATION | | SHARING | |
	Capture	Discovery	Retrieval	Storage	Monitor	Collaboration	Transfer
ARS Remedy			x	x	x		
Netmeeting						x	x
Synera		x	x	x			
80-20 Product Suite		x	x				
Assistum		x					
Correlate K-Map		x	x				
Engenia			x			x	x
Eureka		x		x			
Groove						x	x
Orbis Intelliware	x		x		x		
C-Business Server	x	x		x		x	x
Hummingbird EIP	x			x		x	
Plumtree Portal	x			x		x	
Active Knowledge	x	x	x		x		
AskMe Enterprise	x		x	x		x	
Authorete		x	x				
Autonomy Update		x			x		
BackWeb			x		x		
Collectively Sharper			x				
Communispace	x		x			x	x
Deskartes		x	x				
DocSmart			x	x			
Docushare		x	x	x			
Global Network	x		x			x	
Hyperwave	x		x	x		x	x
InfoImage Freedom		x				x	x
ISYS:Web	x	x	x	x		x	
Kanisa		x	x				
KM Studio			x				
Knowledge XChanger	x		x			x	
KnowledgeMail		x			x		
myLivelink			x	x		x	
Net Perceptions		x	x				
Portal-in-a-Box	x	x	x		x	x	
Practicity			x	x		x	
RetrievalWare	x	x	x				
SageMaker			x				
Semio Map		x	x				x
Semio Taxonomy		x		x			
STRATEGY!			x				
Thinkmap		x					
work2gether			x	x			
ZyIMAGE		x	x				x

METHODOLOGY FOR KNOWLEDGE MANAGEMENT TOOL SELECTION

A methodology was designed that illustrates the factors and issues that can be taken into consideration during the selection of a knowledge management tool. It is important to note that the methodology is not intended as a rigid structure that must be followed without any deviation, as is often the associated meaning where the term 'methodology' is concerned. In fact the opposite is true: the methodology is intended as a guideline and aid that can be adapted according to the requirements of the individual organisation. The remainder of this chapter describes the resultant methodology that was designed for the purpose of knowledge management tool selection.

Designing the Methodology

The information used for designing the methodology was obtained predominantly from three different sources. The first resulted from conducting interviews with people involved with knowledge management tools. Prior to conducting the interviews, questionnaires were used in order to obtain a general understanding of the knowledge management tool and the context in which it was being used. Furthermore, this enabled the questions that needed to be asked during the follow-up interviews to be highlighted. Therefore, in total 58 questionnaires were distributed and follow-up interviews were conducted. The questions used in both, questionnaire and interview, were predominantly of an open-ended nature, and the format of the interviews were unstructured.

The second source of information was from existing methodologies designed for the selection of software. These include two different types: 1) generic methodologies (Curry and Bonner, 1983; Martin and McClure, 1983; Lynch, 1985; Breslin, 1986; Klein and Beck, 1987; Anderson, 1990; Le Blanc and Jelassi, 1991; Sharland, 1991; Montazemi et al., 1996) that can be used for the selection of any software tool and 2) specific methodologies intended for the selection of discipline specific tools. An example of the latter is a methodology that is designed specifically for the selection of educational tools and therefore considers educational requirements (Berryman et al., 1994; Buckleitner, 1999). Discipline-oriented methodologies were investigated to establish how the task of designing a discipline-specific methodology is undertaken and how issues that need to be addressed, with regards to the particular area, were obtained. Furthermore, methodologies designed for areas already existing within the discipline of information systems and computing such as simulation (Hlupic, 1997; Nikoukaran et al., 1998) and computer-aided software engineering (Forte, 1992; Mosley, 1992), were also analysed. The reason underlying this was that, being classified under the same discipline parts of the methodology may also apply to knowledge management tool selection.

The third and final source of information was obtained by consulting the literature related to knowledge management. The purpose of this was to identify the factors specific to knowledge management tools that need to be taken into consideration during the selection process. The results from the three different avenues of information were collated and combined in order to create a methodology for knowledge management tool selection.

The Methodology

The methodology, illustrated in Figure 2, has been designed to aid the selection of knowledge management tools and can be classified under the 'Technology' component of knowledge management. However, Figure 2 demonstrates that the 'Business Processes' and 'Culture' components have also been included within the methodology. The justification for this is to further substantiate the theory that a knowledge management deployment must take into consideration the three components, in combination, as opposed to one in isolation (Davenport and Prusak, 1998; Milton et al., 1999; Trauth, 1999; Vaas, 1999, Duffy, 2001). The methodology consists of five main phases, each of which requires several intermediate stages to be undertaken. In essence, the methodology involves: identifying requirements, creating a short-list of suitable knowledge management tools, evaluating the tools, conducting pilot tests and finally purchasing a tool. The following sections provide a detailed account of each of the five phases and the associated intermediary steps.

Phase I

In order to achieve Phase I, Identify Requirements, it is necessary for a selection team to be formed. The team should consist of a variety of representatives from all levels of an organisation (McDonald, 1996). Ideally this would include: a chief knowledge officer (CKO), technical staff, managers, knowledge librarians, and potential users. The chief knowledge officer, or equivalent, should be a part of the team because their role is to ensure that the knowledge that exists within an organisation is captured and utilised to its maximum potential (Bonner, 2000). The purpose of technical staff being present on the selection team is twofold. Firstly, they need to ensure that the tool that is eventually selected is compatible with the existing infrastructure. Secondly, since they are the ones that will be supporting the tool, their input and advice is vital. The involvement of managers within the selection team is crucial since they have a global view of the particular area that they manage, enabling them to specify broader requirements for the tool in question. It is also important to identify and include, in the selection team, the people that will be maintaining the knowledge once the tool is installed, usually referred to as knowledge librarians. Finally, a number of users should figure in the selection team since, ultimately, they are the ones who will be using the tool on a day-to-day basis (Montazemi et al., 1996).

Figure 2: Methodology for knowledge management tool selection

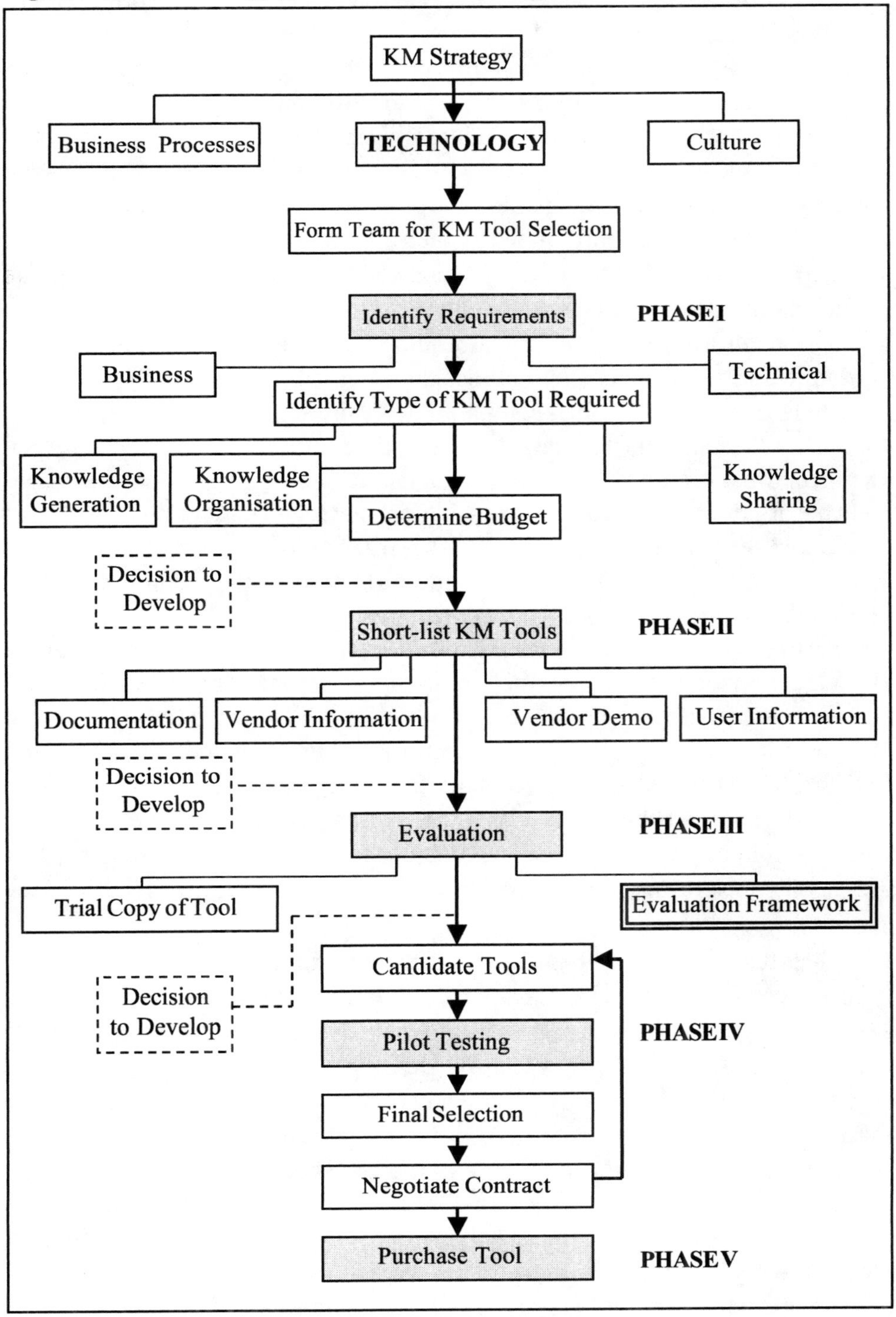

Once a satisfactory team has been formed, their first task is to identify both business and technical requirements (Curry and Bonner, 1983). The former entails specifying the business objectives that need to be achieved, the manner in which each will be addressed and a description of the role of the tool that is to be purchased. For instance, a business objective for an organisation may be to improve customer service. A possible way of addressing this is to reduce the time taken for the Help desk to resolve a query. This could be accomplished by having a system whereby the solutions to queries that have previously been resolved can be easily accessed and used, omitting the need for the same query to be solved time and time again. In light of this, the knowledge management tool required needs to facilitate the storage and retrieval of Help desk queries and their respective solutions.

The identification of the technical requirements consists of establishing what hardware and software currently exists in order to ensure that the purchased knowledge management tool is compatible (Martin and McClure, 1983; Mosley, 1992). Another decision that needs to be considered at this point is if a commercial knowledge management tool would be purchased if it required adapting in order to meet the organisation's requirements. If tools that require adapting are not to be considered, then these need to be discarded from the list of potential tools whenever such a tool is identified. There is no one single point in the methodology that facilitates this consideration since the necessity to adapt may be evident at any number of stages. If the purchasing organisation is prepared to adapt a commercial knowledge management tool, then a number of issues need to be taken into consideration. These include the party responsible for adapting the tool (the vendor or the purchasing organisation), the amount of adaptation required, etc. (Martin and McClure, 1983). If the purchasing organisation is relying on the vendor to adapt the tool, then it needs to be confirmed that the vendor is capable and prepared to do this. If the purchasing organisation has decided to adapt the tool themselves, then they need to ensure that they have the resources and expertise in order to achieve this.

Once the requirements have been established, the next stage involves identifying which of the knowledge management activities need to be supported by the tool. This may include one, two or all three of the knowledge management activities. For instance, referring back to the Help desk example, the knowledge management activities that would be involved are knowledge organisation and knowledge sharing. The former activity will need to be facilitated by the tool in order to store and allow the manipulation of queries and their respective solutions. The latter activity needs to be catered for by the tool so that the knowledge about the queries and respective solutions can be shared between Help desk staff. Having identified the knowledge management activities that the tool is required to facilitate, it is necessary to determine the budget available for purchasing the tool.

In the process of considering this, it is also important to establish whether or not the budget, in addition to the cost of purchasing the tool, will include costs for training, installation, licences, etc. (Mosley, 1992). Once the requirements, the type of tool required, and the budget have been identified, the software market needs to be scoured in order to identify knowledge management tools that meet these criteria. Therefore, prior to preceding to Phase II, a list of all of the knowledge management tools that could potentially be purchased should be created. At this stage it may be indicative that the software market does not provide a knowledge management tool that meets the criteria specified within Phase I. Therefore, it may be decided that the most appropriate option would be to pursue the development angle (Martin and McClure, 1983). This may involve developing the knowledge management tool internally if the expertise and resources are available. Alternatively, a software development company may be utilised to create the required knowledge management tool. Following this route entails a separate study and therefore is not included within this methodology. The boxes in Figure 2 representing the decision to develop are denoted using a dotted line.

Phase II

The aim of Phase II is to take the list created as a result of Phase I of the methodology and produce a streamlined short-list of knowledge management tools. This is achieved by carrying out a sequence of four steps, the objective being to refine the short-list of knowledge management tools with each additional step. The first step involves obtaining an overview and a general idea of the features provided by each of the tools in the short-list. In order to accomplish this documentation, brochures, user manuals and reviews should be gathered and carefully analysed (Sharland, 1991). The tools that are considered unsuitable should be discarded from the list and the remaining tools should be further investigated.

The second step consists of collating information about the actual vendors of the tools. The main aim of this is to ensure, as much as it is possible, that the vendors are reputable and have a stable position within the software market (Martin and McClure, 1983). The level of information gathered during this step depends on the circumstances of the installation and support required for the tool. For instance, if the tool is to be installed, maintained and supported by the purchasing organisation, then the role of the vendor is limited and therefore basic information about the vendor will suffice. However, if the vendor is required to have a major contribution subsequent to the tool being purchased, then a more thorough investigation is required. There are a variety of areas for which information can be collated about the vendor, including the background of the company, contact information and quality of service.

It is important to have some general knowledge about the vendor's background and current stance within the industry to ensure that the vendor is stable and in a position to provide a high-quality service. This may involve gathering information, such as when the vendor was established, whether it is part of another company and a current list of clients. The list of clients can be extremely indicative of the vendor since an association with reputable customers implies the ability to provide a good service (Martin and McClure, 1983). However, it is important to emphasise that the decision of selecting a vendor should not solely be based on the client list. Another way of determining the quality of the vendor by using the client list is to actually contact the vendor's clients and gather their views on the tool and the vendor.

Contact details for the company includes where the vendor is based and the person whom is the main point of reference. The location of the vendor may be important if training is to be conducted at the vendor's site. Consequently the costs of sending employees for training need to be taken into consideration and budgeted for. If possible, it is important to communicate with the same person representing the vendor since this gives the two companies an opportunity to establish rapport. Moreover, the vendor's representative can form a clear idea about the purchasing organisation's requirements (Curry and Bonner, 1983).

The quality of the service provided by the vendor should be continuously recorded, as it is crucial that the purchasing organisation is satisfied and comfortable with dealing with the vendor. Another useful method, recommended by Curry and Bonner (1983), of separating the stronger vendors from the weaker ones is to request the vendor to write a proposal detailing how their particular tool and company can address the purchasing organisation's requirements. According to Curry and Bonner (1983), high-quality and experienced vendors are accustomed to responding to requests for proposals and should do so within a given timeframe (specified by the purchasing organisation). Those that do not respond can be discarded from the short-list.

The third step involves taking the further refined short-list and visiting the vendors of each of the knowledge management tools in order to view a demonstration. Ideally, the demonstration should take place at the vendor site since this provides the purchasing organisation with the opportunity to obtain further insight about the vendor (Curry and Bonner, 1983). During the demonstration of the tool, it is important to ask the vendor to illustrate how to perform functions similar to the ones that the tool is intended to be used for. The responses to these requests can assist the purchasing organisation with determining whether the tool is able to support their needs and how competent the vendor is with the tool. As a result of this step, the tools that appear inappropriate or the vendor that seems weak should be discarded from the short-list.

The final step within Phase II involves contacting actual users of the tools using the clients list that should have been obtained as a part of the second step. The clients should be questioned about the quality of service provided by the vendor and details of any problems encountered. They should also be asked for their opinions with regards to the actual knowledge management tool, and Martin and McClure (1983) suggest approaching the users for their views on how the tool could be improved. After taking all of the information gathered during this step into consideration, a final short-list of knowledge management tools should be drawn up, ready for evaluation. As with the previous phase, the result of this phase may indicate that a suitable knowledge management tool does not currently exist in the software market. Therefore, the option to develop a knowledge management tool may be considered.

Phase III

Phase III of the methodology is concerned with obtaining a trial copy of the tool and conducting evaluation (McDonald, 1996). Therefore, each of the vendors associated with the knowledge management tools contained in the short-list should be contacted and a trial copy obtained. These are usually based on a variation of a limited period of time with access to all features or no time limit but restriction placed on certain features. Once the tool has been installed, it can be explored and experimented with. Trial copies usually come with a tutorial, therefore this is a good place to start becoming accustomed to the tool. Once a certain level of confidence is achieved, a structured and systematic evaluation of the tool should be conducted. For comparison purposes it is advisable to use a framework against which each of the knowledge management tools can be evaluated. An evaluation framework was designed as a broader part of this research and an earlier version of which is published in Patel and Hlupic (2000). The framework is designed to evaluate all aspects of purchasing a commercial knowledge management tool, including areas applicable across all software tools, e.g., costs, training, interface, etc. However, Table 3 demonstrates a small section of the evaluation framework that is applicable to knowledge management tools to enable the understanding of the criteria relevant to this area.

The framework was designed using a similar procedure for data collection as that described in the section about designing the methodology. However, users of knowledge management tools were also interviewed in order to obtain information about criteria that could make up the framework. Furthermore, several knowledge management tools such as those presented in Table 2 were empirically investigated to identify further criteria. As previously mentioned knowledge management tools appear to be designed in order to support one or more of the knowledge management activities. Therefore, the resultant framework was designed to reflect

Table 3: Framework for evaluating knowledge management tools

CATEGORY	CRITERIA		DESCRIPTION
General Criteria			
Type	❏ Generate knowledge ❏ Organise knowledge ❏ Share knowledge		Which of the knowledge management activities does the tool accommodate?
Purpose	❏ General ❏ Specific		Has the tool been designed for a specific area? E.g., help desk
Type of knowledge	❏ Structured ❏ Unstructured		What type of knowledge does the tool facilitate?
Format of data	❏ Numeric ❏ Text ❏ Graphics	❏ Audio ❏ Visual	What format(s) of data does the tool facilitate?
Criteria for Knowledge Generation Tools			
Method	❏ Acquisition ❏ Synthesis ❏ Creation ❏ Search ❏ User profiling ❏ Agents ❏ Clustering	❏ Data entry ❏ OCR ❏ Voice input ❏ Analysis ❏ Web spiders ❏ Data mining ❏ Email	What method(s) is used to generate knowledge?
Criteria for Knowledge Organisation Tools			
Method	❏ Auditing ❏ Categorisation ❏ Manual cataloguing ❏ Auto cataloguing ❏ Filtering ❏ App integration ❏ Portal user interface ❏ Full Text Search ❏ Linking	❏ Indexing ❏ Contextualising ❏ Compacting ❏ Visualisation ❏ Channels ❏ Doc management ❏ Image/video Search ❏ Structured Search ❏ Unstructured Search	What method(s) is used to organise knowledge?
Import facility	❏ Provided ❏ Not provided		Is an import facility provided?
Loading formats	❏ Text files ❏ Databases	❏ Spreadsheets ❏ HTML	If an import facility is provided, what types of files can be loaded into the knowledge base?
Criteria for Knowledge Sharing Tools			
Method	❏ Flow ❏ Push ❏ Communities ❏ App sharing ❏ Conferencing ❏ Bulletin boards ❏ Messaging	❏ Publishing ❏ Notification ❏ Collaboration ❏ Group decisions ❏ Chat ❏ Virtual teams ❏ File transfer	What method(s) is used to share knowledge?

this and consists of four main parts. The first part labelled 'General Criteria' consists of criteria that can be applied to any knowledge management tool regardless of which of the knowledge management activities it has been designed to support. The remaining three parts represent each of the knowledge management activities: knowledge generation, organisation and sharing. The framework can be used in a similar manner to a checklist during the evaluation of the trial copy of the knowledge management tool. This forms a base for the tools to be compared quickly and easily. However, it is important to note that the criteria contained within the evaluation framework are by no means exhaustive and therefore would need updating on a regular basis, particularly considering the frequency of new knowledge management tools appearing on the software market.

Once each of the tools contained in the short-list has been evaluated using the framework, those tools that are considered inappropriate should be discarded. The remaining tools should be listed according to the order of preference. The short-list now becomes a list of 'Candidate Tools' as demonstrated in Figure 2.

Phase IV

This phase involves taking the knowledge management tool positioned at the top from the list of candidate tools and conducting a pilot test (McDonald, 1983). This involves installing the tool in the environment the purchased tool is intended to be used. A selection of users should use the tool for a period of time determined by the purchasing organisation, as though it is a replacement for the existing system. It is probably best, whenever a pilot test is being conducted, to use old data from the existing system so as not to have a negative impact. However, it is important to note that while pilot testing is being undertaken, the old system should continue to support the organisation. In many cases the installation of a knowledge management tool will be a completely new initiative. Under these circumstances the tool should be installed and used by people who intend to use the tool that is finally purchased. If the data for the tool does not exist or is unavailable, then representative test data needs to be created.

Once the time limit for the pilot test is reached, then the users must be questioned about their views and opinions on the tool (McDonald, 1983). If the outcome is positive then the final selection can be made. However, if the outcome of the pilot test is negative then it is necessary to consult the candidate list of tools created as a result of Phase III and the next tool on the list should be pilot tested. If the results from the pilot test indicate an equally divided outcome, then it may be worth extending the testing period and perhaps involving a few more users in the evaluation. This process should be repeated until a suitable tool is identified and a final selection can be made.

Having selected a tool that is approved by both selection team and users, it is possible to approach the vendor to negotiate a contract. Martin and McClure (1983) provide a detailed discussion of what factors to consider when drawing up a contract. In summary, the contract should cover issues such as support, warranties, licences, etc. Furthermore, the contract is likely to be biased towards the vendor. Therefore, it is important to negotiate new terms that favour both parties (Martin and McClure, 1983). If the vendor disagrees to drawing up a new contract, then the purchasing organisation should re-consider carefully another vendor or tool, or both, if necessary. If another suitable vendor that supports the required tool cannot be found, or suitable terms and conditions agreed, then another tool will have to be considered. This involves selecting the next tool from the candidate list produced during Phase III. Once an appropriate knowledge management vendor and contract have been achieved, the tool can be purchased, which is the final phase, Phase V, of the methodology.

Phase V

Purchasing the knowledge management tool is the objective of this methodology and once this is achieved, the procedure concludes. However, at this stage an entirely new procedure begins for the organisation. This involves adapting the tool, if necessary, installing and integrating it into the organisation. This may be done by the organisation itself or the tool vendor. Regardless of who the responsible party is, this can be a long, drawn-out process that may require numerous cycles of testing. Once the knowledge management tool has been integrated, it is necessary to monitor the tool and ensure that it is functioning in the desired manner. It is important to note that this is an extremely brief version of activities that may take place subsequent to the knowledge management tool being purchased. However, the aim of this chapter was to present a methodology for the selection of commercial knowledge management tools, therefore the discussion concludes here.

USABILITY OF THE METHODOLOGY

The methodology presented in Figure 2 can be useful to both industry and academia. The former will be able to use the methodology to facilitate the purchase of a knowledge management tool. This will save them from having to invest time and money developing their own methodology and investigating the knowledge management software market. The latter will benefit because the current literature related to the technical aspects of knowledge management is limited, and this will contribute and help to provide some clarification in the area. The methodology has been used for the evaluation and selection of knowledge management tools by members of the Brunel Centre for Knowledge and Business Process Management (KBM, 2001). Furthermore, companies involved in participating in the interviews in order to share their experiences of evaluating and selecting a knowledge management tool have expressed that had such a methodology been available when they were embarking on purchasing a suitable knowledge management tool, they would have found it very useful.

CONCLUSIONS

In summary, the constant increase in interest in knowledge management has resulted in an overwhelming number of knowledge management tools available in the software market. This presents a problem for purchasing organisations that are required to sift through a vast number of tools. Furthermore, some form of guideline for the selection of knowledge management tools is lacking from the literature. Therefore, the purpose of this chapter was to present a methodology to aid organisations with the selection of an appropriate knowledge management tool. In essence, the methodology aims to identify the organisation's requirements, which are used to select an initial list of knowledge management tools. This list is continually refined until a practical short-list is achieved. A detailed evaluation of each of the tools contained in the short-list is conducted using an evaluation framework. Subsequently, those tools that are considered suitable are ordered according to preference and in turn pilot tested with users. Once the users are satisfied with a tool and a contract negotiated with the vendor, the knowledge management tool can be purchased.

In conclusion, the plethora of knowledge management tools makes a set of guidelines for tool selection essential. The methodology and evaluation framework presented in this chapter achieves this, particularly since no other guidelines for knowledge management tools exist. Furthermore, indications from companies have shown that such a facility would be useful and would be adopted to aid the evaluation and selection process.

REFERENCES

Anderson, E. E. (1990). Choice models for the evaluation and selection of software packages. *Journal of Management Information Systems*, *6*(4), 123-138.

Angus, J. and Patel, J. (1998). Knowledge management cosmology. *Informationweek*, (March 16), 59.

Angus, J., Patel, J. and Harty, J. (1998) Knowledge management: Great concept...But what is it? *Informationweek*, (March 16), 58-70.

Berryman, R., Clark, G. and Ho, A. (1994). An exploration into practices and theories of software evaluation for educational use. *Computers in New Zealand Schools*, *4*(1), 14-19.

Bicknell, D. (1999). Knowledge manager's don't work. *Computer Weekly*, (May 27), 26.

Bonner, D. (2000). Enter the chief knowledge officer. *Training and Development*, *54*(2), 36-40.

Borghoff, U. M. and Pareschi, R. (1997). Information technology for knowledge management. *Journal of Universal Computer Science. Special Issue on Information Technology for Knowledge Management*, 3(8), 835-842.

Breslin, J. (1986). *Selecting and Installing Software Packages*. New York: Quorum Books.

Buckleitner, W. (1999). The state of children's software evaluation: Yesterday, today and in the 21st century. *Information Technology in Childhood Education*, *1*, 211-220.

Curry, J. W. and Bonner, D. M. (1983). *How to Find and Buy Good Software: A Guide for Business and Professional People*. Englewood Cliffs, NJ: Prentice-Hall.

Davenport, T. H. (1993). *Process Innovation: Reengineering Work Through Information Technology*. Boston, MA: Harvard Business School Press.

Davenport, T. H. (1996). We have the techknowledy: New tools for knowledge management. *CIO Magazine*, (September 15). Available: http://www.cio.com/archive/091596/dav.html.

Davenport, T. H. (1997). *Information Ecology: Mastering the Information and Knowledge Environment*. New York: Oxford University Press.

Davenport T. H. and Prusak, L. (1998). *Working Knowledge: How Organisations Manage What They Know*. Boston, MA: Harvard Business School Press.

Duffy, J. (2001). The tools and technologies needed for knowledge management. *Information Management Journal*, *35*(1), 64-67.

Dupuy, A. and Leveson, N. (2000). An empirical evaluation of the MC/DC coverage criterion on the HETE-2 satellite software. *Proceedings from DASC (Digital Aviation Systems Conference)*, Philadelphia, October.

Ferran-Urdaneta, C. (1999). Teams or communities? Organisational structures for knowledge management. *Proceedings of the 1999 ACM SIGCPR Conference on Computer Personnel Research*, 128-134.

Forte, G. (1992). Tools fair: Out of the lab, onto the shelf. *IEEE Software*, (May), 70-79.

Hammer, M. and Champy, J. (1993). *Re-Engineering the Corporation: A Manifesto for Business Revolution*. London: Nicholas Brearley.

Hibbard, J. and Carillo, K. M. (1998). Knowledge revolution: Getting employees to share what they know is no longer a technology challenge–It's a corporate culture challenge. *Informationweek*, (January 5), 663.

Hlupic, V. (1997). Simulation software selection using SimSelect. *Simulation*, *69*(4), 231-239.

Jackson, C. (1999). *Process to Product: Creating Tools for Knowledge Management*. Available: http://www.brint.com/members/online/120205/jackson/.

KBM. (2001). *Brunel Centre for Knowledge and Business Process Management.* Available: http://www.brunel.ac.uk/depts/cs/research/kbm/index.shtml.

Klamma, R. and Schlaphof, S. (2000). Rapid knowledge deployment in an organisational-memory-based workflow environment. In Hansen, H. R., Bichler, M. and Mahrer, H. (Eds.), *Proceedings of the 8th European Conference on Information Systems (ECIS 2000: A Cyberspace Odyssey), 1*, 364-371.

Klein, G. and Beck, P. O. (1987). A decision aid for selecting among information system alternatives. *MIS Quarterly, 11*(2), 177-185.

Kramer, M. (1998). Knowledge management becomes catch phrase but eludes easy definition. *PC Week*, (December 7), 95.

Le Blanc, L. A. and Jelassi, T. (1991). *An Empirical Assessment of Choice Models for Software Evaluation and Selection.* Working Paper, INSEAD No.91/24/TM.

Lennox, G. and McNairn, I. (1999) Making the connection between the mind and the database. *The Original Knowledge Management, 2*(4), 3-6.

Lynch, R. K. (1985). Nine pitfalls in implementing packaged applications software. *Journal of Information Systems Management, 2*(2), 88-92.

Macintosh, A. (1999). *Knowledge Management.* Available: http://aiai.ed.ac.uk/~alm/kamlnks.html.

Martin, J. and McClure, C. (1983). Buying software off the rack. *Harvard Business Review, 61*(6), 32-47.

McDonald, T. (1996). Evaluating primary health care software packages. *ITCH '96 (A Conference Addressing Information Technology Issues in Community Health)*, Victoria Conference Centre, Victoria, Canada, November 3-6.

Milton, N., Shadbolt, N., Cottam, H. and Hammersley, M. (1999). Towards a knowledge technology for knowledge management. *International Journal of Human-Computer Studies, 51*(3), 615-641.

Mosley, V. (1992). How to assess tools efficiently and quantitatively. *IEEE Software*, (May), 29-32.

Montazemi, A.R., Cameron, D. A. and Gupta, K. M. (1996). An empirical study of factors affecting software package selection. *Journal of Management Information Systems, 13*(1), 89-105.

Nikoukaran, J., Hlupic, V. and Paul, R. J. (1998). Criteria for simulation software evaluation. In Medeiros, D. J., Watson, E. F., Carson, J. S. and Manivannan, M. S. (Eds.), *Proceedings of the 1998 Winter Simulation Conference*, 399-406, Washington, DC, USA.

Parnas, D. L., John van Schouwen, A. and Po Kwan, S. (1990). Evaluation of safety-critical software. *Communications of the ACM, 33*(6), 636-648.

Patel, N. and Hlupic, V. (2000). The design of a framework for knowledge management tool evaluation. In Remenyi, D. (Ed.), *Proceedings of First European Conference on Knowledge Management*, 223-230, Bled School of Management, Bled, Slovenia. October 26-27.

Reilly, M., Matarazzo, T. and Ives, W. (1998/1999). Once upon a corporate time: The role of stories in organisational learning. *Knowledge Management, 2*(4), 7-12.

Robson, M. and Ullah, P. (1996). *A Practical Guide to Business Process Re-engineering*. Hampshire: Gower.

Ruggles, R. (1997). *Knowledge Tools: Using Technology to Manage Knowledge Better*. Available: http://www.cbi.cgey.com/pub/docs/KnowledgeTools.PDF.

Sharland R (1991). *Package Evaluation: A Practical Guide to Selecting Applications and Systems Software*. London: Avebury Technical.

Silver, C. A. (2000). Where technology and knowledge meet. *The Journal of Business Strategy, 21*(6), 28-33.

Trauth, E. M. (1999). Who owns my soul? The paradox of pursuing organisational knowledge in a work culture of individualism. *Proceedings of the 1999 ACM SIGCPR Conference on Computer Personnel Research*, April 8-10, New Orleans, LA, USA.

Vaas, L. (1999). Brainstorming: Before opening the floodgates to new KM technologies, IT managers should make sure users are ready, willing and able to share what they know. *PC Week, 16*(22), 65.

Chapter XIII

A Framework for Managing Knowledge in Requirements Identification: Bridging the Knowledge Gap Between Business and System Developers

Wafi Al-Karaghouli
University of Westminster, UK

Sarmad Alshawi and Guy Fitzgerald
Brunel University, UK

ABSTRACT

This chapter reflects on experiences when traditional IT approaches were used to design large IT systems and ended in failure (Etheridge, 2001). The main reflections focus on the reasons for system failure and how they relate to the diversity of knowledge, managing knowledge, and the understanding gaps that may exist between the business and the system developers. The study reveals that the understanding gaps mainly result from lack of knowledge of business operations on the developer side, matched by lack of technical appreciation and knowledge on the user side. To help address the knowledge gap problem, a Knowledge Requirement Framework (KRF), employing soft-systems, diagramming and set mapping techniques, is proposed and described.

INTRODUCTION

This chapter aims to bring together ideas from various disciplines such as Knowledge Management (KM), Information Systems (IS), Software Engineering (SE), Business Process Reengineering (BPR) and Human Computer Interfaces (HCI).

Knowledge and knowledge management fall in the heart of the initial stage (requirements) of the system development process (BS 6719, 1986). The Requirements Engineering Specialist Group (RESG) of the British Computer Society has defined Requirements Engineering (RE) as:

"... the elicitation, definition, modelling analysis, specification and validation of what is needed from a computer system. It is a process which draws on techniques from software engineering, knowledge acquisition, cognitive science and social sciences to improve software engineering practice."

The theme-map of the discussion in this chapter is shown in Figure 1. The diagram illustrates the important role played by knowledge in determining the initial requirement of the information system (IS) required to satisfy business needs. High-quality initial and agreed requirements form the basis of any successful information technology system (ITS) development (Al-Karaghouli et al., 2002).

The area of applied ITS has been enriched both in theory and in practice by the contributions of those in the fields of hard and soft system methodologies (Avison, 1995), and by experiments to improve the quality of designed systems. We quote Lewin's dictum that "the most practical thing in the world is a good theory" which has been practised in its fullest sense by sociotechnical system innovations. Our research is a witness to the fact that applied ITS, e.g., soft system

Figure 1: The role of knowledge in determining agreed requirements

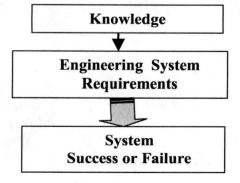

methodology, has made significant progress in contributing to organisational change strategies, and that experiences in soft systems have provided a particularly viable agenda for the future of organisational change. The soft system methodology (Checkland, 1998) is full of success stories that continue to generate enthusiasm among both academics and business practitioners.

However, no work in the applied ITS subject area can ever be completely comprehensive. Therefore, we have chosen to highlight three topics of the field: 1) the points that have been basically responsible for the ITS glitches/failures, 2) knowledge and its role in requirements and 3) the role of business requirements, including the Knowledge Requirements Framework (KRF) and its contribution to ITS developments.

ITS PROJECTS FAILURE

Information Technology System (ITS) still exhibits a significant failure rate (Parker, 2000; Ranger, 2001). For example, a survey (OASIG, 1996) on the eventual outcomes from projects involving investment in IT suggest that: 80% to 90% do not meet their goals, 80% are delivered late and over budget, 40% fail or are abandoned, more than 75% do not integrate business and technological objectives properly and only 10% - 20% meet all success criteria. The report goes on to suggest some of the main reasons why ITS projects seem to fail: Management agenda is too limited in that most ITS project investments are technology led and the main investment motive is only to cut costs. This narrow focus on technical capabilities and efficiency goals means that inadequate attention is given to the human and organisational issues that often determine a project's ultimate success (Gubbins, 2001; Computing, 2001, 1989, 1998). In addition, users don't influence the development process enough, senior managers do not appreciate the links between technical and organisational change, project management techniques and IT approaches seem too technical, and companies fail to organise work or design jobs and roles properly (Hatton, 1999).

Macaulay (1996) argued that some ITS failures are the result of mutual misunderstanding between the customer and the system developers about vital aspects of the project's requirements. It is this area which represents the focus of our research and this chapter.

Getting the customer "requirements" right the first time during the initial stage of the life cycle (*Definition of Requirements*), rather than at a later stage, will save both the customer and the system developer (SD) time and money, and will have a major influence on increasing the success chance of a project (see Ishikawa, 1985; Crosby, 1989; O'Callaghan, 2002). Intensive and continuous communications between the customer and the system developer are extremely important to establish a clear understanding of the business needs which the proposed system must support in order to get things right the first time (Juran, 1989), but in most of the cases this is not happening in the real-world, as has been indicated by Kelly (1999, 2000), who quotes the software guru Ivar Jacobson saying:

"Two generations of developers have been lost to bad habits. They do the coding and then debug. They should get it right from the beginning."

According to O'Callaghan (2002) the requirements should be "signed in blood" to reduce iterations during the requirements stage to speed development and reduce the system development life cycle. High and unrealistic expectations of a system prior to development are well-known problems and can contribute to disenchantment with the system when it is implemented. Customers can get too enthusiastic about technology and over-estimate the technology's capacity to change their world.

THE IMPORTANCE OF KNOWLEDGE MANAGEMENT IN BUSINESS ORGANISATIONS

IT knowledge (technical knowledge) strategy and business knowledge strategy are two sides of the same coin, moving in the same direction to deliver the same goal and to ensure it remains profitable in the face of rapidly increasing competition and pressure to improve efficiency. Yelle (1979) suggested that barefoot KM is about involving the right people (management and users of different departments) to develop an authentic approach to a future system development process that delivers strategy without confusing KM with acquisition of specific information systems (IS). It is important to be clear about agreed business strategy (why, what, where, when and how) between the different users and participants. Creative brainstorming technique needs to be introduced for producing and building good ideas into the process. Also, an overview map of the process (see KRF section) needs to be explained.

The process of managing these knowledge assets creates a dynamic, innovative and agile company (Adler, 1990, 1991; Binney, 2001). Failure to manage information leads to information loss, lessons not learned, work taking longer and trends going unnoticed. Implementing a knowledge management strategy needs an in-depth knowledge of both the business needs of an organisation and the underlying technologies. The emphasis will be on making connections between theory and practice in the following areas:

- Knowledge Management as a strategic issue in determining requirements.
- Groupware and collaborative learning towards better understanding of requirements.
- Barriers to learning and knowledge management.

Business Knowledge (BK) and Knowledge Management (KM) are critical parts of any retail organisation company's role (Computing, 2001). The shared knowledge of the organisation is its most important asset. Disseminating this knowledge is difficult to do in a timely, effective fashion (Argote, 1999). For this reason, communicating the knowledge management process through the development of a systematic knowledge system is indicated. An organised (KRF) knowledge and requirement system will entail the following benefits:

- Detailed, searchable information at the organisation's fingertips.
- Access to all information across the organisation.

KNOWLEDGE DIVERSITY

Acquisition of business and technical knowledge is very important to any organisation. Equally likely, continuous communications (Sturt, 2000; Harrington, 2001) are also vital to the progress of any organisation (Computing, 2001); in most organisations there is a clear division between the customer and users (both business users and end-users) of the proposed system and the developers of the system, i.e., different knowledge and perception of knowledge (see Figure 3).

Usually the developer is the internal IT department, although increasingly it is a third-party organisation, such as an outsourcing vendor or consultancy company. This can exacerbate communication problems due to the physical separation of the organisations. Some organisations claim a more integrated environment where the customer and the developers are not seen as separate elements of the business, but they work seamlessly together with shared objectives. Even in this environment there is usually a separation in the roles of customer and developer; it is just that they work in a coherent team or project (Tenkasi and Boland, 1996; Sieloff, 1999).

For shorthand purposes, we will call the business users and customers of the system, the 'customer,' and the developers of the system, which include business analysts, systems analysts, programmers, software engineers, network specialists, security specialists, etc., shall be called 'developers.' For convenience, we will talk about the two sides, but this terminology should not indicate that there is only one of each or that they are not a diverse set of people and that levels of seniority are not involved. Furthermore, the term customer is usually taken to mean the person or people (internal customers) within an organisation who require the system to support their part of the business (or the business as a whole).

The current concept of a system requirement is ill suited to develop clear "smart" requirements for large systems. The received concept follows a technical rationality, which regards requirements as goals to be discovered and solutions as separate technical elements (Cavell, 1999; Regnell et al., 1995). In contrast, we advocate a view where a requirement specifies a set of mappings between problem and solution spaces, which both are socially constructed and negotiated (Figures 2 & 3).

REQUIREMENTS ENGINEERING: THE CULTURE GAP

The view of two cultures, that of IT and the business, is in evidence in many organisations. The culture of system developers is typically technically oriented and is based on an understanding of technical issues (Price Waterhouse, 1991, 1992). In systems development this is reflected in a focus on issues such as the functionality of the system, its performance, the response rate, the type of programming language that should be used, etc. (Flood, 2000). On the other hand, the organisational culture and focus is rather different and is more concerned with business issues, individual issues and the system as support for business and management processes (Figure 2).

The process of requirements engineering is recommended as follows and is based on business needs.

Figure 2: Requirements engineering framework — knowledge sharing

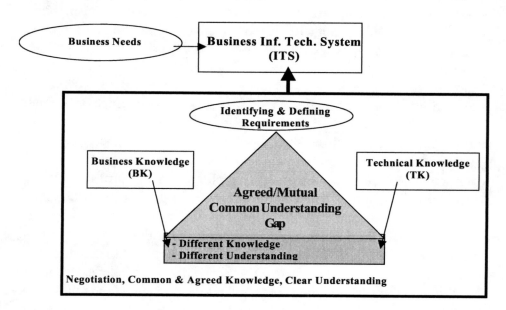

IDENTIFY THE KNOWLEDGE GAP (KG) AND THE UNDERSTANDING GAP (UG)

Intensive and continuous communications between all customers and developers is extremely important to help establish a clear understanding of the needs which the proposed system must support in order to get things as correct the first time as possible. This does not mean that all requirements can be known and elicited. There are clearly some that will only evolve and develop over time, but the objective is to make a better and richer attempt to address those that can potentially be elicited. At this point, it should be stressed that many factors contribute to systems failure (for example, see Myers, 1994), but we believe that improving the initial specification and eliminating errors and problems at an early stage of the design process of software, i.e., the requirement stage in the Life Cycle, will be very beneficial.

The view of two cultures is in evidence in many organisations (Koloszyc, 1998). The IT culture and the business culture view the IT department as a cost centre rather than investment and contributor to the success of the organisation. Therefore different departments in organisations rarely have the chance to talk to one another about their new ITS and suddenly find themselves integrated by the so-called efficiency system. In fact, most of the ITS built in this way has worked against the development of such integrated culture; the reader is referred to Cavell (1999) and List (1999) for work on the implementation of such ITS in the retail sector.

Figure 3: A culture clash — Business knowledge (BK) vs. technical knowledge (TK)

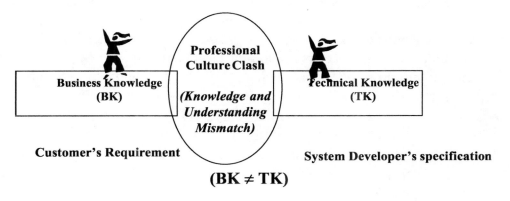

CUSTOMER AND DEVELOPER "KNOWLEDGE" GAP

The emphasis on the customer's business knowledge and acquired knowledge is very important. On the other hand, the developer's technical knowledge is also important, but the knowledge the two parties have is different. This will lead to a mismatch of their interests, which in most cases contributes to the failure of projects. Land (1982) and Glass (1998, 2001) highlight the importance of learning from failures, and of the vital need of the developers to clearly understand the customer's requirements. We take a slightly broader view in that we see the problem not only being that the developers often fail to understand the customer's business and needs, but that the customers in turn often do not sufficiently appreciate the realities of software development, or what the software people are offering. Our aim is to develop techniques to help overcome these problems. On the one hand, we are developing methods to help identify and make mutually apparent the gaps that exist between the understanding that each side in the project has; on the other hand, we have techniques aimed at facilitating and accelerating the generation of understanding to close these gaps (see Al-Karaghouli et al., 1999, 2000).

Even good software, delivered on time to spec., and agreed requirements may still not satisfy the customer. And it may largely be the end user's fault. But why is this so? Human nature is an important and complex factor in the software project. Most of the time, end user expectations can't even be met (Sommerville and Sawyer, 1999; Pressman, 1992).

USING VENN DIAGRAMS FOR IDENTIFYING UNDERSTANDING GAPS

The Venn diagram is being used in a logical sense and is essentially a graphical representation of the situation (Quin and Bronte-Stewart, 1994). Its strength lies in the discussion it provokes and the negotiation between the parties, both in its original construction and then its subsequent re-drawing as understanding and agreement is reached. Normally no attempt at a graphical representation is undertaken in the process of determining requirements. It usually just involves the creation of a specification by the systems developers which the customer is then expected to agree with and too often the fact that the specification was not a good statement of the requirements is not discovered until much later, sometimes only at implementation.

ILLUSTRATIVE CASE EXAMPLE

In the work with the retailers, the authors used Venn diagrams to facilitate discussion and understanding of requirements of a new system that had been agreed in principle to be developed. The case relates to the perceived need to 'enter the Internet world' and to have a web-based information and sales channel for the companies' existing products. Beyond this, the case is simplified and does not reflect the detail of the organisations nor their actual requirements. It is purely illustrative of the situation and the processes.

GRAPHICAL REPRESENTATION OF THE UNDERSTANDING GAP

The Venn diagram of Figure 4 illustrates how set theory can be applied to the understanding of customer requirements (Pisano, 1994).

The two circles represent different areas of knowledge and understanding; one represents the understanding of the system developers, the other the customer. The matching or common understanding of the requirement is where the two circles overlap (RS).

Venn diagrams have been used successfully for some time in management science (Anderson et al., 1995), as well as, of course, in their traditional areas of logic and computing. In this research they were found to be highly effective as a graphical or pictorial technique for illustrating any gaps in understanding that existed at the requirements stage. They are extremely easy to understand and can be manipulated by both sides to make particular points. For example, by re-negotiating the overlaps, it is easy to indicate how good or bad current agreements are on particular matters. The technique can be made more precise and quantitative by, for

Figure 4: Requirements (customer)/specifications (system developer)

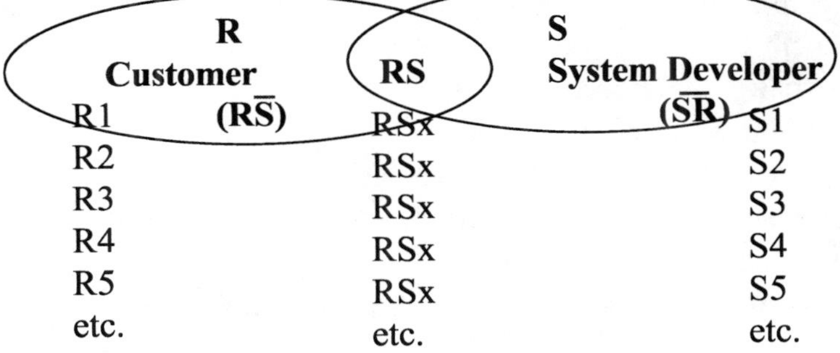

R Customer ($R\bar{S}$)	RS	S System Developer ($\bar{S}R$)
R1	RSx	S1
R2	RSx	S2
R3	RSx	S3
R4	RSx	S4
R5	RSx	S5
etc.	etc.	etc.

example, creating a matching score of specific terms noted in attribute lists drawn up by the two sides.

Illustrative Case – First Stage

Customer Requirements

In the Venn diagram of Figure 4, let (R) denote the set of all possible customer requirements space which contains the individual (fragments) business requirement as sub-sets viewed by the customer:

R contains a set of individual requirements, e.g.:

(The fact that there are 10 instances in this set is purely arbitrary.)

R1 = we would like to offer an e-commerce facility for our external customers.

R2 = the image required for this business is one of trust.

R3 = the new system must be operational by the end of the year.

R4 = the system must be easy for internal and external customers to use.

R5 = the system must provide quick response for customers.

R6 = the system must be totally secure.

R7 = the system must provide enough information for customers so that they do not put an additional burden on the existing help line.

R8 = a maximum of 8 people (from the business side) will be available to support the development of the new system.

R9 = the new system needs to fit very closely with the existing business processes.

R10 = the system should attract additional customers, not just be a different channel for existing customers.

System Developer Specifications

Let (S) denote the set of all possible system developer specifications space which contains the individual (fragments) suggested specification design as sub-sets viewed by the developer:

S contains a set of individual specification elements, e.g.:

S1 = an electronic retail channel is required.

S2 = the development of the system is a major new undertaking for the ITS department.

S3 = the time scale is extremely tight.

S4 = the skill required is in short supply.

S5 = the development environment will be Unix.

S6 = a mirror environment will be required.

S7 = absolute security is impossible.

S8 = the development language will be Java and C++.

S9= response times depend on factors outside of our control.

S10= the system can utilise the existing processing systems for the underlying functions, which will shortcut the development.

Let (R) and (S) be two sets of points (interests) having points in common represented by (RS). Therefore (RS) will represent only the matching (common), and agreed systems functions. They do not necessarily have to equally match the number of requirement elements, e.g., RS= {R1:S1, R9:S10}

In this case the common understanding (overlap) is relatively small and the diagram reflects this. The common factors concern the fact that they are both talking about an Internet channel (R1:S1) and that the existing processes will be utilised which will obviously make them a close fit to the new system (R9:S10). The non-overlapping sector is represented by RS and S2. There is obviously a far greater degree of mismatch than match of requirements between the two parties. The diagram is obviously only illustrative but nevertheless powerful in its ability to convey the size of the gap. In use the diagrams could have the specific elements, i.e., the Rs and Ss written in the appropriate places. However this makes the diagrams rather messy and unwieldy so it has not been included here. When the elements of the gap are discussed in detail and agreements thrashed out, the participants can re-draw the diagrams with the overlap hopefully becoming larger. The point is that the diagram clearly represents the current level of agreed areas of understanding and misunderstanding between the two sides at any stage.

Figure 5: Mapping diagram of R to S (Stage 1)

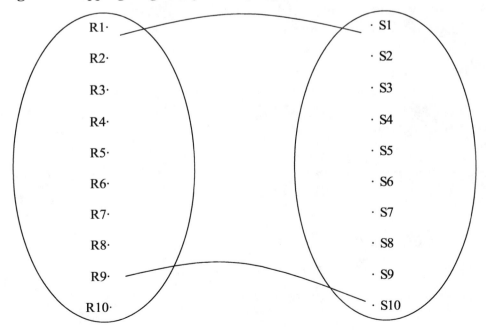

The non-overlapping sector is represented by:
RS = {R2:S2, R3:S3, R4:S4, R5:S9, R6:S6, R7:S7, R8:S8, R10:S9}

The Venn diagram is important in that it helps focus attention on exactly which requirement instances match with which specification instances, i.e., the Rs and the Ss. Figure 5 is the mapping diagram for this first stage of the case.

When the mapping diagram is examined, it can be seen that some instances in one set are mapped to instances in the other set although there are relatively few—in fact only R1:S1 and R9:S10, i.e., RS from the Venn diagram as one would expect. However now the focus is on the instances that do not map. There are some potential matches, for example, R3 and S3 both concern the implementation date. R3 relates to the date the new system is perceived to be required by the Customer, but this is not agreed to by the Systems Developers; they simply state that the deadline is tight (S3) and this certainly does not indicate a meeting of minds as to the likely implementation date. In fact, were this to remain the state of affairs, the project would probably be of high risk of not meeting the deadline simply because the two sides have not really come to a serious agreement on the issue indicated by the fact that there is no mapping on the diagram. Having this highlighted early on is obviously beneficial.

On the other hand the Customer requirement R2, concerning the image of trust, is not really even on the agenda of the developers, as there is really no corresponding element in their set. This is also the case with R4, R7 and R10 where the Software Developers do not seem to have taken any of the implications of these requirements on board. Equally the specification statements of S5 and S8 do not reflect any immediately identifiable requirement of the customer, again indicating a need for further clarification and discussion.

Illustrative Case – Second Stage

The second stage shows (Figure 6) more common and agreed system requirements. Let (R) and (S) be two sets of points (interests) having subsets in common represented by (RS). The intersection is larger than in the first stage, and

Figure 6: Requirements (customer)/specifications (system developer)

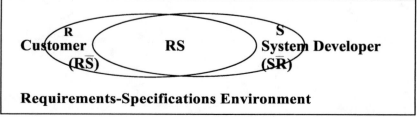

there is a greater degree of overlap indicating a greater convergence of the requirements and the specification.

RS= {R1:S1, R3:S3, R5:S9, R6:S7,R9:S10}

At the end of the second stage, it can be seen that there is a greater degree of overlap indicating a greater convergence of the requirements and the specifications. The issue of time scale has been resolved as a result of it having been highlighted in the first stage. The customer has understood some of the limitations and concerns of the Systems Developers and delayed the deadline by two months (R3). Thus as a result of discussion, negotiation and improved understanding on both sides, the content of the requirement instant has changed. On the developer side the issue of resources has been addressed, project management will be addressed (S3) and new skills are to be brought in (S4). The sides are now in general agreement over time scales and this is agreed as an element of overlap. It should be noted that in this case one requirement instance has mapped to two specification instances, in fact one-to-many, and many-to-many mappings are allowed.

The new mapping diagram (Figure 7) now shows the agreed mappings. The diagram helps the parties to now focus on those instances that are not mapped in each set. These are then reviewed, discussed and negotiated as to what they mean, why they are there and the implications for either side. Ideally a third stage or

Figure 7: Mapping diagram of R to S (Stage 2)

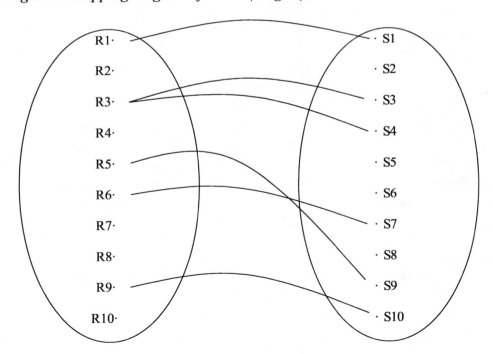

iteration of discussions is undertaken with the objective of mapping all elements in each set.

In this case there are still a number of instances in both sets that have not been agreed and mapped. For example the issue of the image of trust (R2) is still not resolved. It might be that there is nothing on the specification side that can be done to address this. If this is the case then this should be recorded and the requirement instance R2 removed from the diagram. Everybody would now be clear that this is not something that the new system can directly deliver and there are no false expectations. The customer should be made aware of the benefits and limitations of using these development languages. In other words dialogue and negotiation ensue. Compromise and trade-offs are inherent in resolving and illuminating differing perceptions.

The Process

The main feature of the technique proposed is the use of diagrams from set theory; but although the use of the diagrams is important, it is really the negotiation and dialogue processes that present the key issues.

The starting point of the process is arbitrary; it can be after some specifications have been developed or it can be before. There is usually some general agreement that a system of some kind would be beneficial and should be developed. In terms of the systems development life cycle, it is probably most beneficial early in the analysis stage, after feasibility and initial statement of requirements, although there are no hard and fast rules. The stakeholders need to be analysed and the two sides identified (see discussion in Professional Culture Clash section concerning caveats relating to the notion of two sides). It is first recommended that each side independently draw their own list of R or S instances; the number and the way they are described is irrelevant, the important thing is first to get two lists. Then an overlapping Venn diagram is constructed to indicate what they believe the level of mutual understanding to be. This diagram then provides the starting point for further discussion with attention being focused on why there is disagreement between each side's view, and on the nature of the current mismatch between requirements and specification. This discussion should then lead to the development of specific further activities to obtain better understanding so as to increase the overlap and agreement. A scenario approach can be useful to enrich the communications between the parties (Sauer, 1993; Rudelius et al., 1982). Because of the simplicity and clarity of the Venn and mapping diagrams, which is especially helpful to the customer, it is recommended that the above process is repeated frequently throughout the requirements definition stage of the project's life cycle. We have illustrated two stages in the example, but there will probably be more.

The authors suggest that the role of a facilitator in matching and mapping the requirements against the specification is important and will add value to the quality of the final requirement. A facilitator is an independent person who guides the process and helps overcome the various barriers that are in the way and any problems that occur. The facilitator may also arbitrate at times, but ideally should get the parties to agree rather than impose anything.

KNOWLEDGE REQUIREMENTS FRAMEWORK (KRF)

The main aim of the Knowledge Requirements Framework (KRF) is to create a compatible environment during the requirement process, with the principal objective of knowing the customer needs (requirements). Preparing for KRF may involve changing the attitude of both the software engineers and the customers in handling the requirements. The change in attitude should be on the top of the list of anticipated future changes, plus others in the system development process.

Figure 8: Knowledge requirement framework (KRF) architecture

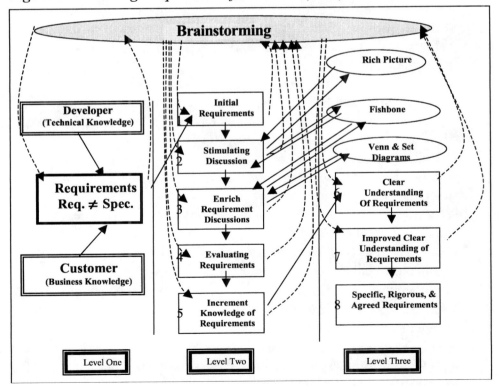

The potency and strength of the KRF concept lies in its experimental approach to organisational change. The ideas generated by ITS experimenters continue to be robust and challenging — robust because they are rooted in continuing efforts to refine variables and rearrange experimental designs, and challenging. In addition, KRF uses knowledge from various disciplines that bear on the issues of the quality of the business sector. KRF represents a powerful paradigm (approach) which combines both management science and software engineering methods and methodologies. Earlier we stressed the important role of knowledge and communication in determining a quality requirement. The KRF architecture (Figure 8) accommodates and provides rigorous, clear and agreed requirements through its different levels, processes, tools and methods used, especially in the first and second levels of KRF.

This description deals only with the first three levels and the techniques used within these levels. KRF is largely a sociotechnical approach dealing mainly with social (human) interactions between customers and developers (Mumford, 1985). After all, the process of customer requirements elicitation involves human-human communications with the aim of achieving a better understanding within organisations and helping elaborate requirements that lead to better systems that better meet the requirements and expectations of the stakeholders. KRF uses several techniques at present, and we are also exploring the use of further methods (Al-Karaghouli et al., 2000). The purpose of all of these tools is to generate, in the various parties involved in a project, the knowledge and understanding needed to create an effective requirements definition.

The knowledge about the customer, from the system developer engineering viewpoint, is often limited. Sometimes system developers take too narrow a focus in terms of the customer requirements, and have different perceptions of the problem during the first stage of the life cycle (O'Brien, 1993).

All techniques used in KRF are based on a workshop-participants scenario (see section — Customer and Developer "Knowledge" Gap). Participants will tackle a set of related questions such as:

- What features of user-developer communication can or should be supported by such representations?
- What properties of a representation contribute to making it an effective communicative aid in system developments?
- How are representations transformed in the course of use for communication?
- What relations are there between effective representational support for communication within user-developer cooperation and for communication outside those collaborative activities, e.g., in communicating the results of their work to system implementers or others who may not have participated in the creation of the representations?

The workshop discussions between user and developer shall provide initial answers to the above questions. They also reveal gaps in our current understanding of the communicative role of representations in systems development and laying the groundwork for a research agenda to produce further answers to these and other questions which arise through the discussions. The workshop discussions should also lead to recommendations for the selection and use of a range to support user-developer communication in systems development practice. This in turn should lead to proposals for technologies to support communication through representations.

KRF ARCHITECTURE

1. Level One (Initial level)
    *   Developer (Technical Knowledge).
    *   Customer (Business Knowledge).
2. Level Two (Negotiation level)
    *   Stage One — Initial Requirements.
    *   Stage Two — Stimulating Discussion.
    *   Stage Three — Enrich Requirement Discussions.
    *   Stage Four — Evaluating Requirements.
    *   Stage Five — Increment Knowledge of Requirements.
3. Level Three (Common Understanding & Agreement level)
    *   Stage Six — Clear Understanding of Requirements.
    *   Stage Seven — Improved Clear Understanding of Requirements.
    *   Stage Eight — Specific, Rigorous and Agreed Requirements.

Many forms of representation have been used or recommended for use in systems development, such as the "Brainstorming" and the "Fishbone" techniques (see Figure 8). These include representations such as:

*   Sketches or storyboards — "Brainstorming" sessions applied curing the whole process (levels 1-3).
*   Paper prototypes or mockups — "Brainstorming" sessions (levels 1-3).
*   Diagrams using prescribed notations — "Fishbone" sessions applied in level 2, stages 2 and 3.
*   Diagrams with dynamically negotiated notation — "Fishbone," "Venn diagrams" and "Set diagrams" applied in level 2, stages 2 and 3.
*   Text in natural, semi-formal and formal languages — "Brainstorming and Audio" applied in level 1 and level 2.

These representational forms may be combined in systems development work, either on a dynamic, ad hoc basis or through a prescribed method. Surveys, case studies and anecdotes all provide illustrations of successes and, too often, failures of these diverse forms of representation in supporting communication among users and developers.

CONCLUSIONS AND FUTURE RESEARCH

In this chapter, we have illustrated the concept of incorporating different knowledge and a different level of understanding to mitigate their effect to the establishment of agreed requirements. Also in this chapter, a model (KRF) was developed to aid the different knowledge and different understanding in managing requirements. In today's rapidly changing international business context, the ability to quickly and effectively manage change is the key to obtaining a competitive advantage. Quality software has become an essential asset, and the IT architecture is an important factor in the business reactivity of the enterprise.

Fragile, rigid systems based on proprietary technology can transform IT into a bottleneck for the business. Organisations need a careful, systematic yet systemic approach to assessing the requirements and impact of IT developments, such as KRF. We consider the business information system (BIT) as a coin, the business requirements (BR) and system development requirements (SDR) are two sides of the same coin, moving in the same direction to deliver the same objectives and goals. The focus on knowledge and knowledge management is not on technology per se but on instigating organisational change. Requirements and knowledge management use technology as an enabler, the value comes in the practices and processes that change the system developers, the organisation culture and practice.

The challenge comes with channelling collective learning both within the business and system developer personnel to satisfy each instance of business need and to manage the different knowledge in the process of system developments.

To manage the requirement you need to manage the knowledge each party possesses, e.g., BK or TK. To combine the two, you need a knowledge management (KM) system to handle, moderate, enrich, etc. this diverse knowledge. KRF handles, moderates and amalgamates both BK and TK. On one hand it will cater for changes in the requirements, while on the other hand it will help to stabilise requirements through the use of different tools and techniques, such as brainstorming, interviews, rich picture, fishbone (Ishikawa), Venn diagrams (Al-Karaghouli et al., 1999), data mapping & set diagrams (Al-Karaghouli et al., 2000), scenarios and joint application design (JAD) (see Avison and Fitzgerald, 1995).

Organisations need a careful, systematic yet systemic approach to assessing the requirements and impact of IT developments, such as KRF. The KRF approach stresses the importance of the analysis phase, involves the client throughout, puts the onus of final agreed requirements and contains frequent progress checks. Using this approach, small to medium sized businesses would be able to identify problems with requirements and go on to acquire and implement more suitable IS/IT systems.

KRF works by creating a business discovery platform between the two parties (the customer and the system developer). KRF represents a step in the development of modern ITS projects, because it is tied directly to business implementations of business service sectors which are growing rapidly (e.g., e-commerce). By developing standards that allow businesses and IT specialists to communicate, our ongoing research addresses other important generalisations of the different knowledge problems identified in this chapter, including the consideration of different understanding problems and the modelled analysis of requirements constraints. The model presented here provides a basis for future generalisations.

REFERENCES

Adler, P. S. (1990). Shared learning. *Management Science, 36*, 938-957.

Adler, P. S. and Clark, K. B. (1991). Behind the learning curve: A sketch of the learning process. *Management Science, 37*, 267-281.

Al-Karaghouli, W., Fitzgerald, G. and AlShawi, S. (2002). Knowledge requirement system (KRS): An approach to improving and understanding requirements-Ch.14. *Knowledge Management in the Sociotechnical World: The Graffiti Continues*. London: Springer-Verlag.

Al-Karaghouli, W., AlShawi, S. and Fitzgerald, G. (2000). Negotiating and understanding information systems requirement: The use of set diagram. *Requirements Engineering, 5*, 93-102.

Al-Karaghouli, W., AlShawi, S. and Elstob, M. (1999). An OR approach to establishing software engineering requirements. *OR41 — Operational Research Society Annual Conference*, September 14-16, Edinburgh, United Kingdom.

Anderson, D. R., Sweeney, D. J. and Williams, T. A. (1995). *Quantitative Methods for Business* (sixth edition). New York: West Publishing Company.

Argote, L. (1999). *Organisational Learning: Creating, Retaining and Transferring Knowledge*. Norwel, MA: Kluwer Academic Publishers.

Avison, D. E. and Fitzgerald, G. (1995). *Information Systems Development: Methodologies, Techniques and Tools*. New York: McGraw Hill.

Binney, D. (2001). The knowledge management spectrum — Understanding the KM landscape. *Journal of Knowledge Management, 5*(2), 33-42.

BS 6719. (1986). *British Standard Guide to Specifying User Requirements for Computer Based Systems*.

Cavell, S. (1999). Salespeople buck the system: Survey finds software fails to take account of culture. *Computing*, (February 25), 16.

Checkland, P. and Holwell, S. (1998). *Information, Systems and Information Systems–Making Sense of the Field*. Chichester, England: John Wiley & Sons.

Computing. (2001). Case study: Tesco–How it can go wrong? (October), 42, UK.

Computing. (1989). Stock exchange kills projects to focus on taurus. (November 2), 1. UK.

Crosby, P. (1989). *Let's Talk Quality*. New York: McGraw-Hill.

Etheridge, M. (2001). Retailer failure. *Computing UK*, July 5, 32.

Flood, G. (2000). Are users satisfiable? *Computing UK*, February 10, 11.

Glass, R. (1998). *Software Runaways: Lessons Learned from Massive Software Project Failures*. Englewood Cliffs, NJ: Prentice Hall.

Glass, R. (2001). *Computing Failure.Com: War Stories from the Electronic Revolution*. Englewood Cliffs, NJ: Prentice Hall.

Gubbins, M. (2001). We can still learn lessons from Leo. *Computing UK*, October 18, 24.

Harrington, A. (2001). Sweet content–Cover story. *Knowledge Management Magazine*, Bizmedia Ltd., Learned Information Europe Ltd. (June), 14-16.

Hatton, L. (1999). Swanwick bug fixes not good enough. *Computer Weekly UK*, (January 7), 11.

Ishikawa, K. (1985). *What Is Total Quality Control? The Japanese Way*. (Translated by D.J. Lu.) Englewoof Cliffs, NJ: Prentice Hall.

Juran, J. M. (1989). *Juran on Leadership for Quality: An Executive Handbook* (fourth edition). New York: McGraw-Hill.

Kelly, L. (1999). Developers bark up wrong tree. *Computing UK*, March 4, 14.

Kelly, L. (2000). Let projects fail says think tank: The government needs to learn from its mistakes. *Computing Public Sector Digest*, (January), 4.

Koloszyc, G. (1998). Retailers, suppliers push joint sales forecasting. *Store*, June.

Land, F. (1982). Adapting to changing user requirements. *Information and Management*, 5, 59-75.

Macaulay, L. A. (1996). *Requirements Engineering*. London: Springer-Verlag.

Mumford, E. (1985). Defining system requirements to meet business needs: A case study example. *The Computer Journal*, 28(2), 97-104.

Myers, M. D. (1994). A disaster for everyone to see: An interpretive analysis of a failed IS project. *Accounting, Management and Information Technology*, 4(4), 185-201.

OASIG Survey. (1996). The performance of information technology and the role of human and organisational factors. Professor C. Clegg, Institute of Work Psychology, University of Sheffield.

O'Brien, J. A. (1993). *Management Information Systems: A Managerial End User Perspective*. New York: Irwin.

O'Callaghan, A. (2002). I think, argo I am. *Application Development Advisor, SIGS, 6*(1), 68-71.

Parker, A. (2000). Commons committee calls for action on IT fiascos. *Financial Times*, (January 5), 2.

Pisano, G. P. (1994). Knowledge, integration, and the locus of learning: An empirical analysis of process development. *Strategic Management Journal, 15*, 85-100.

Pressman, R. S. (1992). *Software Engineering: A Practitioner's Approach* (third edition). New York: McGraw-Hill.

Price Waterhouse. (1991, 1992). The culture gap. *Information Technology Review*, 16-19. London.

Quin, A. J. and Bronte-Stewart, M. (1994). System pictures: A method for capturing clients' views. *Systemist, 16*, 4.

Ranger, S. (2001). State IT failures squander £1bn: Our survey counts the cost of pathway, NIRS2 and the rest. *Computing*, (July 5), 1.

Regnell, B., Kimbler, K. and Wesslen, A. (1995). Improving the use case driven approach to requirements engineering. *Proceedings of the Second IEEE International Symposium on Requirements Eng. (RE'95)*, 41-47, April, York, England.

Rudelius, W., Dickson, G. W. and Hartley, S. W. (1982). *The Little Model that Couldn't: How a Decision Support System for Retail Buyers Found Limbo, Systems, Objectives, Solutions*, 15-124.

Samuels, M. (2001). CRM: Customers are being forgotten. *Computing*, September 6, 29.

Sauer, C. (1993). *Why Information Systems Fail: A Case Study Approach*. Henley-on-Thames, UK: Alfred Waller.

Sieloff, C. G. (1999). If only HP knows what HP knows: The roots of knowledge management at Hewlett-Packard. *Journal of Knowledge Management, 3*(1), 47-53.

Sommerville, I. and Sawyer, P. (1999). *Requirements Engineering: A Good Practice Guide*. Chichester, England: John Wiley & Sons.

Sturt, T. (2000). These craz-e days: Can the right ejargon turn you into a guru? *Computing*, February 10, 80.

Tenkasi, R. and Boland Jr., R. (1996). Exploring knowledge diversity in knowledge-intensive firms: A new role for information systems. *Journal of Organizational Change Management, 9*(1), 79-91.

Yelle, L. E. (1979). The learning curve: Historical review and comprehensive survey. *Decision Science, 10*, 302-328.

Chapter XIV

The Impact of the Knowledge Economy on Leadership in Organisations

Manon van Leeuwen
Foundation for the Development of Science and
Technology in Extremadura, Spain

ABSTRACT

The world economy is in transition. It is moving from the industrial age to a new set of rules — that of the "Information Society" or knowledge economy. This will change everybody's work, affecting the flow of new ideas into enterprises, their management, organisation and procedures. These changes have major impacts on the roles leaders need to play, and on the skills they need. The focus of a leader has shifted towards more intangible issues, being a visionary, a storyteller and a change agent. Leaders need to change and to keep reinventing themselves, they have to be ready to adapt, to move, to forget yesterday, to forgive, and to structure new roles and new relationships for themselves, their teams and their ever-shifting portfolio of partners, and they need to have the capacity to employ more than one style of leadership. The chapter reviews the literature on the skills and abilities leaders need to be successful in the knowledge economy, and describes the way in which they need to manage their organisations by managing the organisation's business model, creating a risk-encouraging culture and by playing different roles.

INTRODUCTION

You think the past five years were nuts? You ain't seen nothin' yet! It's only going to get weirder, tougher and more turbulent. Which means that leadership will be more important than ever — and more confusing (Peters, 2001).

The world economy is in transition. The emerging new economy represents a tectonic upheaval in our commonwealth, a social shift that reorders our lives more than mere hardware or software ever can. It has its own distinct opportunities and its own new rules. Those who play by the new rules will prosper; those who ignore them will not (Kelly, 1998). In an increasingly competitive global economy—one that places a premium on innovation, flexibility and responsiveness—the focus of management's efforts must shift from the more efficient management of tangible resources to the more effective utilization of a firm's intellectual capital and human resources. To compete in the knowledge economy, organisations must increasingly rely on the knowledge, skills, experience and judgment of their people.

This knowledge economy is based on economic values different from those of the "traditional" economy, it has shifted towards intangibles and increasing value by incorporating knowledge into services and products. A greater proportion of economic output will be based on information and knowledge. A recent OECD study points out that "more than half of the total GDP in the rich economies is now knowledge based, including industries such as telecommunications, computers, software, pharmaceuticals, education and television. High-tech industries have nearly doubled their share of manufacturing output over the past two decades, to around 25 percent, and knowledge-intensive services are growing even faster. Knowledge workers...from brain surgeons to journalists...[now] account for eight out of 10 new jobs."

The next major business transformation is represented by seven megatrends, all due to the new technologies; most of them already have become potent forces for business change. Taking advantage of these trends can offer great competitive advantage to organisations:

I. *New information and communication technologies, coupled with the increased speed of scientific and technological advance, are forcing*

Figure 1: The shift from industrial to knowledge-based econony

Industrial Economy	Knowledge Economy
Wealth comes from leveraging machines, cash, raw materials– tangible assets	Wealth comes from leveraging people, partners, suppliers, competitors and customer experience, know-how and knowledge–intangible assets
Organisational Power	*Employee Empowerment*
Source: Auckland, 2000	

companies to transform themselves, rethinking their strategies, organisations and business models. The extended enterprise concept of electronically networking customers, suppliers and partners is now a reality. In fact a study of IDC shows that almost 80 percent of European executives recognise that the greater flexibility obtained by the implementation of the Information Society Technologies is a decisive factor in the competitive battle.

II. *New channels are changing market access and branding* and causing disintermediation in traditional channels. Since companies can now build real-time, close relationships with their customers, they are often cutting out the intermediaries—and improving service and reducing costs at the same time. Retailing has become e-tailing, a term that applies both to conventional store-based retailers that embrace the Internet, such as for example GAP, that combines previewing and ordering goods online with recollection of the items at the store, as well as new players based purely on e-tailing, as for example Amazon.com, the virtual bookstore.

III. *The balance of power is shifting to the customer*. With unlimited access to information afforded by the new technologies, customers are much more demanding than before. The *"Cluetrain Manifesto"* states that "markets are conversations: business look at their marketing missions as doing demo-graphic segmentation, slicing and dicing and delivering the message down a one-way pipe to passive individuals, but what's happening with the new technologies is something much more human to human, people talking to other people, and this should be the way in which businesses interact with their customers" (Locke, 2000). We are entering an era of unprecedented consumer power; if knowledge is power, then consumer knowledge about products and profit margins will turn things around. The credo is "what I want, where I want it, when I want it and how I want it " (Loewe and Bonchek, 1999). Customer loyalty instead of customer satisfaction is the key to success.

IV. *The face of competition is fundamentally changing*. Not only are new competitors coming out of the woodwork, but traditional competitors are exploiting the new technologies to become much more innovative and efficient. Global competition has redefined who competes, on what basis and in which markets. The relationship of one organisation to the other may simultaneously contain elements of competition, cooperation, supplying and buying. Forging partnerships of convenience that move on when the benefits dry up is the key, a good example is the PowerPC of IBM and Apple, old enemies.

V. *The pace of business is moving to "warp speed."* Planning horizons, information needs and the expectations of customers and suppliers are reflecting reductions in time. Speed is shortening the product life cycles from years to months or even weeks. Speed is reducing the time lapse between producing and selling, and purchasing and delivery has been reduced enormously; in Tokyo a customer can order a customised Toyota on Monday and drive it on Friday.

> *Speed*: It took the telephone 40 years to get into 30% of all homes in the United States, it took the television 17 years; it took the Personal Computer 13 years; and it took the Internet 7 years.

VI. *The new technologies are pushing enterprises past their traditional boundaries.* Traditional enterprise boundaries between companies and their suppliers are a thing of the past, as are internal boundaries separating processes, functions and business units. Cisco Systems maintains a strong web of strategic partnerships and systems integration with suppliers, contractors and assemblers. Its alliance partners are an integral component of the company and are treated as such.

VII. *Knowledge is becoming a key asset and source of competitive advantage.* No longer can organisations account for intellectual capital in a "goodwill" category. In the majority of the larger industrial companies in the United States, intangible assets are worth double the tangible assets; in service and high-tech companies this rate increases to 5 to 15 times over. Organisations must increase the rate of knowledge transfer and knowledge transformation, that is transforming knowledge into forms which allow the organisation to more effectively profit from it (Ridderstrale and Nordström, 2000).

The new knowledge-based economy is really about three things (Enriquez, 2001):

1. *Expansion of individual opportunity* — After decades of thinking that "Business" was synonymous with "the corporation" and that workers were anonymous pieces of a giant machine, now the unit of analysis for creating value, making change and producing results is the individual worker. Or to put it in an extreme way, "Karl Marx was right," as his view was that the workers should own the major assets of society, the critical means of production. They do now, as in a modern organisation 70 to 80 percent of what people do is done by way of their intellects (Ridderstrale and Nordström, 2000).

2. *Disruptive energy of ceaseless innovation* — The era of stable, predictable competition is over; the only way to stay in business nowadays is to be open to new ideas, new practices and new opportunities.

3. *Transformative power of information technology and communications* — These technologies remain a powerful force that changes the environment in which organisations operate.

As enterprises worldwide are awakening to the opportunities of the digital economy, there is a growing realisation that the transition has barely started and that a vast number of challenges remain to be addressed before potential benefits

> *Exhibit 1: Impact of a leader's behavior and style on the performance of the organisation*: The leadership style applied to a specific work situation or job creates the climate in which people work. The climate has a direct impact on bottom-line performance, affecting growth, sales, productivity, efficiency and customer service. Climate counts for up to 25% of the variances in performance. *Source: Hay Group*

materialise to the fullest (European Commission, 2000), and giving European businesses a competitive edge.

The strategic emphasis shifts from the efficient management of mass markets and tangible assets, to innovation and the effective utilisation of knowledge and human capital resources. As a result of this, organizations and their leaders must also change (Picken and Dess, 2000). The challenges of today and tomorrow demand new ways of leading organisations, building collaborations and creating communities. In the new world of business defined by accelerating change and unforgiving competition, new models of how to organise and compete are essential.

A NEW ORGANISATION

The traditional organisation of work, based on the ideas of mass industrial production, has been questioned more and more, leading to the implementation of team work, just-in-time systems, quality circles and others, as an attempt to improve productivity. In parallel, a fundamental change in the organisation of work is taking place, a shift from fixed systems of production to a flexible, open-ended process of organisational development. This new concept of a process of continuous change is sometimes described as "the flexible firm" and the workplace a high trust and high-skill workplace. There is no one model, but an infinite variety of models, which are constantly being adapted to the circumstances of the individual firm and its workers. New innovative business models require a shift from a functionally based way of doing things to one that is based on agility, flexibility and responsiveness. It is not enough to simply apply the Information Society Technologies to the rigid structures and systems of the "old" economy; an adaptation of management of relationships, processes and transactions throughout the whole organisation is needed (Ginige et al., 2001).

Organisations used to be perceived as giant pieces of engineering, with largely unchangeable human parts. Their structures and their systems were described in inputs and outputs, the control devices, and their management as if the whole was one large factory. Today the language is not that of engineering but of politics, with talk of cultures and networks, of terms and coalitions, of influence of power rather than control, of leadership not management (Handy, 1989).

When large business first emerged throughout the industrial world around 1870, they did not emerge out of the small businesses of 1850 — it emerged independently. The only model available, the most successful organisation of the 19th century, was the Prussian Army, which had just been reorganised and had learned from the inability of the Americans in the Civil War to organise, transport and communicate with masses of people. It was the first modern organisation. It defeated the Austrians in 1866, who had a much larger and better-armed army, and then, four years later, defeated the French, who were even better armed. The Prussians succeeded because they had created an organisation. They were the first ones to use modern technology effectively, which in those days meant railroad and telegraph. Businesses copied the command and control structure of the Prussian army, in which rank equalled authority. We are now evolving towards structures in which rank means responsibility but not authority and in which the job is not to command but to persuade.

ORGANISATIONAL CHANGE

The new network technologies reverse the traditional relationship "the organisation determines the task" into: "The nature of the task and the needs of those involved can now determine the organisational form adopted." It is not a question of technology or power, but of relationships. In organisations integrated by networks, authority does not work anymore as a base for labour relations. A revolution is taking place in the way that work is organised within companies. New organisation structures, corporate cultures, working methods, training programmes and motivation and reward systems are being introduced in companies. The new organisational structures are focused on process-based and market-oriented organisations, team working and flatter decentralised structures with more empowerment and devolved responsibility.

New corporate cultures include greater trust, more participation, greater personal autonomy, better alignment of employee and business objectives, increased consultation, and greater focus on the customer and quality. These cultures are characterised in most companies by:

1. *A strong people orientation* emphasising greater trust, increased participation by staff at all levels, and greater autonomy and accountability. Communication and consultation processes are used to stimulate the creativity of all the components of the organisation and to focus on the development of the individual. Companies have realised that their stron-

gest asset is their human capital, and this is also demonstrated by the training and career development programmes that have become an integral part of human resource management.

2. *Greater focus on customer, service and quality*: The emergence of Customer Relationship Management is an example of how companies realise that the customer is their "raison d´être."

New organisational structures characterised in most companies by the implementation of the following actions:

1. *Market-oriented or process-orientated business units or divisions*: Moving to business units that focus on different parts of the market on critical processes, improving in this way its customer focus, or to put in a bold way: "Hierarchy is an organization with its face toward the CEO and its ass toward the customer" (Ridderstrale and Nordstrom, 2000).

2. *Semi-autonomous work teams*, with high accountability and independence.

3. *Reduction in the number of functions*, emphasising team work and structures more than individual recognition.

4. *Reduction in management layers*, as hierarchical structures have been removed by flatter and more horizontal ones, creating new roles for management.

New, more flexible and less hierarchical working methods include more flexible working time, working patterns, job groups and job content, multi-skilling, greater use of part-time workers and new management models based on coaching and supporting. The most common forms of implementation of these new methods are:

Figure 2: Modes of work

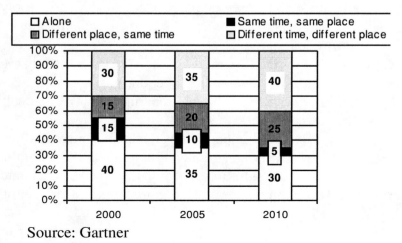

Source: Gartner

1. *More flexible working hours*: New annual work contracts and new shift patterns that permit adaptation to seasonal flows and irregular demand fluctuations, while maintaining competitiveness,

2. *Multi-skilling and job rotation*: Traditional boundaries between functions and job categories have disappeared and the people in the organisation are encouraged to widen their skills (and acquire new ones) and work in a more flexible way (often in combination with the set-up of semi-autonomous teams).

New performance measurement techniques are shared through the company and designed to focus both employees and managers on long-term drivers of competitive success as well as traditional financial results. The above changes have been accompanied by new ways of measuring performance, among which the most common ones are:

1. *The use of financial and non-financial performance measures*: Companies have realised that performance is not only based one their financial success, but also on non-financial measures such as customer satisfaction, organisational learning and employee satisfaction.

2. *Objectives for teams and individuals*: Connected with the new organisational structures, objectives are set for teams and for individuals, making them an integral part of the realisation of the objectives of the company as a whole.

3. *More open information systems*: More open and transparent communication and information flows can be found throughout the organisation, enabling teams and individuals to make the right decisions based on the relation of these decisions to their overall performance. At the same time they enable management to obtain more accurate information about the organisation and what is living among their employees (an important issue for human capital management).

4. *Use of new information sources*: The fact that different items are being measured (e.g., for performance) has consequences for the way they are measured; advanced performance measurement systems, such as market research, benchmarking and direct customer response complement the internal sources.

5. *Changes in individual appraisals*: As performance measures and structures change, individual appraisals changes also; staff is now assessed by means of specific performance targets (linked to the objectives set) and horizontal assessments by colleagues, with the objective of tracing individual career development plans. These changes in turn have led to the implementation of new reward systems, such as a greater use of profit sharing, bonuses and other types of sharing mechanisms, relating part of the rewards to performance.

These changes in the working environment create a need for a great cultural revolution inside an organisation. Changes to roles, jobs, business processes and the collective sharing of information must be addressed and any difficulties overcome. The organisation as a whole needs to create a new cultural framework that is strong enough to replace hierarchy.

This framework will depend on the strength of social and knowledge relationships that are much more fluid and much less prescribed than in a traditional command-and-control environment. Three parties must coordinate their roles. *Workers/employees*, who fulfill objectives or deliver tangible services or output, apply their unique blend of knowledge, expertise, education, intuition and skills to unique situations and deliver solutions in a unique fashion. *Leaders* provide purpose, direction and behavioural role models. They share ideas with, walk among and listen to members of the enterprise, customizing the message and sensing employees' understanding of enterprise direction. *Managers* perform a middleman role, reinterpreting the enterprise vision and mission in a way that makes sense and resonates with employees. They guide performance and offer suggestions for corrective action. Managers who are accustomed to directing rather than guiding people's actions will be uncomfortable in a setting that is essentially improvisatorial.

As management faces greater and greater levels of volatility and uncertainty, it will instinctively try to implement yet more control. The only way to deal with this new business environment will be to relinquish complete control by: understanding

Figure 3: Three coordinated roles

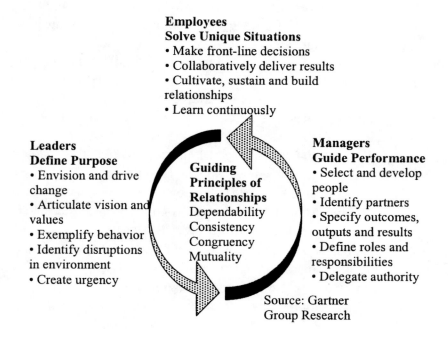

Employees
Solve Unique Situations
• Make front-line decisions
• Collaboratively deliver results
• Cultivate, sustain and build relationships
• Learn continuously

Leaders
Define Purpose
• Envision and drive change
• Articulate vision and values
• Exemplify behavior
• Identify disruptions in environment
• Create urgency

Guiding Principles of Relationships
Dependability
Consistency
Congruency
Mutuality

Managers
Guide Performance
• Select and develop people
• Identify partners
• Specify outcomes, outputs and results
• Define roles and responsibilities
• Delegate authority

Source: Gartner Group Research

the nature of chaos and complexity; accepting complexity but not adding to it; measuring the immeasurable; trust, tolerance and cooperation; and looking outwards.

For successful leadership in this new working environment, managers must adopt new approaches in four key areas: managing information, managing people, managing teams and managing facilities, but the most important issue is to manage themselves.

Leaders operate in four dimensions: vision, reality, ethics and courage. The power of strategic vision lies in how it is used, an effective strategic vision is clear, compelling and communicated in a way that motivates and inspires. The visionary leader thinks big, thinks of new things ahead….reality is the opposite of vision, the leader as a realist faces reality as it is, not as he wants it to be. A survey conducted by CIMA as part of Global Business Management Week 2000, among business leaders from Asia, the United States, the Middle East, the UK, France and Germany, showed leadership as the most important skills for business leaders of the future. Visionary leaders combine "softer skills" such as vision and communication with more technical capabilities and know how (Chartered Institute of Management Accountants, 2001). In formulating a strategic vision, leaders should take input from employees and their concerns should be addressed in such a way that the strategy becomes a *shared vision* or *shared ambition* (Ghoshal and Bartlett, 1997). The ethics dimension refers to basic human values and represents a higher level of development; courage is the realm of will, it involves both the ability to make a stand and the internalisation of personal responsibility and accountability. The challenge for a leader is to develop all dimensions at the same time, and fulfill their full potential instead of limiting themselves.

The task of management will to a lesser degree become managing and controlling, and to an increasing degree become inspiring and motivating: it is spiritual management. Real leaders communicate, then communicate the same thing again, and again and again. Communicating a vision not only involves repetition and a carefully distilled message, it demands the ability to tell a story … metaphors and language are incredibly powerful for transferring a message.

LEADERSHIP IN THE NEW ECONOMY

There are three historic sources of authority and a brand new one coming out of the Information Age: charisma and tradition led the nomadic age cultures, force ruled in the agricultural age, rule of law dominated the industrial age and shared purpose of the new authority in the information age. Napoleon Bonaparte believed that a leader was "a dealer in hope;" according to leadership guru, Warren Bennis, "managers do things right," while "leaders do the right thing;" and Harold Geneen, Chief Executive of ITT during the sixties and seventies noted how "leadership is practised not so much in words as in attitude and in actions." Former UK Prime Minister Margaret Thatcher once said that a leader was "someone who knows what they want to achieve and can communicate that." The question arises if the old ideas and definitions of leadership, as it fitted into the 20th century, still work in today's new business environment.

Leadership is about making things happen and getting things done. Leaders need to understand and master traditional leadership skills, understand and be able to use the information and communication technologies, and understand and be able to work effectively in a digital environment. In the new business patterns, emerging from the knowledge economy, there seems to be enough evidence to suggest that strong leaders will become even more indispensable. The new world of business demands a new way of working, one that is primarily characterised by its responsiveness to change.

Nearly everyday we are reminded that the future core competence of companies will be in their ability to continuously and creatively destroy and remake themselves in order to meet new demands. Real change leaders have a sustained commitment to change and drum up courage in those around them, to challenge the status quo and to gain a commitment to a better way of doing things. They see change as pebbles dropped in a pond, creating expanding waves of energy that spread around to impact people at all levels; the real change leader is the pebble that makes these waves (Katzenbach, 1996).

This new way of working is also characterised by the importance it gives to recruiting the right people. The shift to knowledge-intensive economy means that individuals are much more expensive to replace. Skilled staff can move jobs relatively easily, which in turn means they require more than financial rewards to

Figure 4: Hierarchy of needs

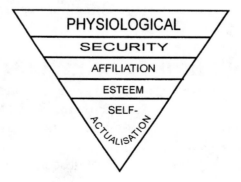

keep them motivated. They need to feel a sense of value, fulfilment and — above all — belonging if they are to stay. It looks almost as if Maslow´s Hierarchy of Needs has been turned upside down (Figure 4).

But it is not only about the people in the organisation; leaders themselves will have to acquire new skills in order to steer the business of tomorrow. They will have to lead at a distance, so to speak, as outsourcing and home working become more common. They will need to learn to 'lead out' teams of distant workers over whom they might not have any direct supervisory power. In addition, they will have to act a lot faster if they are to keep up with the pace of change.

Some believe that not much has changed from the Old Economy. A study among more than 1,300 U.S. executives shows that according to them, the management skills and personal attributes necessary for successful leadership, although acknowledging the impact of new technologies, are solidly grounded in traditional skills and qualities. The managerial skills necessary for success in the digital or knowledge economy, according to this study, are the ability to develop and implement business strategy (mentioned by 76%), operational management skills (59%) and understanding emerging technologies (53%). The personal attributes that are still relevant today are, among others, communication skills,

---

Exhibit 2: Leadership attributes according to Federal Express

Charisma: Instills faith, respect and trust; has a special gift of seeing what others need to consider. Conveys a strong sense of mission.

Individual consideration: Coaches, advises and teaches people who need it. Actively listens and gives indications of listening. Gives newcomers a lot of help.

Intellectual stimulation: Gets others to use reasoning and evidence, rather than unsupported opinion. Enables others to think about old problems in new ways. Communicates in a way that forces others to rethink ideas that they had never questioned before.

Courage: Willing to stand up for ideas even if they are unpopular. Does not give in to pressure or to others' opinions in order to avoid confrontation. Will do what's right for the company and for employees even if it causes personal hardship.

Dependability: Follows through and keeps commitments. Takes responsibility for actions and accepts responsibility for mistakes. Works well independently of the boss.

Flexibility: Functions effectively in changing environments. When a lot of issues hit at once, handles more than one problem at a time. Changes course when the situation warrants it. Reaches sound and objective evaluations of alternative courses of action through logic, analysis and comparison. Puts facts together rationally and realistically. Uses past experience and information to bring perspective to present decisions.

Integrity: Does what is morally and ethically right. Does not abuse management privileges. Is a consistent role model.

Judgment: Reaches sound and objective evaluations of alternative courses of action through logic, analysis and comparison. Puts facts together rationally and realistically. Uses past experience and information to bring perspective to present decision.

Respect for others: Honours and does not belittle the opinions or work of other people, regardless of their status or position.

integrity, ability to coach and mentor, and creativity (Kearney, 2000). The American company Federal Express thinks that the traditional leadership skills are still valid in today's world and has identified nine personal attributes shared by the best leaders, that are used to rate aspiring leaders on whether they possess these attributes (see Exhibit 2).

But Digital leadership demands more than the application of the skills of the Old Economy; it requires new ones that enable speed, flexibility, risk-taking, an obsession with customers and new levels of communication inside the organization are needed.

Citrin and Neff's six augmented qualities of leadership in the Knowledge-based Digital Economy are as follows (Citrin and Neff, 2000):

1. *Obsessing about the customer*: No business can succeed without customers. The Knowledge-based Digital Economy inverts the traditional relationship between the company and the customer, dramatically lowering customer's costs in switching suppliers; therefore customer obsession is a critical leadership characteristic in today's world.

2. *Building a flat, cross-functional organisation*: As mentioned before the command and control style of management was the rule in the Industrial Economy, a style that has now given way to greater organisational flexibility. As the Chairman of General Electric, Jack Welch, once said, "The key to organisational success going forward will be to have the right person solving the most important business problems, no matter where they are located in the company hierarchically, organisationally or geographically."

3. *Managing via business model*: The difference between developing and maintaining a winning strategy, an essential element of leadership, in the Old Economy and the Knowledge one, is the strategy development process.

4. *Evangelising and generating positive buzz*: Organisations have always had to communicate effectively with their employees, but in the Knowledge Economy, effective communication has to go a step further; an organisation needs to be able to "evangelise" the company and to generate public relations buzz, as a first step to success. As mentioned before, management becomes increasingly inspiring and motivating, and the key for being effective is the ability to tell a story. Stories can transfer knowledge, embody tacit knowledge and nurture community in ways other forms of communication cannot, as it involves the creating of meaning for the members of the organisation.

5. *Encouraging risk-taking for real*: The innermost mechanism of human progress is called failure; therefore leaders need to make risk-taking a reality, not just talk, making it less risky to take risks.

6. *Rolling up the sleeves and working hard*: Of course all the above mentioned won't make a difference if it is not combined with hard work and commitment.

Some of the issues mentioned by Citrin and Neff (2000) may have been around for some years, for example the importance of the customer or building a flat organisation, but have gained an enormous importance in the new environment businesses operate in, as the speed of change is urging them even more to focus on the demands from their clients, and to respond to these needs in the shortest time possible by having a flexible organisation. Two aspects, though, are more specific for the new knowledge-based economy: managing via business model and encouraging risk-taking for real.

Managing via Business Model

The knowledge-based economy prioritises intangible assets, such as "organisational capital," which involves a process of knowledge management and knowledge creation, and its deployment for organisational change and continuous adaptation of business models. A real business model is the organization's core logic for creating value, or in other words: the set of value propositions an organization offers to its stakeholders, along with the operating processes to deliver on these, arranged as a coherent system, that both relies on and builds assets, capabilities and relationships, in order to create value.

It is business model innovation that is the key determinant of success, creating a drive towards innovation and the creation of organisational structures that enable to take advantage of the opportunities of the new economy (Bounfour and Damaskopoulos, 2001). These new business models need to move beyond cost control to address the issue of how to create value (Tapscott, 1997).

Relationships in the knowledge-based economy are much more fluid and multidimensional, and as a result, leaders, rather than managing via a detailed annual strategic planning process, manage via a strategic framework, or business model, using scenarios to test assumptions on future developments. The nature of creating strategic advantage today has changed. More than a decade ago innovation started with a strategy, which then moved on to a description of the process and the implementation of information technologies (IT), the use of information technologies super-imposed on rigid structures and systems. The next development focused on change leadership, the starting point being strategy. In today's complex and fast-changing environment, organisations need to be adaptive, and the innovation process can start in any part of the organisation.

The implementation approach of new business models should integrate elements of strategy, process, organisation, partner relationships and technology, as these cannot be separated. The success depends on an integrated approach that ensures technology capabilities are fully understood and utilised, and that the company can take strategic advantage of them (Figure 5). Successful organisations will be those that excel in building networked business models, realise sustainable

Figure 5: Changes in the innovation process

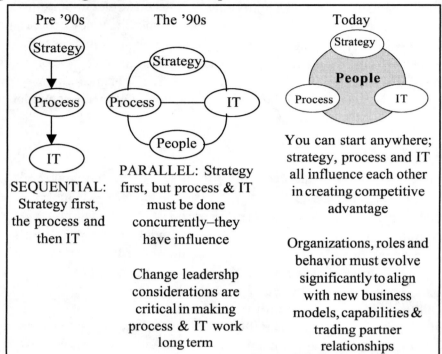

Pre '90s	The '90s	Today

SEQUENTIAL: Strategy first, the process and then IT

PARALLEL: Strategy first, but process & IT must be done concurrently–they have influence

Change leadershp considerations are critical in making process & IT work long term

You can start anywhere; strategy, process and IT all influence each other in creating competitive advantage

Organizations, roles and behavior must evolve significantly to align with new business models, capabilities & trading partner relationships

economies of scale (both on an individual as on a networked basis), focus on core competency, and forge trusted relationships between partners and customers.

Leadership is concerned with both the choice of an appropriate model and with making the transition. There are five levels at which high-quality leadership is relevant (Tate, 2000):

1. *Choosing the right business model for the company's future*: There is no right paradigm; a particular form of business model may or may not be appropriate for a company, given its heritage and its generic framework.

2. *Understanding the company's present business model*: That is understanding the generic framework—of commitments, expectations, values and norms—that arise from its location in a given society at a given time.

3. *Leading the company on a journey from the present to the future*, as leading the transition must take account of where the company is coming from as well as where it is going to.

4. *Running the company successfully within the framework of the chosen business model.*

5. *Continually monitoring the model in a dynamic competitive, technological and social environment.*

Exhibit 3: The Post-It Product

Dr. Spencer Silver was working in the 3M research laboratories in 1970 trying to find a strong adhesive. He developed a new adhesive, but it was even weaker than what 3M already manufactured. It stuck to objects, but could easily be lifted off, it was super weak instead of super strong. But, what to do with it? For the next five years, Silver gave seminars and buttonholed individual 3Mers. Then four years later, another 3M scientist named Arthur Fry was singing in the church's choir. He used markers to keep his place in the hymnal, but they kept falling out of the book. Remembering Silver's adhesive, Fry used some to coat his markers. Success! With the weak adhesive, the markers stayed in place, yet lifted off without damaging the pages. 3M began distributing Post-It Notes nationwide in 1980–ten years after Silver developed the super weak adhesive.

Encouraging Risk-Taking for Real

In the Digital Economy where barriers to entry are low and the rewards for success huge, continuous innovation and new approaches are needed to gain, or maintain, a competitive advantage. An innovative environment must have an exceptionally high tolerance for mistakes, as innovation requires experimentation. Leaders of the future need to have an experimental mind set. Some decisions will work, some won't. Some projects will pay off, some won't. In other words, facing reality means facing up to mistakes and failures, nobody gets it right the first time. Winston Churchill said: "success is the ability to go from failure to failure without losing your enthusiasm." Minneapolis-based 3M's culture is filled with storytelling on how risk taking and failure led to success; probably the most famous story is the Post-It product.

Different industries and different business circumstances demand different levels of risk-taking, but still some suggestions can be made for encouraging risk-taking:

1. *Actions speak louder than words*: Senior management must be the first to model risk-taking behaviour by sharing their mistakes and what they have learned.

2. *Develop skills*: Some individuals fear risk-taking because they lack the skills or experience to make sound decisions; intensive training and job coaching are essential in this case.

3. *Recognise/reward risk-taking*: Too often the only recognition for risk-taking is punishment when things have gone wrong. The stigma attached to failed risk-taking must be eliminated, and those who take risks and succeed should be recognised and rewarded.

In between all the turbulence, three common tendencies in leadership can be seen:

1. *From strategist to visionary*: People do not establish strong emotional bonds with strategies; they do not compromise them as they respond to the what-question and not to the why-question, and to know the why is much more important… Vision is "a shared image on what we want organisations to be or to become" (Albrecht, 1994); creating a vision means being brutally honest about yourself and what you want to be, as well as what the organisation is and what it wants to be. In other words, having a personal vision convincing enough for others to share, to express what others could not express. A good example is Walt Disney's vision: "Make people happy."

2. *From commander to storyteller*: Strategic leaders can control and command, while visionary leaders stimulate and "seduce." Gardner (1996) states "the key to leadership is the effective communication of a story," and these are accepted more easily if they are of the "Star Wars" type, simple histories that contrast the good and the bad. Not only the form is important, but also the content, therefore leaders need to dominate rhetoric, including the use of metaphors and rhythm.

3. *From system architect to change agent*: The leaders prepared for the new economy force people to think and prepare for an uncertain future; they concentrate less on managing and controlling employee behaviour and more on the development of their abilities for initiative and the support of their ideas; the leader opens up the way for the others.

CONCLUSIONS

The new economy is about reinventing how business is conducted, in every single job and in every single organisation; there is a revolution going on. None of the historical references on understanding the world, the marketplace and work apply anymore: "Speed is the holy grail"(Miller, 2001). There will be more confusion in the business world in the next decade than in any decade in history. And the current pace of change will only accelerate. It is only going to get weirder, tougher and more turbulent, which means that leadership will be more important than ever and more confusing. Leadership will emerge as the most important element of business—the attribute that is highest in demand and shortest in supply.

In the organizations that have adapted successfully to the new knowledge-based economy, everyone is a leader, responsible for creating an environment for collective gain and success. The main characteristic of a leader will be to create other leaders within the organization, and thus building management strength to achieve change throughout the organization, imperative in a world where organizations no longer have the time for day-to-day decisions to go up and down the hierarchy. Choosing the right business model is essential, and its implementation should integrate elements of strategy, process, organization, partner relationships and technology. Those organizations that excel in building networked business models realize economies of scale, focus on core competency, and forge trusted relationships between partners and customers, will be successful. An exceptionally high tolerance for mistakes in these organizations creates an innovative environment in which leaders have to have an experimental mindset.

It is about influencing the organization to face its problems and to live up to its opportunities; therefore successful leaders will be the ones that are able to mobilise and motivate their people to tackle tough challenges. A leader needs to create the vision and put the mechanisms into place, so that the people in the organisation can produce the results. They have to have a personal vision convincing enough for others to share, they stimulate and "seduce," using stories as effective communication means, not only focusing on content but also on rhetoric. Leadership in the new environment should not be seen as a "position" based on power and authority, but as a "function" based on principles and personal abilities, as well as on the capacity to involve others to reach consensus on critical decisions and on problem solution, developing the abilities for initiative of their employees. Leaders must consciously build trust linkages among employees at all levels, and with partners. Only this level of trust and the resulting productivity will offer the company a clear competitive advantage. Leaders trust trust: every word, every action, every initiative they realise must build trust: According to Carly Fiorina, Hewlett Packard, "You have to be conscious about your behaviour, because everyone else is."

Leadership is an improvisational art; there is no one-size-fits-all approach. The game keeps changing, competition keeps changing, therefore leaders need to change and to keep reinventing themselves; they have to be ready to adapt, to move, to forget yesterday, to forgive, and to structure new roles and new relationships for themselves, their teams and their ever-shifting portfolio of partners. And most important they need to have the capacity to employ more than one style of leadership. According to Richard Leider (2000), founding partner of the Inventure Group, leaders need to realise that "people don't leave companies—they leave leaders." Moreover, all important business gurus agree, failure is a necessary experience to become a leader; you have to learn not to be careful.

But some things will never change: successful leadership still remains the result of hard work and commitment, and just as in this century and the last, the same will most probably be true in the next.

REFERENCES

Albrecht, K.(1994). *The Northbound Train: Finding the Purpose, Setting the Direction, Shaping the Destiny of your Organisation.* New York: Amacom.

European Commission. (2000). *New Methods of Work and Electronic Commerce.* February.

Auckland, M. (2000). *Achieving European Competitiveness in a Knowledge Based Economy: E-Business, Key Issues, Applications, Technologies.* Amsterdam: IOS Press.

Bounfour, A. and Damaskopoulos, P. (2001). Managing organizational capital in the new economy: Knowledge management and organizational design. In Stanford-Smith, B. and Chiozza, E. (Eds.), *E-Work and E-Commerce, Novel Solutions and Practices for a Global Networked Economy.* Amsterdam: IOS Press.

Boyett, J. and Boyett, J. (1998). *The Guru Guide.* New York: John Wiley & Sons.

Bullón, P. (2001). e-Organización: Internet marca pautas a las empresas tradicionales. Lideres.com, September.

Chartered Institute of Management Accountants. (2001). Leadership skills, an overview. *Technical Briefing Developing and Promoting Strategy,* May.

Citrin, J. M. and Neff, T. J. (2000). Digital leadership. *Managing, 18,* 42-50.

Collins, J. (2001). Good to great. *Fast Company,* (October) 90-104.

Denham, M., Dickhout, R. and Blackwell, N. (1995). Shaping a strategy for change. Available at: www.mckinseyquarterly.com. *McKinsey Quarterly, 2,* 181-183.

Dichter, S., Gagnon, C. and Alexander, A. (1993). Leading organizational transformations. Available at: www.mckinseyquarterly.com. *The McKinsey Quarterly, 1,* 89-106.

Drucker, P. (1996). The organization of tomorrow and the executive of tomorrow. Available at: www.mckinseyquarterly.com. *Leader to Leader Magazine,* 1.

Deloitte Consulting and Deloitte and Touche. (2000). e-leadership? Beyond the hype: Perceptions vs. reality about e-leadership. *e-view Deloitte Research.*

Enriquez, J. (2001). There is a battle underway to define the past, present and future of the new economy. *Fast Company, 50,* (September) 102-104.

European Commission. (2000). Challenges for enterprise policy in the knowledge-driven economy. *COM(2000) 256 final/2, 2000/0107 (CNS).*

Future Unit. (1999). *Work in the Knowledge Driven Economy.* Department of Trade and Industry, United Kingdom.

Gardner, H. (1996). *Leading Minds, An Anatomy of Leadership.* New York: Basic Books

Ghoshal, S. and Bartlett, C. A. (1997). *The Individualised Corporation.* Michigan: Harper Business.

Ginige, A., Murugesan, S. and Kazanis, P. (2001). A road map for successfully transforming SMEs into e-businesses. *Cutter IT Journal*, 5 (May), 39-51.

Häcki, R. and Lighton J. (2001). The future of the networked organization. Available at: www.mckinseyquarterly.com. *McKinsey Quarterly*, *3*, 26-39.

Handy, C. (1989). *The Age of Unreason*. New York: Business Books.

Hay Group/*Fortune Magazine*. (1999). What makes great leaders: Rethinking the route to effective leadership. *Hay Executive Briefing*.

Hope, J. and Hope, T. (1997). *Competing in the Third Wave*. Boston, MA: Harvard Business School Press.

Jackson, P. and Harris, L. (2000). E-Business and organisational change. In Stanford-Smith, B. and Kidd, P. (Eds.), *E-Business: Key Issues, Applications, Technologies, 76-82*. Amsterdam: IOS Press

James, K.(2000). *Leadership and Management Excellence; Corporate Development Strategies*, Available at: www.managementandleadershipcouncil.org. Council for Excellence in Management and Leadership.

Katzenbach, J. (1996) Real change. *McKinsey Quarterly*, *1*, 148-163. Available at: www.mckinseyquarterly.com.

Kearney, A. T. (2000). *Digital Economy May Change, but Attributes of Leaders Don't*. November, Survey.

Kelly, K. (1998). *New Rules for the New Economy: 10 Ways the Network Economy is Changing Everything*. London: Fourth State Limited

Kerr, J. and Klasson, K. (Eds.). (1999). New economy primer. *New Economy White Papers*. Available at: www.ctp.com. Cambridge Technology Partners

Klasson, K. (1999). Business models for the new economy. *New Economy White Papers*. Available at: www.ctp.com Cambridge Technology Partners.

Kostner, J. (1996). *Virtual Leadership, Secrets from the Round Table for the Multi-Site Manager*. New York: Warner Books.

Leeuwen, M. van (2001). The impact of the digital economy on leadership in organizations. In Stanford-Smith, B. and Chiozza, E (Eds.), *E-Work and E-Commerce, Novel Solutions and Practices for a Global Networked Economy*. Amsterdam: IOS Press

Locke, C., Levine, R., Searls, D. and Weinberger, D. (2000). *The Cluetrain Manifesto: The End of Business as Usual*. Perseus Printing.

Loewe, P. and Bonchek, S. (1999). The retail revolution. *Management Review*, April.

Mahoney, J., Hayward, S., and Mingay, S. (2000). The new synergy: People, systems, settings. *Gartner Symposium ITxpo 2000, Conference Proceedings [CD-ROM] Cannes*, France, November 6-9.

McFarland, L. J., Senn, L. E. and Childress, J. R. (1994). *21ˢᵗ Century*

Leadership: Dialogues with 100 Top Leaders. New York: The Leadership Press, McGraw Hill.

Means, G. and Schneider, D. (2000). *Metacapitalism: The E-Business Revolution and the Design of 21st Century Companies and Markets*. New York: John Wiley & Sons.

Miller, S. (2001). Smart steps. In Canabou, C. and Overholt, A. (Eds.), *Fast Company Magazine, 44* (March), 91-93.

Mintzberg, H. (1991). *Mintzberg over Management*. Uitgeverij Contact.

Neilson, G., Pasternack, B. and Viscio, A. (2000). Up the (e)-organization: A seven-dimensional model for the centerless enterprise. *Managing, 18*, 52-61.

Peters, T. (1997). *The Circle of Innovation: You Can't Shrink Your Way into Greatness*. New York: Alfred A. Knopf, Inc.

Peters, T. (2001). Rule #3: Leadership is confusing as hell. *Fast Company, 44* (March), 124.

Picken, J. C. and Dess, G. G.(2000). Changing roles: Leadership in the 21st century. *Organizational Dynamics, 28* (January),102-109.

Ridderstrale, J. and Nordström, K. (2000). *Funky Business: Talent Makes Capital Dance*. Bookhouse Publishing.

Tapscott, D. (1997). Strategy in the new economy. *Strategy and Leadership*, (November/December).

Tate, W. V. (2000). *Futures Project, Implications of Future Studies for Business, Organisation, Management and Leadership*. Council for Excellence in Management and Leadership.

Thomas, R. and Bennis, W. (2001). Speed leading: Qualities of successful leaders in the digital age. Accenture Institute for Strategic Change, *Research Note 2*, May.

Winter, P. De (2001). MT interview met Mickey Huibregtsen. *Management Team*, 13, (August).

Chapter XV

The Role of Teams in Business Process Change

Jyoti Choudrie
Brunel University, UK

ABSTRACT

The concept of reengineering teams is not new to business process change practice and research. However, frameworks that describe the organisational changes that have to be undertaken in order to establish reengineering teams, in particular, are novel. By having such a framework, practitioners and academics alike can determine beforehand what to expect before the actual team is formed. This in turn allows organisations to prevent disastrous consequences, something that can occur if information is not available. Additionally, the chapter describes the characteristics that surround the planning and design of reengineering teams. This can be used as a suggestion for organisations in order to decide if they do have the appropriate numbers of individuals within a team. From these explanations it can then be stated that this chapter can serve as a directive that organisations undertaking business process change in the future can use as guiding information.

INTRODUCTION

The normative literature on business process change (BPC) emphasises the role of reengineering teams; however, when investigated in detail it can be found that there is minimal literature about their formation, tasks and so forth. In particular, when BPC was being introduced, Davenport (1993) and Hammer and Champy (1993) stressed that the implementation of BPC is better if a reengineering team is established to undertake the management change approach. However, after examining to this issue, there was little detailed information about the manner that they could be formed, and what are their constituents. BPC is defined as the *"radical rethinking of business processes to achieve dramatic improvements in critical contemporary measures of performance such as cost, quality and speed"* (Hammer and Champy, 1993).

BPC is a management change approach that still holds the interest of both academics and practical researchers (Willcocks and Currie, 1996). This can be confirmed by determining the number of articles still being published about the topic both within academic journals and projects on BPR being funded by various research bodies and reports.

This research has attempted to fill some of the gap regarding reengineering teams by providing a framework that illustrates and describes the organisational changes that can be expected to occur when a reengineering team that has undertaken BPC is formed. This framework is based upon an original one that examined the impact of organisational change by the adoption of CASE tools. It has to be remembered that this framework applies to the reengineering teams when the project is at the planning and analysis stages. The teams at these stages do not require the assistance of information systems (IS) to a large extent, hence the minimal emphasis upon IS.

To describe and understand the research discussed in this chapter, the following section first begins by describing some of the theory surrounding organisational change. This was important to identify how the research can proceed. This is followed by a description of the research methodology, which allowed the capturing of the data. An explanation about the framework is then provided, which is then closely followed by the application of the framework in practice using the case study undertaken for this research. Following this a discussion about the implication and limitations of this research is offered. Finally, the chapter draws conclusions from the discussion afforded in the chapter.

BACKGROUND OF ORGANISATIONAL CHANGE

In this section a background of the normative organisational change literature is provided. This allows the reader to obtain a better perspective of the approach that is of interest to this research. When examining BPC, it has been found that the approach falls within the vicinity of organisational change. There are several forms of change within the organisational change area, but the one being emphasised in this chapter is the change model of Lewin (1947). There have been several methodologies that have been developed in recent years to investigate the process of organisational change, but ultimately their foundations are underpinned by the most famous and established Lewin's (1947) model. With change occurring more often, present-day researchers have begun to find ways to form their own impressions of the changes taking place, thereby extending the theoretical foundations of Lewin's (1947) model (Orlikowski and Hoffman, 1997; Armenakis et al., 1999).

Lewin (1947) contends in the model that that there are two sets of opposing forces that exist within a social system — the driving forces that promote change and the resisting ones that want to maintain the status quo. Lewin's model has three stages that an organisation undergoes to obtain organisational change: *unfreezing, changing and refreezing* (Jones, 1968). *Unfreezing* is the stage at which there is a recognised need for change, and actions are taken to unfreeze the existing attitudes and behaviour. This is viewed to be essential to obtain employee support and reduce the resistance to change. Once the actions have been recognised, the organisation moves toward *changing* to the desired state. After the change has taken place, then the final stage of *refreezing,* whereby a positive reinforcement of desired outcomes to promote the new behaviours and attitudes, occurs (Dawson, 1994). Although this step is viewed to take place, it is seen to last for only a short while before the organisation has to prepare to unfreeze once again, particularly as the environment is rapidly changing and organisations have to change in order to survive or operate in the present market. Having provided the background of the model, the chapter now offers a description of the research methodology used.

RESEARCH METHODOLOGY

The data collected for this research was interpreted using the 'grounded theory' method (Strauss and Corbin, 1990). Since the research is contemporary and little information regarding the area was obtainable, this was the best method to pursue. Grounded theory was most applicable after the data was collated and analysed. The results were coded and it became apparent that they were best suited to a framework similar to that proposed by Orlikowski (1993).

However, it has to be understood that the theory developed in Orlikowski's (1993) case was for adopting and using case tools as organisational change. This research on the other hand is investigating the issues with regards to reengineering teams in obtaining BPC. By doing so, an understanding about the way that reengineering teams, an essential component for the implementation of BPR when obtaining business process change, is achieved. It also describes the changes that occur within the organisation and environment in order to operate and obtain the required results.

One of the initial steps to be undertaken for the development of the framework was to form a research question. In the face of the method being used, the research question formed was: *What are the critical issues that shape the organisational changes associated with the adoption and use of reengineering teams in the context of business process change?*

The analysis of the data was undertaken using a combination of face-to-face and Telephone interviews. The total numbers of interviews undertaken were approximately 90. The interviews were undertaken upon individuals from various levels of the organisational, that is, directors, senior managers and middle-level managers were interviewed. This was to obtain a more unbiased viewpoint and to provide rigour to the data. Additionally, a mixture of the strategy of open- and close-ended questions was applied. To verify that the data was appropriate and applicable to the organisation, a triangulation of methods that mainly consisted of data, methodological and theory was utilised.

EXPLAINING THE FRAMEWORK REGARDING REENGINEERING TEAMS

To understand how the framework regarding reengineering teams works, the following description is offered. Before that an assumption about the organisational process is provided. The organisational process followed is influenced by the structuration theory of Giddens (1984). The theory is based upon the premise that interaction between the human actions and institutional contexts take place over time. Therefore, the two areas — human actions and institutional contexts — are no longer two separate areas of investigation having no impact upon one another. Instead they do have a relationship with one another, but over a length of time. Thus making the assumption that human actions and institutional contexts have a relationship over time, the research then determined how the institutional context could be influenced by the actions of competitors or clients. Having described the theory that developed the framework of Orlikowski (1993), the chapter now describes the details and operations of the framework in terms of this research.

RELATING THEORY TO PRACTICE

In this section the results of the conceptual framework are described in real-life terms. This was achieved by using the data collected from a case study, and it was decided that a public sector organisation that had recently undertaken BPC would be used. This organisation is called People Care[1] and in the following sub-section, the background of the organisation and the changes that it underwent when BPC was introduced are provided.

Institutional Context

Clients

People Care is a public sector organisation—local authority—that is fully funded by the government. This means that it is accountable to various people, but mainly, the members of the public and the government. When identifying the clients, it was apparent that they varied, from members of the public, the government, other local authorities and other public sector organisations, such as fire stations. When deciding upon the services to be provided to the members of public, the organisation has to be considerate of the other government-funded organisations that are dependent upon People Care for their funds. For instance, there are schools within People Care's domain that have to be allocated funds. In this case, People Care receives the funds and has the added responsibility of distributing them in a fair and efficient manner. As such, People Care also provides funds from the government to the organisations that are dependent upon the government.

People Care serves the members of the public in its vicinity by providing various services, including highway maintenance, strategic planning, traffic, social services, housing and education. Presently, the organisation employs thousands of people within its region and beyond to provide the required services and products, and the trend is viewed to continue.

People Change is undertaking business process change in several stages and is currently still in the midst of a business process change. The change is being undertaken within stages; the first stage involved the development and implementation of a call centre.

Competitors

Since People Care is a publicly funded organisation, its competitors are limited to other publicly funded organisations. Overall, it was found that competition occurs from other large local authorities and government-funded organisations. However, it was stressed that since members of the public and their needs were foremost for the organisation, competition did not always enter into the picture. Instead, service and provision of delivery were of utmost importance.

Organisational Context

Corporate Strategies

This was an unusual organisation in that earlier training to undertake the project was not really provided; instead teams were formed by selecting individuals who were experienced and had the existing knowledge and skills that were required to undertake the project. When working for the local authority, individuals are expected to undertake training courses related to their daily jobs.

The teams usually worked within their daily functional areas as it was felt that the individuals should be close to their daily tasks and attend to the duties from the project. During the earlier analysis periods, external consultants were employed to assist the planning, analysis and design team; however, once that task was completed, they were also left out.

Structure and Culture

The authority is a traditional organisation with several hierarchies in its structure and these include the first line managers, senior officers and steering committees. Control of the organisation is undertaken by the central government funding body. There are several locations of the organisation since so many personnel are employed by the organisation.

The culture of People Care is a flexible and innovative one, which recognises and encourages career development and the quality of working life. Individuals are encouraged to undertake further studies. As explained earlier, People Care recognises not only educational benefits, but also family responsibilities. Allowing individuals to work on a flexible hours scheme achieves this. This means that when a certain number of hours of the working week are completed, then the individual has the choice to work over the amount and take the extra hours off from their coming work week schedule.

Career development is usually a rigid path with a graduate beginning at a level of the organisation that allows progression to a good managerial position after several years of employment. Career is usually assessed using appraisal schemes, where the responsibilities of an individual as well as the career development are assessed. This is usually in the form of an interview between the manager and the individual. However, this is in the instance of progressing up a scale on the progression ladder. There are instances when the end of a scale is reached and to progress to the next level, a formal interview by a panel of executives is undertaken.

From these discussions it can be seen that the actions within the institutional context influence the conditions required by management for adopting and using the reengineering teams (arrow 1). The information that is given in the conditions required by management for adopting and using reengineering teams in turn, influences the institutional context (arrow 2) and is illustrated in the following description.

Figure 1: A framework describing the theory about reengineering teams used in the planning and analysis stages

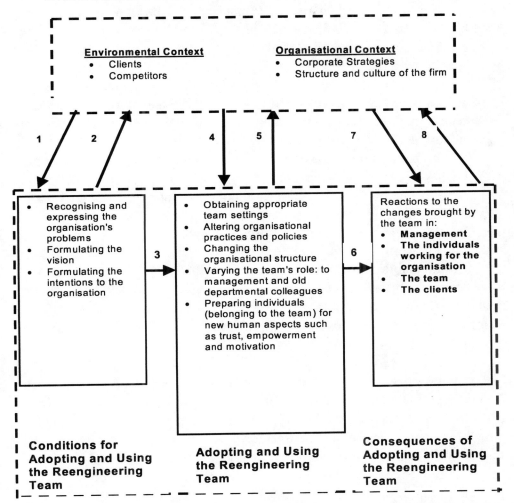

INSTITUTIONAL CONTEXT FOR ADOPTING AND USING TEAMS

Environmental Context
- Clients
- Competitors

Organisational Context
- Corporate Strategies
- Structure and culture of the firm

1   2   4   5   7   8

Conditions	Adopting	Consequences
• Recognising and expressing the organisation's problems • Formulating the vision • Formulating the intentions to the organisation	• Obtaining appropriate team settings • Altering organisational practices and policies • Changing the organisational structure • Varying the team's role: to management and old departmental colleagues • Preparing individuals (belonging to the team) for new human aspects such as trust, empowerment and motivation	Reactions to the changes brought by the team in: • **Management** • **The individuals working for the organisation** • **The team** • **The clients**

3   6

Conditions for Adopting and Using the Reengineering Team

Adopting and Using the Reengineering Team

Consequences of Adopting and Using the Reengineering Team

STRATEGIC CONDUCT IN ADOPTING AND USING THE REENGINEERING TEAM

Conditions Required by Management for Adopting and Using the Teams

The three actions undertaken by management assisted the team with the task at hand in this category. They were crucial for the project as they relayed the expectations of management to the team. If they were not there, the team would not be able to form impressions and views about the problems facing the organisation at present and what was required of it.

Recognising and Expressing the Problems Faced by the Organisation

The government feels that "while many of England's councils are actively tackling the need to review structures and methods, many have become out of touch and irrelevant to the lives of local people" (Management Report). With IT becoming readily available, it was within reach of many organisations and members of the public and was flexible enough to deal with many different situations. This was viewed to be particularly important as everyone could obtain and use the desired IT. The present government is also very interested to develop the potential of IT and the benefits offered by it. Also the government's new initiative on 'best value' and other recent reports that conveyed similar messages made almost all the existing local authorities consider change.

People Care conducted research and found that the residents of the county were not happy with the services being provided. For instance, if an individual required information about schools in the county, various individuals had to be contacted and there was still no assurance that the required information would be obtained. With technology being widely available and being able to provide various different services to individuals, the organisation then considered a change that could be obtainable with the assistance of IT. For this the ideal was viewed to be a call centre which would be a central system allowing calls to be handled by a multi-functional group of people, rather than the present situation where questions were being unanswered since knowledge in the area is limited.

Formulating a Vision

A number of core processes were identified at the early stages of the project. The initial planning, analysis and design team conducted this task with the assistance of external consultancy firms. The initial results of the conducted analysis included an estimate of the costs involved in transforming the processes from their annual budget. Additionally, some support processes such as the people, money and Information Technology underpinning the core processes were identified, but providing an in-depth analysis about them was not an issue considered by the team. A report was compiled that included a description of the analysis as well as the impact of the expected change and presented to the steering committee. The core processes that were identified are described below:

- "Engaging and managing the democratic process,
- Generating information and intelligence about People Care,
- Developing a statement of intent (of vision, direction and priorities across the County),
- Determining what to deliver and method of delivery,
- Monitoring and evaluating delivery."
  (People Care, Draft Report)

A vision that listed the members of the public and the organisation's expectations regarding service not being met, and being below the organisation's 'ideal,' was initially formed. Encompassed within the vision was also the note about how the organisation would meet the challenge with confidence and obtain business benefits both for the organisation and its customers. However, due to the vision, there were other expectations that were formed during the initial stage and these expectations were relayed to the team when the team began its tasks.

Formulating the Intentions of the Organisation to the Team

In order to determine the progress of the team, new strategies, review of the existing ones, progress and strategy meetings were arranged. Fortnightly meetings to provide updates to the whole of the team were held. It was necessary for all the team members to attend. If it was not possible to do so, then prior notice was provided and updates of the work were sent to the team and in exchange, the team leader sent e-mails with the decisions and updates made in the meeting. The meetings were held for approximately an hour and within the project manager's offices. The offices are located within the authority's premises and are usually used for the purposes of holding meetings. As such, they are equipped with flip boards (that were used for purposes such as writing brief points), drawing diagrams, conference tables and chairs. Other meetings were also held to provide the steering committee with an update and obtain their feedback on their undertaken work. When a thorough analysis of the work was required, a day away from the organisation was organised. This was to prevent distractions from their daily jobs and to have a 'change of scenery.'

It can be interpreted that the actions undertaken at this stage are affected by the institutional context, particularly the organisational context one, since the information for the tasks undertaken at this step is obtained from that particular area. Once these three actions are undergone, management's next task is to form the team (arrow 3) and for that certain changes have to occur that are described as follows.

Adopting and Using the Reengineering Teams

The team was formed as a result of well-thought processes and activities, and they are described as follows:

Obtaining the Appropriate Team Settings

The original reengineering team that was responsible for planning, designing and analysing the change consisted of approximately 10 individuals, all retaining positions of high authority within the hierarchy of the organisation and belonging to various departments within the organisation. The team members were individuals whose decisions were carried out rather than waiting for approval from senior managers. The only approval sought was that of the Board. They were also responsible for providing reports of their discovery to a steering committee that consisted of members of the Board, who were elected members of the council. This team was unlike the implementation teams, as this was a self-directed one that was formed for the purposes of determining whether BPC was actually the management change approach that was desirable for the local authority.

A corporate director within the local authority devised the plans for BPC and thereafter, sought approval from members of the Board. After a deliberation period, approval towards the project was given. Once the decision to undertake BPC was made, the next step was to form the implementation teams to undertake the project. The number of implementation teams that were formed varied between 8 to 10. In some instances, the teams were disbanded as soon as a task was completed. The process of forming these teams was a long one, as many individuals had to be selected since it was felt that this was not a job for one individual.

The implementation teams usually consisted of between 10 to 12 individuals. The individuals ranged from graduates, accountants and holders of national vocational qualifications, certification received as a result of attending courses set up to improve the knowledge and experiences of the individuals in the organisation. Rather than having a random selection process, and not providing anyone with the opportunity to express an interest in the occurrences of the organisation, advertisements describing the roles and responsibilities of the newly formed vacancies were placed within the departments. Selection was made based upon the knowledge, skills and attributes of the individuals. When examining the knowledge area, emphasis was placed more upon how familiar to the organisation and to their own departments the individuals were. This was the main criterion utilised. The skills searched for were team development, writing and presentation ones, and the attributes were flexibility, diplomacy and dedication.

From there, the managers were informed of the decision and appropriate measures to assist the individual were taken. For instance, a majority of the team members were middle managers holding responsible jobs that required their full attention. To assist them with their daily tasks, they were provided with assistants or in other instances, secondments were provided.

This was an unusual organisation in that earlier training to undertake the project was not really provided; instead teams were formed and, from the experiences that each individual had and the existing knowledge and skills, were expected to undertake the project. When working for the local authority, individuals are expected to undertake training courses related to their daily jobs.

If individuals felt the need to obtain more knowledge on the project management area, they could have requested to attend a course that involved some of the issues related to project management or other areas that could have an impact upon the project. It was assumed that the members would have many of the team building skills since they were viewed to be experienced in their fields. As a result of this and the team devoting all their attention to project deadlines, an understanding of issues such as conflicts and not having a suitable balance in the team development occurred. This will be demonstrated in the proceeding sections.

The teams usually worked within their daily functional areas as it was felt that the individuals should be close to their daily tasks and attend to the duties from the project.

During the earlier analysis periods, external consultants were employed to assist the planning, analysis and design team; however, once that task was completed, they were also left out.

Altering the Organisational Working Practices and Policies

After forming the team, management had to allow a change in the working practices and policies within the organisation. Prior to working in the team, the individuals had knowledge only about their own departments, thus it was considered to be a rather closed system. Information about other departments, including the workings or operations of other departments, was not known. Being part of the team allowed the members to form a broader perspective of the organisation.

To demonstrate that there was trust in the team and to expedite the decision-making techniques within the organisation, the members were 'empowered' with more decision-making authority. The original planning, analysis and design team formed in 1997 was provided with a lot of power. The power designated to them was to scrutinise departments and their operations, and analysing documents held within the departments. This was a new phenomenon since previously, access was usually restricted to the individuals working within the departments. Therefore, prior to BPC, department heads usually interacted with members of their department, and if interaction with individuals from other departments was required, prior permission had to be sought. As a result of the occurring changes, the ability to move around freely within organisations was allowed. This also meant that the individuals after deliberations among themselves, proposed changes that affected not only their departments, but the others as well. However, not all the proposed changes were accepted and this also proved to be a source of conflict between the steering committee and the team.

The newly found power and responsibilities were meant to allow the team to progress with the work at a much faster rate than if approval from the steering committee at every major point was required. As a result, targets were met and the team members were happy with the newly assigned responsibility. These members were individuals holding responsible positions within the organisation and were particularly selected for this trait. They were the ones who assisted in amending and forming some of the original vision of the whole BPC project. Empowerment was not a gradual process in this instance; instead as soon as the teams were formed, the individuals were informed of the new powers and expected to work well with their newly placed responsibility, which they did. This was determined by the results that were formed later on by the implementation teams.

The implementation teams that were formed later had empowerment instilled gradually, in comparison to the earlier planning and analysis team. When the teams formed, they were informed of their newly assigned responsibilities and expected to undertake their work with this new form of power; and there was a lesser role for the project manager. A particular example described to demonstrate the point was that of the training group. The manager who was responsible for the training to be provided to the users was introduced to the implementation teams at a later stage. To assist the instructor in ensuring that the information being relayed was being received in the correct sense, extra powers such as a different form of thinking that was beneficial for the organisation and not to be constrained in any way were afforded. Initially, enforcement of the new forms of thinking at the time that the team was formed was avoided. Gradually it became apparent that the power was required and began to be employed. The new responsibility was particularly helpful when thinking of ways to relay the information from the training manager to the teams or expecting certain tasks to be completed.

There were no formal rewards and recognition systems established for the team. Since funding is limited due to the allocation funds provided by the central government, People Care does not have an established rewards system, but individuals are still praised for their efforts. Some individuals placed high value upon this recognition of their efforts and, despite there not being directly evident reward systems, continued to display enthusiasm and excitement for the project.

Changing the Organisational Structure and Culture

For the team to work together, departments also had to endure change in practical terms. In some instances, temporary promotions were assigned and if this involved a shift from an ordinary, daily chore to a decision-making one, changes in responsibility also occurred. In diagrammatic, hierarchical terms, the change was not evident. The change was assumed to be a temporary one; therefore, the modifications in the organisational chart did not have to be shown.

In order to assist the team with suitable completion dates and to provide the organisation with a better picture of when the several stages were to be completed, project milestones were formed. However, the plans were not always stuck to and in such circumstances, extensions were sought. In such instances, management was informed of a decision and a new date of completion would be stated.

Varying the Role of the Team with Regards to Management and Old Departmental Colleagues

Contact with the old colleagues during the work hours was reduced. As mentioned, it was meant to keep the team concentrated upon the task at hand and preventing the influence of external factors (such as queries from the departments).

The relationship with management changed as a result of an individual being part of the reengineering team. Prior to BPC, the individuals may have been recognised and known within the department, but with the organisation being a large one, they were not known to management. In this new role, the team members became known to management and not only that but they were in a capacity of decision making in their own right, which was an implausible situation before BPC.

Preparing Individuals (Belonging to the Team) for the Human Aspects Such as Trust, Empowerment and Motivation

There was no formal training for the human aspects issues of trust, empowerment and motivation. Trust was viewed to exist without it being illustrated. *"If there was no trust, there would be no way that we would have worked together. We were allocated duties at the beginning of the project, and there was the feeling that it would be completed. This is how I would describe that there was an element of trust"* (Human Resources Manager).

Conflict was an issue that was apparent within the implementation teams then any of the other teams formed during the project and was dealt with in the earlier stages of the project: *"Towards the end, our attention was upon completing the project on time, and all the conflicts that erupted were put on the side. In fact, we made sure that attention was not doted upon conflict"* (Project Manager). The ignorance was attributed to conflict due to less time being available and explained, *"During the earlier periods, we could afford to deal with the issues. Deadlines were matters of concern, but not to such an extent."* It was also found that the conflict was more tasks related than personal and dealt with at the time it became apparent, as opposed to setting a day for the issues to be dealt with.

An example of conflict being dealt with at the moment was that between the Information Technology 'technicians' (providing the information base) not understanding the 'librarians' (the people looking after the contents base). The original intention was to have the two sides working together to form a suitable database that could be utilised easily by the individuals within the council. However, what occurred was that the two sides remained separate. Several attempts at mediation by the project manager were made, and efforts to make the two sides work together

•

as a team rather than two separate entities were undertaken, but the target was not completely obtained. Several attempts were made to overcome this problem and at the end it came down to getting on with the job and meeting the set deadlines. Therefore, conflict was not really well handled at this organisation.

The other behaviour mentioned is motivation, and although it is considered to be an inner feeling of an individual, it is also instigated by external factors such as pay or recognition, which then obtains feelings of esteem and belonging (as explained by Maslow, 1943). In this case motivation was promoted by the fact that the members had the privilege of being part of this historical and large project. There were no financial incentives and so the esteem and belonging issues seemed to be more prevalent.

From this discussion it can be noted that the actions taken by management when forming the team were influenced by the institutional context (arrow 4), particularly the organisational context. In turn, the actions taken at the box labelled 'Adopting and using the reengineering team' have an impact upon the organisational context (arrow 5), for instance upon the organisational structure and practices.

The activities undertaken to adopt and use the reengineering team consequently resulted in various outcomes on the different stakeholders of the team (arrow 6), and this issue is dealt with in the box labelled 'Consequences of adopting and using the reengineering teams.' The impact upon management, the team, clients and individuals of the organisation is dealt with at this point.

Since the ideas expressed in structuration theory are being used, it is shown that the actions taken when adopting the team have been influenced by the institutional context; therefore, when examining the consequences, the institutional context has to be placed in the picture (arrow 7). The consequences in turn affect the institutional context, both the external environment and the organisational one (arrow 8).

Consequences of Adopting and Using the Teams

The consequences of the adoption and use of the teams was assessed in terms of the client, management, individuals working within the organisation and the team's reactions.

Client Reactions to the Consequences of Adopting and Using the Teams

The organisation had managed to ensure that the absence of the individuals involved in the projects was not felt. Secondments or temporary promotions managed to overcome any gaps. The interviewed individuals all displayed a sense of pride that the organisation had managed to bring about such a good team to overcome any problems.

Management's Reaction to the Consequences of Adopting and Using the Team

The team did consist of some personnel who belonged to the management board of the organisation. Due to this, management was supportive of the actions undertaken by the team.

The Organisation's Reactions to Adoption and Using of the Team

The members of the organisation who replaced the team members obtained a learning experience of a different job to their own. The organisation was aware that there were going to be changes within it that was going to have an impact upon them. Some people were apprehensive about the results, particularly with regard to their own jobs and the changes that were coming alongside. However, the findings showed that there were few reductions in the workforce, and the organisation had responded positively to the undertaken changes.

The Team Members' Reactions to Adopting and Using the Team

Generally the team members were enthusiastic about the project and this was a major factor for the motivation in the project. Reflecting back to the period, it was noted that new forms of skills such as team development skills, and the experience of working with a change management approach that brought a lot of attention, were some of the benefits of working in the team. On the other hand, the disadvantage of being removed from the daily workings of the original department was acknowledged, but it was not a major issue of concern.

This concludes the discussion regarding the newly formed theory. In the next section, the implications and limitations of this research are presented.

IMPLICATIONS OF THE RESEARCH

This research was begun because it was found that researchers in the BPC area claimed that reengineering teams are critical for the implementation of BPC; however, there was very little information regarding the teams. Attempts to overcome the gap began by firstly identifying some issues that could be associated with such teams. Issues such as the size, interaction among the teams in terms of conflict and development of the teams were analysed to obtain a detailed overview of the area. However, the question that still remained to be understood is the role of the reengineering team in the context of business process change.

By using the ideas expressed by Giddens (1984) and Orlikowski and Robey's (1991) structuration theory, it was shown that the aforementioned claim made by the BPR researchers is valid. Thus the theory shows teams as change agents who fulfill management's expectations, and the several activities and issues that need to be considered when forming the team. It also verifies the claims made by the established researchers in the BPR area by demonstrating their application in practice (using the case study). By undertaking this research, BPR researchers can now point to some theory that will demonstrate the process of organisational change that is assumed to be an underpinning of the area and other issues related to the formation of the theory.

LIMITATIONS OF THE THEORY

A limitation of this research was that it was difficult to generalise from one case study. However, the same can also be said of experiments conducted in a laboratory, as the variables utilised for one experiment may not be the same for another; therefore, it would be difficult to generalise. This deficiency has been noted in the IS area by Walsham (1995) who also noted that it is difficult to generalise from a small sample. However, the limitation that such situations form was overcome upon the reasoning that attempts to compensate for this problem are made by "drawing on other literature and case material, ..." (Walsham, 1995). Similar reasoning was used in this research; however, since this is an initial attempt into the research area, the findings from other literature has been used to overcome this problem in this research.

Although generalisations are difficult to obtain with case studies, the method allows an in-depth understanding and that is something that experiments or the survey questionnaires lack. This was an issue that was emphasised when describing the reasons for undertaking case studies. The above limitations have also been observed in other undertaken research and are something that is considered in theory and also observable in practice. The following have been limitations that the researcher had personal experiences of when conducting the research and include, among others, limited access to reference materials, and other individuals within the organisation.

This concludes the discussion part of this research. In the next section, the conclusions formed as a result of this research are described.

CONCLUSIONS

A framework that can be utilised to understand the relationship between organisational change and the reengineering teams that undertake business process change was proposed and formed. Such a framework can assist organisations by making them aware of some of the issues to deal with, particularly in the face of organisational change. The framework also demonstrates the importance of reengineering teams in the implementation of BPC.

The traditional models for determining organisational change do not address the events that occur as a result of change. Instead they treat change as a sequence of events without determining in detail what is involved in the process. For instance, a traditional model such as Lewin's (1947) organisational change model proposes the three forms of change — unfreeze, refreeze and change — but what exactly happens at each of the stages is missing from literature. The framework proposed in this chapter describes the actions that occur when reengineering teams are formed at the analysis and planning stages. By detailing the events, researchers are provided with a solid understanding rather than having ideas about the occurrences of business process change and reengineering teams.

Having a framework such as the one described in this chapter, it will assist organisations to prepare a plan of action and determine in advance what can be done in order to have reengineering teams forming within their organisation. Although there may be certain details to the framework that are common knowledge within researchers, for instance, forming of the vision, they have not been detailed in any way and this research intends to fill such a gap.

ENDNOTES

1 To ensure anonymity of the organisation that assisted with the research, the name People Care was used.

REFERENCES

Armenakis, A., Harris, S. and Field, H. (1999). Paradigms in organisational change: Change agent and change target perspectives. In Golembiewski, R. (Ed.), *Handbook of Organisational Behaviour*. New York: Marcel Dekker.

Davenport, T. H. (1993). *Process Innovation: Reengineering Work Through Information Technology*. Boston, MA: Harvard Business School Press.

Dawson, P. (1994). *Organisational Change: A Processual Approach*. London: Paul Chapman Publishing Ltd.

Giddens, A. (1984). *The Constitution of Society*. Berkeley, CA: University of California Press.

Hammer, M. and Champy, J. (1993). *Reengineering the Corporation*. New York: HarperCollins Publishers, Inc.

Lewin, K. (1947). Frontiers in group dynamics. *Human Relations*, *1*, 5-41.

Orlikowski, W.J. (1993). CASE tools as organisational change: Investigating incremental and radical changes in systems development. *Management Information Systems Quarterly*, *17*(3), 33.

Orlikowski, W. J. and Robey, D. (1991). Information technology and the structuring of organisations. *Information Systems Research*, 2(2), 143-67.

Strauss, A. and Corbin, J. (1990). *Basics of Qualitative Research*. Newbury Park, CA: Sage Publications.

Willcocks, L. P. and Currie, W. L. (1996). Information technology and radical reengineering: Emerging issues in major projects. *European Journal of Work and Organisational Psychology*, 5(3), 325-350.

About the Authors

Vlatka Hlupic received a DiplEcon and an MSc in Information Systems from the University of Zagreb, and a Ph.D. in Information Systems at the London School of Economics, UK, as well as a CEng from the UK Engineering Council and Eur Ing from the European Federation of National Engineering Associations. She is a Senior Lecturer at Brunel University, at the Department of Information Systems and Computing, and a Director of the Brunel Centre for Knowledge and Business Process Management (KBM). Dr. Hlupic has published over 100 papers in journals, books and conference proceedings, mainly in the areas of knowledge management, business process change and simulation modelling. As a European Engineer and Chartered Engineer, she acts as a consultant for a variety of service and manufacturing companies, as well as having managed various research projects. Her current research interests are in discrete-event simulation, knowledge management, business process reengineering and software evaluation. Dr. Hlupic is an Associate Editor of *Simulation*, and a member of various journal editorial boards and conference organising committees.

***

Wafi Al-Karaghouli lectures in Information Technology and Quantitative Methods at the Westminster Business School, University of Westminster in the UK. He holds a BA and a MPhil from London University, and was previously employed in database consultancy in London and linear programming consultancy in a Blue-chip Company in Surrey. His research interests are in finding ways to improve the use of Information Technology Systems (ITS) in business. Research interests include the application of ITS in organisations, LP and developing an understanding of TQM to system development. Current research topics include system failures, especially requirements engineering, KM and benchmarking in relation to system development.

Sarmad Alshawi has more than 15 years of academic experience and currently holds the position of Courses Director in the Department of Information Systems and Computing, Brunel University. UK. Dr. Alshawi is an active member of research groups at Brunel, with research in data management, business intelligence and information systems development. Dr. Alshawi has written in internationally refereed journals, spoken at conferences worldwide and has guest-edited many special issue journals. He has participated in several large and medium-sized research projects funded by various UK research funding bodies.

Dee Alwis trained and qualified as a management accountant and is an associate member of the Chartered Institute of Management Accountants (CIMA), UK. She has held various management and financial accounting positions within international companies. Ms. Alwis obtained a Master of Science degree in Information Systems at the Brunel University in 1998/99. Currently reading for a PhD at Brunel, her main research interests include knowledge management and corporate memory.

Robert O. Briggs is director of Methodology and Process Tools at GroupSystems.com, and is research coordinator in the Center for the Management of Information at the University of Arizona. He explores the theoretical foundations of joint effort, and designs technology to improve the performance and satisfaction of teams working toward a common goal. He has published more than 50 scholarly works on technology support for teams. He is currently researching the use of thinkLets to create repeatable, predictable patterns of group interaction and the use of technology-supported methodologies to create predictable success on cognition-intensive tasks. He earned his doctorate in Management Information Systems at the University of Arizona, and holds BS and MBA degrees from San Diego State University.

Vlatko Ceric is a Professor and Head of the Business Computing Department at the Graduate School of Economics and Business, University of Zagreb. His research interests are simulation modelling, decision support systems, information retrieval, electronic commerce and operations management. He has published over 80 papers and several books in this field. He also led several research and application-oriented projects. He was the Editor-in-Chief of the international *Journal of Computing and Information Technology*, Head of the International Programme Committee of the international conference *Information Technology Interfaces* and a member of programme committees of several international conferences. He reviews papers for several international journals and conferences.

Jyoti Choudrie is an Assistant Professor of Information Systems and Organisational Information Management in the Department of Information Systems and Computing of Brunel University. She has a master's degree in Information Systems and a PhD in Information Systems from Brunel University. Her main research interests include evaluating the organisational change and the human aspects that occur when the implementation of information systems occurs, business process change/

reengineering, Internet abuse and e-commerce security. Currently she is developing an interest in the implications of broadband upon policy making. She has published in the *Journal of Cognition, Technology and Work, Journal of Intelligent Systems* and in numerous proceedings of international conferences on information systems, in particular the Americas Conference on Information Systems and Bled Conference of Electronic Commerce.

Tony Cockett (BSc, MSc, MTech, PhD) is a Cybernetician and Lecturer in Multimedia Design at Brunel University, London. Dr. Cockett has a background in Cybernetics and has spent several years establishing the undergraduate subject of Multimedia Design at the University. He was for nearly 20 years Head of the University Department of Business. Also, he has spent nearly 15 years in industry where he worked as a designer.

Wendy L. Currie is Professor and Director of the Centre for Strategic Information Systems in the Department of Information Systems and Computing at Brunel University. Her research interests are IT strategy and outsourcing, the strategic positioning of suppliers in the software and computing services industry, managing large-scale IT projects and the development of electronic commerce high-tech start-ups. She recently completed a large-scale research project on IT outsourcing in the U.S. and Europe, and now consults widely in this area. She is currently Postgraduate Director at Brunel, and is responsible for three MSc degree courses. Her recent books include: *The Global Information Society* (Wiley), *New Strategies in IT Outsourcing in the U.S. and Europe* (Business Intelligence Ltd) and *Rethinking MIS* with Professor Bob Galliers (Oxford University Press). Other books include: *Management Strategy for IT* (Pitman) and *The Strategic Management of Advanced Manufacturing Technology* (CIMA). Professor Currie has published in numerous journals, including *OMEGA, British Journal of Management, Long Range Planning.* She is on the editorial board of the *Journal of Information Technology* and is an Associate Editor of *the European Journal of Information Systems.* She is an Associate Faculty Member of Templeton College, University of Oxford and Henley Management College, and a member of the Association for Information Systems (AIS), the UK AIS and the British Academy of Management.

Gert-Jan de Vreede is an Associate Professor at the Faculty of Technology, Policy, and Management of Delft University of Technology in The Netherlands. He received his PhD in Systems Engineering from the same university. His research interests include the application of collaborative technologies to facilitate organizational design activities, and the adoption and diffusion of GSS in both western environments as well as developing countries. His articles have appeared in various journals, including *Journal of Management Information Systems*, *Journal of Decision Systems*, *Journal of Creativity and Innovation Management*, *Holland Management Review*, *Database*, *Group Decision and Negotiation*, and *Journal of Simulation Practice and Theory*.

Charles Dennis is a Chartered Marketer and a Lecturer in Marketing and Retail Management at Brunel University, London, UK. Originally a Chartered Chemical Engineer, his early career included some years in engineering and technical posts, with a 'marketing' emphasis in the latter. Industrial experience was followed by seven years with 'Marketing Methods,' including as an Institute of Marketing approved consultant, leading to training and then lecturing. He has been full time in this current post since 1993.

John S. Edwards is a Reader in Operational Research and Systems at Aston Business School, Birmingham, UK. He holds MA and PhD degrees from Cambridge University. His principal interests are in knowledge management and decision support, especially methods and processes for system development. He has written more than 30 research papers on these topics, and two books, *Building Knowledge-Based Systems* and *Decision Making with Computers*. Current work includes the transferability of best practices in knowledge management, linking knowledge-based systems with simulation models to improve organisational learning and a study of the relevance of knowledge management to management accounting.

Guy Fitzgerald is Professor of Information Systems at Brunel University. Prior to this he was at Birkbeck College, University of London. He has also worked in the computer industry with companies such as British Telecom, Mitsubishi and CACI Inc., International. His research interests are concerned with the effective management and development of information systems (IS), and he has published widely in these areas. He is co-author, with David Avison, of *Information Systems Development: Methodologies, Techniques and Tools,* and he is founder and co-editor of the *Information Systems Journal (ISJ)* from Blackwell Science.

Petros A. M. Gelepithis is Leader of Complex Intelligent Systems Research at Kingston University. His personal research programme is the development of a Unified Theory of Mind. His first volume on Intelligent Systems was published in 2001. Dr. Gelepithis has been the Principal Investigator of a major EU grant, Consultant to the HOLIST Programme Director and holder of a BT research fellowship. He is a Fellow of the Cybernetics Society, Assessor for the Directorate of Community Support Framework, Ministry of National Education, Greece, and has been invited to give lectures in the United States, England, Greece and The Netherlands. Dr. Gelepithis is on the Editorial Board of *Cognitive Systems* and of *Neural, Parallel & Scientific Computations*.

George M. Giaglis is Assistant Professor of Information Systems in the Department of Financial and Management Engineering of the University of the Aegean, Greece. He also teaches at the executive MBA programmes of the Athens University of Economics and Business, Nottingham Trent University, and Henley Management College (UK). His research interests lie in the areas of business modelling, eBusiness and mBusiness, information systems evaluation and knowledge management. He has published more than 50 papers in journals such as the *International Journal of Electronic Commerce, International Journal of Information Management* and others. He is also working closely with the Commission of the European Communities as an independent expert on new technologies and electronic commerce.

John B. Kidd was educated in the UK and worked for several major UK organisations before returning to university scholarship. In the universities of Birmingham and now Aston Business School, his research focused on the development of IT use in SMEs, the management of projects and the softer management issues that concern multi-national joint ventures. He has held visiting professorships in several European Universities, and in the China Europe International Business School, Shanghai. His recent books on Asian matters, Co-Edited with Li Xue and Frank-Jürgen Richter, are *Maximising Human Intelligence Deployment in Asia: The 6th Generation Project* and also *Advances in Human Resource Management in Asia* (London & New York: Palgrave, both 2001).

V. P. Kochikar has anchored the organization-wide Knowledge Management initiative at Infosys Technologies since its inception, as Principal Knowledge Manager. He has published in the areas of knowledge management, software project management, object technology, systems modeling and related areas of software engineering in several international conferences and journals. He has also lectured in a guest capacity at various business schools and industry in India, the U.S. and the UK. He serves on the panel of reviewers for various international journals and conferences. Dr. Kochikar has been profiled by *Knowledge Management Review* magazine, and interviewed by, among others, BBC Radio, *Business Today* magazine and *Computers Today* magazine. He holds a BTech and PhD from the Indian Institute of Technology, and an MTech from the Indian Institute of Science. Dr. Kochikar is a member of the IEEE Computer Society.

Kavi Mahesh is the Technology Manager in the Knowledge Management Group at Infosys Technologies, and has been primarily responsible for building the technology architecture for KM. He was earlier a Principal Member of Technical Staff with the Server Technologies Division of Oracle Corporation in California, USA. Before joining Oracle, Dr. Mahesh was a Research Faculty Member and an Adjunct Assistant Professor of Computer Science at New Mexico State University. His areas of interest include text processing, information classification and retrieval, ontologies, and knowledge-based design and development. Dr. Mahesh has an engineering degree from Bangalore University, an MTech in Computer Science from the Indian Institute of Technology, and MS and PhD degrees in Computer Science from the Georgia Institute of Technology.

C.S. Mahind is the Research & Content Manager in the Knowledge Management Group at Infosys Technologies. He has played a key role in defining the KM architecture for Infosys. His research work ranges from behavioral aspects to measurement of benefits in KM. Prior to joining Infosys, he had a 10-year long career in academia. He holds bachelor's and master's degrees in Engineering.

David Marsland (MA, PhD, FRSH) is a graduate of Cambridge University and LSE. Through the center for Evaluation Research at Brunel University (London, UK), he is working on a program of research on the modernization of public and private sector organizations. His latest book, *Welfare or Welfare State?*, was published by Macmillan in 1996. He is currently completing a textbook on research methods.

Jay F. Nunamaker, Jr. is Regents and Soldwedel Professor of MIS, Computer Science, and Communication, and Director of the Center for the Management of Information at the University of Arizona, Tucson. He has over 40 years of experience in developing collaborative information systems. He has served as a Test Engineer at the Shippingport Atomic Power facility, as a member of the ISDOS team at the University of Michigan and as a member of the faculty at Purdue University prior to joining the faculty at the University of Arizona in 1974. Dr. Nunamaker received his PhD in Systems Engineering and Operations Research from Case Institute of Technology, an MS and BS in Engineering from the University of Pittsburgh, and a BS from Carnegie Mellon University. He has been a registered professional engineer since 1965.

Nicole Parillon was born in London in 1962. She has held administrative and accountancy positions in various industries, including pharmaceutical, banking and television in both Basel and Zurich, Switzerland. Currently, she is completing her degree in Computer Information Systems Design at Kingston University. Her dissertation "A Knowledge Management Strategy for WS Atkins" grew out of her interest in issues surrounding knowledge modelling. She is planning to do her doctorate in Complex Intelligent Systems, contributing to a Unified Theory of Mind by studying human perception, motivation and emotions, and how they can be modelled in robots.

Nayna Patel received a BSc (Hons) in Computer Science and an MSc degree in Information Systems from Brunel University. She worked as a consultant in the area of BPR as well as having held several teaching posts. She has published her research work in various international journals and conference proceedings. Her current research interests include simulation, business process reengineering and knowledge management.

Athanasia (Nancy) Pouloudi is an Assistant Professor in the Department of Management Science and Technology at the Athens University of Economics and Business (AUEB). She holds a first degree in Informatics (Athens University of Economics and Business), and MSc and PhD degrees in Information Systems (London School of Economics). Her research focuses on strategic and social issues in information systems, specialising in electronic commerce, knowledge management and stakeholder issues with more than 50 publications in these areas. She has acted as the Associate Director for research in electronic commerce at the Centre for Strategic Information Systems at Brunel University (UK). Her work included leading an EPSRC grant (GR/N03242) on "Human Factors in Electronic Commerce: A Stakeholder Approach." She has also taught information systems at Brunel University (as lecturer) and the London School of Economics and Political Science (as teaching assistant), and held visiting positions at Erasmus University (The Netherlands) and the Athens Laboratory of Business Administration (Greece).

Angeliki Poulymenakou is a Lecturer in Information Systems in the Informatics Department of the Athens School of Economics and Business. Prior to that she has worked as a Lecturer in Information Systems in the London School of Economics and Political Science. She holds a first degree in Mathematics (Athens), and MSc and PhD degrees in Information Systems (London School of Economics). Her current research focuses on information technology-enabled organisational capability development where she studies in particular organisational processes related to knowledge management adoption. Overall, her published research work addresses three areas of interest: analysis practices for knowledge-intensive systems, the management of ICT projects (and the study of project failure) and socioeconomic impact of ICTs with a specific emphasis on ICT-enabled organisational change and electronic commerce. Her several publications in international journals and conferences draw from the full range of activities outlined above. She has served as a member of the scientific committee of four international conferences in information systems (ICIS, ECIS, IFIP 8.2 and 9.4) and has acted as a referee in several international journals in the field.

Sajda Qureshi is Assistant Professor in the Department of Decision and Information Sciences in the Faculty of Management at Erasmus University Rotterdam in The Netherlands. She holds a PhD in Information Systems from the London School of Economics and Political Science at the University of London in the United Kingdom. She has been Coordinator of the Commonwealth Network of Information Technology for Development, and she has lectured at the University of Arizona in the USA. Her work has been published in journals such as *Group Decision and Negotiation, Information Infrastructure and Policy* and *Communications of the ACM,* and in books published by Prentice Hall, Springer-Verlag, Chapman and Hall and North-Holland. She has performed editorial work for *DataBase, Electronic Journal of Information Systems in Developing Countries, SIGGroup01*, and *HICSS.*

George Rzevski is Emeritus Professor of the Open University, Visiting Professor in Intelligent Systems at Brunel University and Chairman of MagentA Corporation plc, a software development company specialising in multi-agent systems for knowledge management, real-time logistics and e-commerce. Professor Rzevski has extensive experience in research and consulting related to networked organisations and advanced IT.

Konstantinos Samiotis was born in Athens, Greece. He holds a first degree in Informatics and an MSc in Information Systems from the Athens University of Economics and Business. Currently he is working on his PhD research in the field of *Organisational Knowledge Management,* specifically focusing on the impact of novel knowledge management technologies on the capabilities and competences of organisations. The context of application is primarily service industries. Besides his research, he is also engaged in the management of several European R&D projects. Part of his professional background consists of executive teaching, consulting for policy making in e-Business, and working experience in large Greek companies.

Manon van Leeuwen obtained her University Degree in Business Economics at the University of Tilburg (The Netherlands), specialising in Organisational Processes (with a focus on culture, structure and internal communication). She obtained a master's degree from the European Community of the University Pontificia Commillas, ICADE Madrid, and PhD in New Tendencies in Company Management at the University of Valladolid (Spain). She is currently Director of Information Society at Fundecyt and President of RedWise Extremadura, a regional network of women in the information society. She has participated as a speaker at conferences and courses on issues related to the new forms of work organisation and new organisational models.

Index

A

abilities 236
acquisition 75
activities 195
affinity credit card 156
application domain 86
artificial intelligence (AI) 54, 76
attractiveness 157
attribute evaluations 158
automobile manufacturing 128

B

behaviour 244
benefit to customers 94
body of knowledge (BoK) 85
brand manager 96
Brunel attractiveness index 164
business knowledge (BK) 219
business models 236, 238
business process change (BPC) 257, 261
business process reengineering (BPR) 34, 37
business processes 104, 117, 196
business transformation 237
business units 239

C

capabilities 98
capability development 98
capability maturity model 88
case study 136
case study results 140
change agent 252
change leaders 246
change management approaches 33
characteristics of business processes 123
codification 121

codified knowledge 20, 101
collaborative context 172
collaborative culture 174
collaborative technologies 173
collective effort 175
collective human knowledge 73
common knowledge 101
communication 71, 245
communities of practice 128, 147
competitive advantage 237
components 195
composite KCU rating 90
concerted effort 175
consumer power 238
content architecture 89
coordinated effort 175
core competences/competencies 123
core processes 123, 264
corporate cultures 241
corporate knowledge base 136
corporate yellow pages 146
courage 245
creation 75
critical mass 96
cultural change 118
culture 86, 118, 142, 196
customer and developer knowledge gap 221
customer database 155
customer relationship management (CRM) 153, 154
customized services 173

D

data mining 24, 153
databases 139
deep Web 24
demand-side view of knowledge 124
designing organisational memory 136

diagramming 216
digital environment 246
digital technologies 23
digitisation 23
discovery 21
disintermediation 238
distance 118
diversity of knowledge 215

E

e-commerce 51, 58
education & research (E&R) 85
electronic collaboration 172
embodied knowledge 101
ethics 245
European Projects 1
evaluation framework 195
expert/knowledge-based systems 119
explicit knowledge 137
extended enterprise 238
external knowledge 148

F

failure 248
firewall 95
framework 136

G

general electric 127
generic model of knowledge processes 119
goal congruence 174
group support systems (GSS) 177
growth 85

H

half-life of knowledge 128
hard research 4
hierarchy of needs 246
HTML 85
human resource management 125
human resources 21

I

identification 75
importance motivation 162
incentive schemes 142

incremental change 124
individual appraisals 243
individual knowledge 73
information and communications
    technology 16
information system (IS) 52, 216, 258
information technology system (ITS) 216
innovation 16
intangibles 237
integrated programme portfolio analysis
    (IPPA) 6
intellectual property issues 95
intellectual property rights (IPR) 85
intellectual resources 173
intelligent agents 51
internationalisation of operations 118
intranet 85
IT knowledge 218
ITS failures 217

J

just-in-time (JIT) 34, 36

K

KCU score board 89
KM deployment architecture 88
KMM 83
know-how 20
know-what 20
know-who 20
know-why 20
knowledge 16, 68
knowledge and information management
    (KIM) 1
knowledge assets 16
knowledge availability 128
knowledge creation 27
knowledge currency units (KCUs) 84
knowledge discovery in databases 24
knowledge dissemination 26
knowledge distribution 26
knowledge drift 124
knowledge economy 16, 236
knowledge gap (KG) 220
knowledge generation 196
knowledge hierarchy 86, 89
knowledge-intensive companies 136

knowledge life cycle 87
knowledge management (KM) 1, 34,
    44, 51, 68, 82, 117, 218, 137
knowledge management activities 196
knowledge management components 196
knowledge management maturity model 83
knowledge management processes 119
knowledge management research 10
knowledge management tools 195
knowledge market 68
knowledge measurement 27
knowledge networking 77
knowledge organisation 196
knowledge portal 84, 90
knowledge processes 119
knowledge requirement framework (KRF)
    216
knowledge sharing 122, 186, 196
knowledge shop (KShop) 84, 90
knowledge summits 94
knowledge transfer processes 120
knowledge transmission 26
knowledge workers 148
knowledge-sharing practices 94

L

leaders 236, 244
leadership 236
leading organisations 240
learn once, use anywhere paradigm 83
learning enactment 98
limits of management 68
limits of technology 68
Lotus Notes 122
loyalty schemes 156

M

management 236
management panaceas 34
managers 243
managing knowledge 172, 215
manufacturing 122
mapping techniques 216
market awareness 84
meaning 71
measurement of KM benefits 93
methodology 86, 194

model 173
most admired knowledge enterprises 95
motivation 241
motivation clusters 159
multi-agent software 58
mutual benefit life insurance 128
myKShop 91

N

NetMeeting 186
networked business models 249
networking 23

O

objective corporation 127
organisation of work 240
organisation structures 241
organisational capital 21
organisational change 241, 257
organisational knowledge 73
organisational learning 117
organisational memory 73, 136
organisational structure 122
organizational knowledge 98
outsourcing 246

P

patents 21
people-knowledge map 91
performance appraisals 95
performance measurement techniques 243
primary activities 123
primitives 72
process architecture 93
process innovation (PI) 34
process knowledge 104
project management 86
project reviews 95
project snapshots 93
psychic distance 129

Q

qualities of leadership 248
quality 84
questionnaire 140

R

radical change 124
realisation process 124
reality 245
reengineering teams 257, 260
repositories 146
requirements engineering (RE) 216
requirements engineering specialist group
     (RESG) 216
research and development 139
resource constraints 174
revenue productivity 84
reward systems 241
risk reduction 84
risk-encouraging culture 236
risks 248
roles 236

S

satellite repositories 92
scope and limits of technology 68
selection of a knowledge management tool
     194
shared spaces 174
sharing culture 96
sharing of knowledge 75
'shopping' and 'service' motivations 159
shopping centers 153
shopping motivations 159
simulation modelling 33
skills 236
social knowledge 101
soft research 5
soft-systems 216
softer skills 245
software 18
speed 237
spiritual management 245
storytelling 128
style of leadership 236
supply chain 129
supply-side view of knowledge 123
system developer (SD) 217
system development 216

T

tacit knowledge 20, 137
taxonomy 1
teams 236
technical aspect of knowledge management
     195
technology 86, 196
technology architecture 90
telecommunications domain 95
tendencies in leadership 251
the flexible firm 240
theory of knowledge 72
thought leadership 95
total quality 34
total quality management (TQM) 34
training programmes 241

U

understanding 70
understanding gaps 215
Unisys Corporation 127
Uppsala model 129

V

value chain 123
virtual classroom 87
virtual teamwork 85
vision 245
vital knowledge 137

W

Web mining 24
Web technologies 85
work practices 98
workers/employees 244
working methods 241

NEW Titles
from Information Science Publishing

- **Web-Based Education: Learning from Experience**
  Anil Aggarwal
  ISBN: 1-59140-102-X: eISBN 1-59140-110-0, © 2003
- **The Knowledge Medium: Designing Effective Computer-Based Learning Environments**
  Gary A. Berg
  ISBN: 1-59140-103-8; eISBN 1-59140-111-9, © 2003
- **Socio-Technical and Human Cognition Elements of Information Systems**
  Steve Clarke, Elayne Coakes, M. Gordon Hunter and Andrew Wenn
  ISBN: 1-59140-104-6; eISBN 1-59140-112-7, © 2003
- **Usability Evaluation of Online Learning Programs**
  Claude Ghaoui
  ISBN: 1-59140-105-4; eISBN 1-59140-113-5, © 2003
- **Building a Virtual Library**
  Ardis Hanson & Bruce Lubotsky Levin
  ISBN: 1-59140-106-2; eISBN 1-59140-114-3, © 2003
- **Design and Implementation of Web-Enabled Teaching Tools**
  Mary F. Hricko
  ISBN: 1-59140-107-0; eISBN 1-59140-115-1, © 2003
- **Designing Campus Portals**
  Ali Jafari and Mark Sheehan
  ISBN: 1-59140-108-9; eISBN 1-59140-116-X, © 2003
- **Challenges of Teaching with Technology Across the Curriculum: Issues and Solutions**
  Lawrence A. Tomei
  ISBN: 1-59140-109-7; eISBN 1-59140-117-8, © 2003

Excellent additions to your institution's library! Recommend these titles to your librarian!